HOW TO RUN A
Successful
HOME INSPECTION BUSINESS
by NICK GROMICKO

How to Run a Successful Home Inspection Business

Generate a steady pipeline of profitable leads
and get really, really rich as a property inspector

A Publication of the
International Association of Certified Home Inspectors

This manual is designed to help inspectors create, sustain and grow their companies. For both business veterans and those who are just starting out in the inspection industry, this book will help guide you through the step-by-step process of setting up a business that's both ethical and profitable.

Good marketing is the foundation of a solid business, and this publication outlines tried-and-true techniques for performing easy marketing tasks that will distinguish you from the competition, as well as tips on how to court and secure high-end inspections that will put you on another level of earning.

Author:
Nick Gromicko

Contributors:
Kate Tarasenko; Ben Gromicko; Chris Morrell; Mark Cohen, Esq.;
Joseph Ferry, Esq.; Kenton Shepard; Michelle Thakur; and Kelsea Lewis

Editor:
Kate Tarasenko/Crimea River

Design & Layout:
Jessica Langer

Graphics:
Levi Nelson; Erica Saurey; Erik Gromicko; and Chris Krowiak

www.NACHI.org

Preface

When I was a boy back in the 1990s, my dad, Nick Gromicko, would take me with him on his home inspections around Philadelphia. For most boys my age, going to work with their dad is a lot of fun. It was thrilling for me to be appointed as my dad's helper. I wasn't exactly sure what a home inspector did, but I was going to learn everything about it that I could so that I could be one, too, when I grew up.

It was during these exciting excursions that I was able to witness that there were different people who were at these appointments for different reasons—real estate agents, home buyers, and home sellers. They all seemed friendly, but anxious. They followed my father as he made his way through the house, watching his every move, and hanging on his every word. I knew that they were looking to him for information, but I could also sense that they were hoping for his reassurance, too. At the end of the appointment, whether he gave them good news or bad, these people seemed extremely grateful, shaking my dad's hand and thanking him profusely for telling them things that apparently no one else had.

On our rides to and from these appointments, I was filled with questions I wanted to ask and observations I wanted to share, just as any boy would. The first question I remember asking my dad was whether he was the only home inspector, or if there were others like him—people who did what he did. He confirmed that there were others. So, although my regular interrogations over the years about his process were informed by the fact that he represented an entire profession, I continually peppered him with questions to find out in what ways his methods were superior to those of other home inspectors.

One of my earliest observations was that he always spent a lot of time and took such great care with everything related to his job. He washed his truck at the end of the day, and charged his flashlight batteries. He confirmed his appointments the night before. And he checked his gear again in the morning. Once we arrived at the appointment, he carefully organized his tools and supplies in his pockets and tool belt, and then greeted his clients enthusiastically—all at what seemed like a breakneck pace, although he always looked relaxed and had a smile on his face. I followed him closely while he then methodically worked his way through the house, knowing where to find exactly what he was looking for.

All his energy and daily momentum made me realize early on that because he worked on his own, without a boss telling him what to do, my dad had to have developed his own reliable structure—and maybe even some secrets—for his success. And I was determined to learn what they were.

I remember when he figured out how to create his reports using the photos he'd taken during his inspections with his new digital camera. He was very excited, he told me, because he was the only home inspector in the area whose reports had integrated photos with the text. It was such a simple thing, and yet even I knew that it was special—that it was exactly what an inspection report should be, both descriptive text and actual pictures of the property. I asked him if there was a way that other inspectors could create their reports with photos as easily as he did. "No, not yet," he replied.

As I began using our home computer for school assignments and hobbies, I became aware of the various types of newsgroups forming online. It wasn't too hard to find others connected to the Internet who shared my interests. Although the early online forums were bare-bones, it was a revelation to me to be able to float my questions out into the ether and eventually find someone—and usually several someones—willing to answer me with clear instructions and helpful advice. I remember asking my dad if there was something like that for home inspectors. I had accompanied him on enough inspections by then to know that every house was different, and a lot of them had unusual and unique problems. Was there one place on the Web where inspectors could find each other and ask for help and support if they needed it? "No, not yet," he answered.

It also occurred to me during this time that home inspectors probably needed classes or some type of instruction on how to inspect homes, just like I needed to attend classes in the various subjects I had to learn in order to graduate. I asked my dad if there was a special place where inspectors could go to learn about houses and the home inspection process. Was there even a place online where they could learn all they needed to know? "No, not yet," he said.

When my dad created his own logo for his own brochures and business cards, I was impressed by how professional-looking they were. They really made his business stand out. I wondered out loud if there was a way that other inspectors could get these items made so that they could look as professional as he did. Again he told me, "No, not yet."

Through the years, my questions became even more specific and sophisticated. What about commercial properties—was there some protocol for inspecting them? I continually asked my dad if we had this or that for home inspectors to make the inspection process easier, faster, safer, and more standardized, as well as modern and as cutting-edge as possible. He never said, "No." He always answered, "No, not yet."

As my dad founded and built the world's largest trade association for inspectors, I heard "No, not yet" become "Yes, we have that at InterNACHI."

I've been witness to his dedication to innovation for the benefit and betterment of home inspectors and an industry that has been more than just his career.

I'm honored to present his latest edition of "How to Run a Successful Home Inspection Business." This new expanded version is filled with groundbreaking tips and advice that every residential and commercial property inspector should embrace. If there was ever a how-to manual for starting an inspection business and making it succeed beyond your greatest expectations, this book is it. It's the industry bible, plain and simple.

—**Nikolai Gromicko, Owner**
Inspector Outlet

Foreword

I often see inspectors marketing when they have extra money, and not marketing when money is tight. This is upside-down thinking. Your marketing decisions should not be based on your cash flow.

Some inspectors say things like, "I've been slow this month, so I'm not going to spend much on marketing." This strategy causes the inspector's worst fear to become reality.

If you aren't inspecting today, work on building your business.

Regardless of the current state of your inspection business, you've come to the right book. In it, you'll find straightforward talk and more than 200 tips you can implement TODAY that are designed specifically for inspectors who want to dominate their market, raise their fees without regret, and build and sustain the type of business that will make them the envy of the local competition, as well as the first—and last—inspector their customers call.

—**Nick Gromicko, Founder**
InterNACHI

Table of Contents

Introduction

For all the diversity among inspectors—as defined by age, education, cultural background, home town, family makeup, work history, experience, income level, and even work ethic—there are some basic qualities that most of us have in common. We share the hallmarks of the classic entrepreneur. We prefer to work for ourselves and be our own bosses. We appreciate the challenges that confront our expertise on the job. We take pride in the fact that if we don't have the answer at hand, we are, at the very least, resourceful enough to find it. We make the regular commitment to expand our reach by seeking out the advice and fellowship of our colleagues. We are always learning. We exert the discipline required to increase our education. And we welcome the greater tests ahead so that we can exercise our latest knowledge. For all our varying degrees of perspective, we are a community. Providing for our families, taking pride in our work, making a daily investment in ourselves and in our clients, and enjoying the subsequent rewards of our labor are what form the foundation of our working lives. Can there be a greater ambition?

Success, then, seems already threaded through our business. It may be modest in terms of finances. But those rewards are available, too. There's more to our work ethic and earning potential as inspectors than being a reliable expert on the job. Our name is always working for us (or against us!) even off the job, and that's where many inspectors seem to give short shrift to the regular care and feeding of their inspecting enterprises. Treating this dual aspect of entrepreneurialism with anything less than equal effort will inevitably drive your business under as surely as making a habit of performing haphazard inspections.

Marketing is often seen as a chore—'the work that you have to do when you're not working'—and the less-than-enthusiastic result barely goes beyond a sign on the truck, a box of business cards, and a list of contacts. But our success depends on marketing not just our services, but also ourselves. Our credibility is our true calling card, and it's important to get our reputation out there so that it's as obvious as that sign on the truck. It's our first and most important marketing tool because without it, we are nothing.

The good news is: Just as there are logical ways to perform a property inspection, there are equally logical and common-sense marketing tips and techniques that will put us on a trajectory to a greater level of achievement and expectation in our inspection businesses. We have to approach marketing as deliberately as we do our training, education, and even our property inspections themselves. Pinning our hopes on random jobs each day is no way to build a business. And for as many inspectors as may populate the town we live in, we're not so much in competition with them (or each other) as with our own limitations. Our unwillingness to market ourselves is an unacceptable obstacle that puts a fatal limit on what we can become. Overcome that obstacle, and the competition won't matter.

These success tips are the culmination of years of training, education, experimentation, argument, failure, and breakthrough—all the building blocks of success. In them, you'll find dozens of straightforward strategies that will have you nodding, perhaps disbelieving, but, ultimately, becoming seriously motivated—perhaps for the first time in a long time—to move up to the next level in your career as an inspector.

"Great progress comes about by constantly making small improvements."

—Japanese concept of Kaizen

To succeed at anything, be it landing on the moon or building a successful inspection business, you have to do many little things properly. Always work on building your business. If you're not at the jobsite, be marketing your business, learning more, and improving your services. Remember that if you're a good inspector, you have a moral obligation to let as many people as possible know about and benefit from your good work.

Your Mission Statement

Every inspection company should have a mission statement. Mission statements are not just for big corporations or charitable organizations or political parties. Even your one-man inspection company should have one. A mission statement helps define what a company is and what it offers, and clarifies the company's goals to keep it on the path of service and success.

"If you think you can do a thing or think you can't do a thing, you're right."

—Henry Ford

A good commercial mission statement spells out not just the purpose, but also the priorities of the company, which, obviously, go beyond "I've put years into my training and education, and I need to support my family"—that part is understood. It also explains what you esteem, and how you intend to achieve your business goals of serving your clients, based on your values and priorities.

Sample Mission Statement:

[Your Company]'s mission is to provide the highest-quality work possible. We succeed at this because of the integrity of our staff, our commitment to a solid work ethic, and our passion for staying current with the newest innovations of our industry, with consideration for the environment and our local community.

[Your Company] is an inspection business incorporated in [state or province] in [year] by [principals]. Our staff brings years of experience to bear in residential and light commercial building inspections.

Our employees have been chosen based on their ability and level of competence, as well as their personal qualities and values.

Our pride and personal involvement in the work we perform result in superior quality and service. This attitude is also directly reflected in our employees' level of responsibility, professionalism and competency.

Basically, a mission statement should state:

1. what you do;
2. how you do it;
3. why you do it;
4. who you do it for; and
5. how you succeed at it each day.

Don't let a blank screen or piece of paper intimidate you; it doesn't have to be Shakespeare, but writing down the answers for these points is a great exercise for crystallizing why you're doing what you're doing and how you're doing it. It also may help you decide whether you need to change any of it. Your mission statement should guide your company's actions and move you forward every day.

Once you've got these points written down on paper, consider hanging it on your wall so that you can see it every day. If you're not happy with it, hang it up anyway and tweak it as you go.

A good mission statement isn't just an excellent marketing component; it helps clarify for you (and your employees, if you have any) exactly what your goals are each and every day. It's easy to lose sight of why you became an inspector when you're booked solid and rushing from one appointment to the next. Sometimes, providing excellent customer service may be done more from memory than passion.

Building Your Business Identity

Ask yourself exactly what you do to help improve your business on a regular basis, and write those things down. Do you take special training and Continuing Education courses? Do you belong to the International Association of Certified Home Inspectors and attend chapter meetings and special events? An important element in defining your professional identity—which is reflected by your mission statement—is belonging to a supportive association and being in regular contact with your fellow members.

Attending industry events will help you stay current with:

- changes in codes and standards;
- new developments in inspection products and practices;
- safety training; and
- innovative marketing and business success tips.

By exchanging your experiences and ideas with other inspectors through online forums and at industry events, you'll expand your own pool of ideas, as well as learn from the mistakes of others.

Aside from peer input, do you get customer feedback that tells you whether you're on the right track—the one that you've set for yourself? Your mission statement is what you tell the world you are, but it's also important to find out whether the world agrees with you!

Your Mission Statement (and Mission) Refined

Once you've finalized your mission statement, display it in a prominent place where you (and your staff) can see it every day, such as on your office wall or in a common area. Reading your mission statement regularly is sort of like a coach giving his/her team a pep talk; you may have heard it a hundred times, but it helps to reinforce just why you're doing what you're doing, and that's great for personal morale, as well as for expanding your vision for achieving your business goals.

Once you're satisfied with your mission statement, have it added to your brochure. A client will value someone who knows who s/he is and what his/her goals are, and how s/he achieves them. Putting that into words can make a confident and powerful statement that guides your company on a trajectory of success.

"If you're waiting for a freak time in the free market to go into business, when the demand for your product or service is much greater than your would-be competitors' ability to supply that demand, you probably shouldn't go into business."

—Nick Gromicko, founder of InterNACHI

Forms of Business Ownership

One of the first questions you'll have to address as a business owner is how the company should be structured. Your decision will have long-term implications, so consult with an accountant and an attorney who can help you select the form of business ownership that's right for you.

In making your determination, you'll want to consider the following factors:

- your vision regarding the size and nature of your inspection business;
- the level of control you wish to have;
- the complexity of the structure you're willing to deal with;
- the business's vulnerability to lawsuits;
- the tax implications of the different ownership structures;
- the expected profit (or loss) of the business;
- whether you'll need to re-invest your earnings into the business; and
- your projected need to take cash out of the business for yourself.

Sole Proprietorship

The vast majority of inspection businesses start out as sole proprietorships. These types of businesses are typically owned by one person who has the day-to-day responsibility for running the business. Sole proprietors own all the assets of the business, as well as the profits generated by it. They also assume complete responsibility for its liabilities and debts. In the eyes of the law and of the public, the inspector and the business are one and the same.

Advantages of a Sole Proprietorship:

1. It is the easiest and least expensive form of ownership to organize.
2. Sole proprietors are in complete control and, within the dictates of the law, may make decisions as they see fit.
3. Sole proprietors receive all income generated by the business to keep or re-invest.
4. Profits from the business flow directly through the business to the owner's personal tax return.
5. The business is easy to dissolve, if desired.

Disadvantages of a Sole Proprietorship:

1. Sole proprietors have unlimited liability and are responsible for all debts against the business. Their business and personal assets are legally exposed.
2. Owners may be at a disadvantage in raising funds, and are often financially limited to using funds from personal savings or consumer loans.
3. Owners may have a hard time attracting high-caliber employees and additional inspectors, and those who are courted are motivated by the opportunity to own a part of the business.
4. Some traditional employee benefits, such as the owner's medical insurance premiums, are not directly deductible from business income (and only partially deductible as an adjustment to income).

Partnership

In a partnership, two or more people share ownership of a single business. Like proprietorships, the law does not distinguish between the business and its owners.

The partners should have a buy-sell agreement that sets forth how decisions will be made and how much time and capital each will contribute to the business, as well as questions of salary, how profits will be shared, and even supervisory oversight and separate everyday duties, etc. This agreement should also describe how future inspectors will be admitted to the partnership, how disputes will be resolved, how partners can be bought out, and what steps will be taken to dissolve the partnership, when needed. Similar to a pre-nuptial agreement that must be signed before the wedding, it's hard to think about a "breakup" when the business is just getting started. But many partnerships split up at times of crisis, and unless there is a defined process, there will be even greater problems.

Advantages of a Partnership:

1. Partnerships are relatively easy to establish; however, time should be invested in developing the partnership agreement.

2. With more than one owner, the ability to raise funds may be increased.

3. The profits from the business flow directly through the business to the partners' personal tax returns.

4. Prospective inspectors may be attracted to the business if offered the incentive to become a third partner.

5. A business usually benefits from partners who have complementary skills.

Disadvantages of a Partnership:

1. Partners are jointly and individually liable for the actions of the other partner(s).

2. Profits must be shared with others.

3. Since decisions are shared, disagreements can occur.

4. Some employee benefits are not deductible from business income on tax returns.

5. The partnership may have a limited life; it may end upon the withdrawal or death of a partner.

Types of Partnerships:

- General Partnership: Partners divide responsibility for management and liability, as well as the sharing of profits and losses, according to their internal agreement. Equal shares are assumed unless there is a written agreement that states differently.

- Limited Partnership and Partnership with Limited Liability: "Limited" means that most of the partners have limited liability (to the extent of their investment), as well as limited input regarding management decisions, which generally encourages investors for short-term projects or for investing in capital assets. This form of ownership is not often used for operating inspecting businesses. Forming a limited partnership is more complex and formal than a general partnership.

- Joint Venture: This type is similar to a general partnership, but is clearly for a limited period of time or for a single project, such as a commercial inspection. If the partners in a joint venture repeat the activity, they will be recognized as party to an ongoing partnership and will have to file as such and distribute accumulated partnership assets upon dissolution of the entity.

Corporation

A corporation, chartered by the state in which it is headquartered, is considered by law to be a unique entity, separate and apart from those who own it. A corporation can be taxed, it can be sued, and it can enter into contractual agreements. The owners of a corporation are its shareholders. The shareholders elect a board of directors to oversee the major policies and decisions. The corporation has a life of its own and does not dissolve when ownership changes.

Advantages of a Corporation:

1. Shareholders have limited liability for the corporation's debts and any judgments against the corporation.

2. Generally, shareholders can only be held accountable for their investment in stock of the company. However, officers can be held personally liable for their actions, such as the failure to withhold and pay employment taxes.

3. Corporations can raise additional funds through the sale of stock.

4. A corporation may deduct the cost of the benefits it provides to officers and employees.

5. A corporation can elect to file for S-corporation status, if certain requirements are met. This enables the company to be taxed similarly to a partnership. (It is designated an S-corporation for Subchapter S of Chapter 1 of the Internal Revenue Code.)

6. It's easier for shareholders to sell their shares in the inspection business—and the business itself—when they want to retire.

Disadvantages of a Corporation:

1. The process of incorporation requires more time and money than other forms of organization.

2. Corporations are monitored by federal, state and some local agencies, and there may be more paperwork to fill out in order to comply with regulations.

3. Incorporating may result in higher overall taxes. Dividends paid to shareholders are not deductible from business income, so the income can be taxed twice.

4. There is a potential loss of control over the business and decisions regarding its direction, etc.

S-Corporation

A tax election only, this enables the shareholder to treat earnings and profits as dividends or distributions and have them pass through the business and directly to his/her personal tax return. The catch here is that if the shareholder is an employee of the company and the company makes a profit, s/he must pay him/herself wages that meet standards of "reasonable compensation." This can vary by geographical region (as well as by occupation), but the basic rule is to pay yourself what you would have to pay someone else to do your job, as long as there is enough profit. If you don't do this, the IRS can re-classify all of your earnings and profits as wages, and you'll be liable for all the payroll taxes on the total amount.

Limited Liability Company (LLC)

The LLC is a type of hybrid business structure. It's designed to provide the limited liability features of a corporation and the tax efficiencies and operational flexibility of a partnership. Formation is more complex and formal than that of a general partnership. The owners are members, and the duration of the

LLC is usually determined when the organization papers are filed. The time limit can be continued, if desired, by a vote of the members at the time of expiration.

In summary, deciding the form of ownership that best suits your inspecting business should be given careful consideration. Use your key advisors to assist you in the process.

"I formed a corporation or limited liability company. Now what?" or Asset Protection for Inspectors

by Nick Gromicko and Mark Cohen, Esq.

An asset is anything of value in your name, such as a house, a vehicle, your business, and even your bank account. Unfortunately, if you are successfully sued by someone who is unhappy with the results of the work you performed—regardless of whether the lawsuit has merit—attempts will likely be made to tap some of your assets as compensation if you wind up on the losing side. In order to protect your home and personal property from being exposed to such liability, along with your business assets beyond your E&O insurance, it's important to safeguard all your assets through a collection of techniques known as asset protection. Taking some of these urgent precautions will ensure that, in the event that you lose a lawsuit brought against you and your inspection business, your home, personal vehicle, and other personal property will be exempt from garnishment, repossession or seizure. It will also provide you with the opportunity to rebuild your business.

Approximately 50,000 lawsuits are filed daily in the United States, which equals one lawsuit for every 17 Americans, annually. In professions that are predisposed to litigation, such as home inspection, medicine, law and business, the chances of being sued are considerably higher, although unscrupulous opportunists may target anyone who they perceive as having deep pockets. And there are plenty of ways besides litigation that unprotected assets can be taken away, such as through identity theft, divorce, death, healthcare costs, probate, auto accidents, home fires, floods and bankruptcy, to name a few. Any of these events can ruin someone's finances if they lack proper asset protection.

The first things every new small business owner should consider include the following.

First, incorporate. Incorporating a business limits the owner's personal liability in lawsuits filed against the business because a corporation or LLC, under Western legal systems, is considered under the law to be a separate legal entity from its owners. Therefore, the owners of an entity are not personally liable for the debts of the entity. This limited liability is an inherent purpose for incorporation. However, this protection is not absolute. Employing a remedy known as "piercing the corporate veil," a court may disregard the separateness of a corporation or LLC when failure to do so would bring about an injustice, or when it can be proven that the business owners did not obey corporate formalities.

Typically, courts will not allow the corporate veil to be pierced, except in certain factual circumstances.

Courts consider a variety of factors to determine whether the corporate form should be disregarded, including:

- whether the corporation is operated as a separate entity;
- commingling of funds with other assets;
- the failure to maintain adequate corporate records;
- the nature of the corporation's ownership and control;
- the absence of corporate assets and under-capitalization;
- the use of the corporation as a mere shell;

- the disregard of legal formalities; and

- diversion of the corporation's funds or assets for non-corporate uses.

Generally, if an entity looks like it is not the alter ego of its owner(s), the courts will treat it as a separate entity. While every case is different, there are steps the inspector may take to reduce the risk that a court might pierce the corporate veil of the inspector's business entity.

The following strategies are recommended:

1. Obtain a separate Employer Identification Number (also known as an EIN or Taxpayer ID number) from the IRS. Corporations are required to do this, but LLCs with a single owner are not because a single-member LLC owner may use his or her Social Security Number. Nevertheless, we recommend that single-member LLCs obtain their own separate EIN.

2. Open a separate bank account for your corporation or LLC.

3. Do not mix personal money and business money.

4. Do not pay personal expenses from a business account.

5. Do not pay business expenses from a personal account.

6. File the required annual report with the Secretary of State in your jurisdiction.

7. File required tax returns for your business.

8. Title business property in the name of the entity.

9. File business property tax returns if required by your state.

10. Prepare minutes of meetings of shareholders and directors (for corporations), and minutes for annual meetings of members (for LLCs).

11. If the corporation or LLC has more than one owner, make sure there are written bylaws (for a corporation) or a written operating agreement (for an LLC).

12. Keep licenses and insurance in the name of the entity.

13. Make sure the public knows your business is a corporation or LLC. If a customer knows he or she is doing business with a corporation or LLC and voluntarily chooses to do so, the customer is not in a good position to ask a court to pierce the corporate veil. On the other hand, if the customer has no knowledge of the existence of a separate entity, a court may determine that equity requires it to pierce the corporate veil. Therefore, the wise inspector puts the public on notice by including "Inc." or "LLC" on the inspector's website, advertisements, forms, and business cards.

14. Use a family limited partnership (FLP). Family limited partnerships are specially designed partnerships that consist of general and limited partners. The FLP allows an individual to maintain full control and enjoyment of their property while separating themselves from actual legal ownership. A creditor of a single partner cannot reach the assets owned by the partnership because the partnership, as an entity, owns the asset. This does not prevent the partnership from being sued, but it will keep certain assets separate and unexposed to legal liability or claim.

15. Purchase professional liability or errors and omissions (E&O) insurance. The cost of insurance premiums is generally small compared to the cost of defending a lawsuit.

16. Keep major assets encumbered. If you own property free and clear, you can imagine how attractive that is to a judgment creditor. Many inspectors lease their company vehicles to prevent them from becoming a target.

17. Check your state's homestead exemption. Homestead property protection laws help protect your home from creditors, as well as help provide survivors with a home after the death of the primary wage-earner.

If you think this is all just abstract legal theory, you might read the opinion of the Indiana Court of Appeals in ABC Home & Real Estate Inspection, Inc. v. Plummer, 500 N.E.2d 1257 (Indiana App. 1987). In that case, the inspector's corporation never issued stock, the inspector advertised himself as the "owner" of the business, and the inspector kept his contractor's license in his name rather than in the corporation's name, so the trial court determined that the inspector's corporation was a "sham" and was the mere "alter ego" of the inspector. The inspector appealed, but the Indiana Court of Appeals determined that the trial court properly pierced the corporate veil, and the inspector was personally liable to the home buyers.

To be effective, asset protection should be performed years before you find yourself in financial trouble. Any transfer of ownership of property after the emergence of a significant claim may be deemed fraudulent, which can result not only in seizure of the asset anyway, but significant civil penalties. After a claim arises, you need debtor and possibly pre-bankruptcy planning, as asset protection becomes more difficult as legal proceedings progress. Most importantly, have an attorney and an accountant guide you through the process of asset protection. You need these experts to make sure that asset-protection planning is performed competently and within the parameters of the law. Professionals will make sure that you use appropriate legal structures to safeguard your assets without deliberately defrauding creditors.

In summary, inspectors should invest in legal asset-protection strategies to keep their business assets separate from their personal assets, and also to ensure that, should they face a tough legal battle, they will be able to re-establish themselves after the dust settles.

Mark Cohen is General Counsel for the International Association of Certified Home Inspectors.

Code of Ethics

"Being good is good business."

—Anita Roddick,
founder of The Body Shop

Every inspector should have his/her own Code of Ethics. Consumers look for licensing in their inspectors (if required by their state), but remember that licensing is just a minimum requirement. What will separate you from your competitors is your customer service, and part of that is spelling out who you are. A code of ethics is similar to a mission statement in that it articulates and crystallizes who you are as a businessperson based on the standards you embrace. But it focuses more on your duty to your clients and to your industry. Regardless of whether your state licensing authority and any associations you have membership in have their own code of ethics that binds you, your own code of ethics, posted on your website (and, optionally, in any marketing materials), is a declaration of self-accountability that you share with the people who are deciding whether to hire you.

To follow are some suggestions for categories and items you can consider and adapt in creating your own business Code of Ethics. You can make your Code as brief or as elaborate as you want, but make it easily readable and readily understandable.

Avoid being redundant; opt for brevity. Format it so that it's user-friendly. Finally, incorporate items that describe what you're committed to doing, including the standards of behavior and business practices that you would expect of your inspector if you were the client.

(Remember that your Code of Ethics applies to any staff and crew in your employ. They should be made aware of what it means to uphold it, as well as any consequences for violating it.)

InterNACHI's International Code of Ethics for Home Inspectors

The International Association of Certified Home Inspectors (InterNACHI) promotes a high standard of professionalism, business ethics and inspection procedures. InterNACHI members subscribe to the following Code of Ethics in the course of their business.

I. Duty to the Public

1. The InterNACHI member shall abide by the Code of Ethics and substantially follow the InterNACHI Standards of Practice.

2. The InterNACHI member shall not engage in any practices that could be damaging to the public or bring discredit to the home inspection industry.

3. The InterNACHI member shall be fair, honest, impartial, and act in good faith in dealing with the public.

4. The InterNACHI member shall not discriminate in any business activities on the basis of race, color, religion, sex, national origin, familial status, sexual orientation, or handicap, and shall comply with all federal, state and local laws concerning discrimination.

5. The InterNACHI member shall be truthful regarding his/her services and qualifications.

6. The InterNACHI member shall not:

    a. have any disclosed or undisclosed conflict of interest with the client;

    b. accept or offer any disclosed or undisclosed commissions, rebates, profits, or other benefit from real estate agents, brokers, or any third parties having financial interest in the sale of the property; or

    c. offer or provide any disclosed or undisclosed financial compensation directly or indirectly to any real estate agent, real estate broker, or real estate company for referrals or for inclusion on lists of preferred and/or affiliated inspectors or inspection companies.

7. The InterNACHI member shall not release any information about the inspection or the client to a third party unless doing so is necessary to protect the safety of others, to comply with a law or statute, or both of the following conditions are met:

    a. the client has been made explicitly aware of what information will be released, to whom, and for what purpose, and;

    b. the client has provided explicit, prior written consent for the release of his/her information.

8. The InterNACHI member shall always act in the interests of the client unless doing so violates a law, statute, or this Code of Ethics.

9. The InterNACHI member shall use a written contract that specifies the services to be performed, limitations of services, and fees.

10. The InterNACHI member shall comply with all government rules and licensing requirements of the jurisdiction where s/he conducts business.

11. The InterNACHI member shall not perform or offer to perform, for an additional fee, any repairs or associated services to the structure for which the member or member's company has prepared a home inspection report for a period of 12 months. This provision shall not include services to components and/or systems that are not included in the InterNACHI Standards of Practice.

II. Duty to Continue Education

1. The InterNACHI member shall comply with InterNACHI's current Continuing Education requirements.

2. The InterNACHI member shall pass InterNACHI's Online Inspector Exam once every three years.

III. Duty to the Profession and to InterNACHI

1. The InterNACHI member shall strive to improve the home inspection industry by sharing his/her lessons and/or experiences for the benefit of all. This does not preclude the member from copyrighting or marketing his/her expertise to other Inspectors or the public in any manner permitted by law.

2. The InterNACHI member shall assist the InterNACHI leadership in disseminating and publicizing the benefits of InterNACHI membership.

3. The InterNACHI member shall not engage in any act or practice that could be deemed damaging, seditious or destructive to InterNACHI, fellow InterNACHI members, InterNACHI employees, leadership or directors. Accusations of a member acting or deemed in violation of such rules shall trigger a review by the Ethics Committee for possible sanctions and/or expulsion from InterNACHI.

4. The InterNACHI member shall abide by InterNACHI's current membership requirements.

5. The InterNACHI member shall abide by InterNACHI's current message board rules.

Members of other associations are welcome to join InterNACHI, but a requirement of membership is that InterNACHI must be given equal or greater prominence in their marketing materials (brochures and websites) compared to other associations of membership.

Read InterNACHI's COE online at www.nachi.org/code_of_ethics

The Code of Ethics for commercial property inspectors, as outlined in the **International Standards of Practice for Inspecting Commercial Properties (ComSOP)**, is similar:

9. Ethics

Inspectors performing inspections in accordance with this Standard must maintain a high level of business ethics.

9.1 Duty to Client

9.1.1 The inspector shall substantially follow this Standard unless the Scope of Work indicates otherwise.

9.1.2 The inspector shall not engage in any practices that could be damaging to the client or bring discredit to the inspection industry.

9.1.3 The inspector shall be fair, honest, impartial, and act in good faith in dealing with the client.

9.1.4 The inspector shall not discriminate on the basis of race, color, religion, sex, national origin, familial status, or handicap, and shall comply with all applicable federal, state and local laws concerning discrimination.

9.1.5 The inspector-member shall be truthful regarding his/her services and qualifications.

9.1.6 The inspector shall have no undisclosed conflict of interest with the client, nor shall the inspector accept or offer any undisclosed commissions, rebates, profits or other benefit, nor shall the inspector accept or offer any disclosed or undisclosed commissions, rebates, profits or other benefit from real estate agents, brokers or any third parties having financial interest in the sale of the property, nor shall the inspector offer or provide any disclosed or undisclosed financial compensation directly or indirectly to any real estate agent, real estate broker or real estate company for referrals or for inclusion on lists of preferred and/or affiliated inspectors or inspection companies.

9.1.7 The inspector shall not communicate any information about an inspection to anyone except the client without the prior written consent of the client, except in cases when the information may affect the safety of others, or violates a law or statute.

9.1.8 The inspector shall always act in the interest of the client, unless doing so violates a law or statute.

9.1.9 The inspector shall use a written Scope of Work Agreement that specifies the services to be performed, the limitations of services, and fees.

9.1.10 The inspector shall comply with all government rules and licensing requirements in the jurisdiction where he/she conducts business.

9.1.11 The inspector shall not perform or offer to perform, for an additional fee, any repairs or repair-associated services to the structure for which the inspector or inspector's company has prepared a commercial inspection report for a period of 12 months. This provision shall not include services to components and/or systems which are not included in this Standard.

Read the Code of Ethics online at www.nachi.org/comsop.htm#9

Read the ComSOP in its entirety at www.nachi.org/comsop

Inspector Selection: A Real Estate Agent's Duty

It doesn't hurt to remind the real estate professionals you deal with that you both are ethically bound to serve the interests of your clients. But that doesn't mean they should suggest that their clients hire the cheapest or "softest" inspector. Here's an article to pass along to them.

The seller has accepted your clients' offer and now, with your help, your clients must choose a home inspector. Should you steer them toward the inspector who writes the softest reports? Should you steer them toward the inspector who pays to be on your office's preferred vendor list? Should you help them find the cheapest inspector? The answers to these questions are of course No, No, and Hell, no.

You have a fiduciary duty to your client and, therefore, must recommend the very best inspectors. If you recommend a "patty-cake" inspector, an inspector who indirectly pays for your recommendation, or a cheap inspector, you violate your fiduciary duty to your client.

The National Association of REALTORS® defines your duties in their Code of Ethics. Article 1 requires you to protect and promote your clients' interests. Article 6 requires you to disclose any financial benefit you may receive from recommending related real estate services (this also includes any benefit to your broker).

Because most real estate agents get paid only if the real estate transaction successfully takes place, your personal interests and your fiduciary duties already conflict. Don't make your situation any worse. The best way to avoid negligent referral claims, to operate ethically, and to fulfill your fiduciary duty is to help your client find an inspector based solely on merit. And although no real estate agent can guarantee the thoroughness of any particular inspector, there is a strong correlation between an inspector's fees and his/her competence (in other words, you get what you pay for). Helping your client find a cheap inspector for the purchase of their lifetime is a violation of your fiduciary duty. When in doubt, shop price, and seek out the most expensive inspectors for your clients.

Tip: Use the article "How Agents Can Limit Their Liability" at www.nachi.org/agenthelp to help real estate agents limit their liability with regard to inspections.

Advanced Tip: Get your favorite agents to register for and receive free negligent referral protection from claims by homeowners at www.nachi.org/agent-indemnification

Almost Everything You Do Can Generate Leads

Like it or not, marketing is crucial to any successful inspection business. The strength of your marketing program can make or break your company because the object of all of your marketing is lead generation.

Inspectors often complain that they have too much work or not enough work. Creating a steady pipeline of leads will end these complaints. Once you do this, you'll have quality leads that will allow you pick and choose the projects you want, attract the types of clients you want to work for, and pre-sell your services before you even book the job. Almost everything you do can generate leads—that's the goal. But have you thought about where you're at now?

"The leads are weak? The [bleeping] leads are weak? You're weak."

—Alec Baldwin as Blake in "Glengarry Glen Ross"

Every successful enterprise started by defining its mission. So, that's where we'll begin.

At the Tone, Please Hang Up and Call My Competitor

You've probably done a lot of marketing to get your phone to ring. Don't let it all go to waste. Convert every call into a scheduled appointment. Make sure someone who can convert or sell is actually answering your business phone. If your potential customers are reaching voicemail, an answering service, or an untrained employee or spouse, you are probably not converting many of them into appointments.

Many inspectors refuse to allow their cell phones to interrupt them at a job. This is a mistake. The client you're performing work for is already sold. His/her money is in the bank. The prospect calling you is new money. Get that new money.

The Red Phone

All inspectors should have a dedicated phone number—and even a dedicated phone—that's used only for new business. In fact, this dedicated phone should be red in color (which you can easily make by using a basic colored cell phone cover). An actual red phone is your instant reminder that there is no phone call that you'll answer all day that's more important than a call for new business. This red phone should have the phone number you would list in any and all advertising that's designed to acquire new clients, such as emails and newsletters to new potential customers, print ads, truck signage, yard signs, billboards, brochures and direct mail.

You can use a different "main" number for vendors, in your contracts, and for general business use. That way, you or your staff can man the red phone and leave the other phone number to be used primarily for everyday, routine business. The red phone should always be manned because it means new business, and you should never let new business slip away under any circumstances.

If you're a one-person operation, be sure to ask your clients whether they'd mind if you took calls during your meeting with them; most of them won't object if you ask in advance. Let your everyday phone calls go to voicemail if you're busy, but always answer your red phone. Prospective clients won't be interested in leaving you a voicemail; they'll just move on to the next inspector. If you carry both phones with you out in the field, make sure your everyday phone is turned off during meetings. Make both your phones' ringtones different so that you know which phone is ringing, alerting you to pick up any red-phone calls. Again, if you're meeting with a client, ask for permission to answer your phone during the meeting. Your client's confidence in you will increase if s/he sees that you are in demand from other consumers trying to hire you.

Tip: Think of a phone call the way a football receiver thinks of a pass and try to "catch the call."

Toll-Free Numbers

Avoid using toll-free numbers. Unless you're a national company, you'll only be working locally, so why offer the illusion that you're saving your prospective clients any money with a simple phone call? Besides, customers will choose the local inspector with the local area code. They want to talk to the actual inspector who'll be working for them. A toll-free number implies an impersonal, non-local corporation that will send someone out whom the client won't get to speak to beforehand. A few very cheap customers appreciate toll-free numbers to save a few pennies. Let your competitors have those customers.

Vanity Numbers

Don't use alpha-numeric phone numbers, such as "1-800-INSPECTOR," unless you also display the numbers in parentheses after it. No one enjoys having to decipher a clever vanity number.

The one exception to this rule is the phone number you have on a vehicle sign. You may have only an instant to make an impression, so a word as the phone number (or partial phone number) is actually easier for people to remember.

After Hours

If you accept new business calls after hours, keep your red phone on and your other phones off. One way to prevent website visitors from hesitating to call you after hours is to add something along the lines of the following sentence under your red phone's phone number: *"Please don't call after 9:30 p.m."* Many consumers are on your website in the evening and this sentence will let them know that it's OK to call you at 8:15 p.m. It also implies that they will get YOU—the inspector, in person.

Receptionist's Flowchart

Whoever answers your phone better be a polite, efficient, natural-born salesperson. Your receptionist is more important than anyone else in your company. Your receptionist is on the front line of the battle.

Create a flowchart for your receptionist that helps him/her respond appropriately, reminds him/her to emphasize certain points with the caller, and to collect certain information from the caller. The flowchart can be referred to each time a call veers off into unexpected territory. Your receptionist should alert you every time s/he is unsure of how to respond to a caller who takes the conversation in a different direction so that the flowchart can be updated.

Tip: Have someone call your company regularly and secretly brief you on their experience. Did a live person answer your phone? How many rings did it take before the call was answered? Did the receptionist ask for the caller's contact information?

Inspection Sales Script Generator

Create a customized inspection sales script by checking off boxes and filling in blanks. It includes all the pertinent details to automatically generate an inspection sales script that will be optimized to make you appear to be the perfect choice of inspector. Visit www.nachi.org/script to learn more.

The SoundSmart Call Converter

You only get one chance to make a good first impression. Keep the SoundSmart page open in a window of your computer and ready to use to convert incoming callers into scheduled inspections.

Consumers often have particular concerns that they reveal when they call. Simply click on the issue and SoundSmart will provide you with short, concise talking points while you're on the phone. It's like having a little helper on your shoulder, whispering in your ear!

Each set of talking points is followed by useful, related links. Both the talking points and the links are ordered by their usefulness.

You can also print particular articles that SoundSmart provides links to. You can then review these articles before the inspection, give copies of the articles to your clients, and include the articles as attachments to your inspection reports. These copyrighted articles are free for InterNACHI members' use. Members may use them as they wish.

You can also email your potential client the links to these articles. An easy way to do this is to ask for the caller's email early in the conversation and compose and send an email that includes the links to choice articles.

You can also use the Inspection Fee Calculator to bid the inspection project. A link to open it in a new window from SoundSmart is provided. The fee is based on a Base Price, a Mileage Factor, an Age Factor, and a Size Factor. Then enter the home's distance, age, size, and how busy you are in order to calculate the inspection fee.

You can also use the Inspection Time Slot Estimator found at www.nachi.org/time-slot (don't forget to set up the light gray box first!) to schedule the inspection project. A link to open it in a new window from SoundSmart is provided. The time slot estimate is based on Base Time, Occupied Status, Client Accompanying Status, a Distance Factor, an Age Factor, a Size Factor, and Ancillary Services Time (all of which you pre-set in the light gray box). Then, enter the home's distance, whether it is occupied or not, whether or not your client will be accompanying you, the age of the home, the size of the home, and any ancillary inspections ordered to calculate the time slot estimate.

You can also sign the caller up for your Home Maintenance Newsletter. A link to open it in a new window from SoundSmart is provided.

Once you sell the inspection project, you might want to use InterNACHI's free, Online Inspection Agreement System.

And, finally, SoundSmart provides a link to a list of technical refresher articles at the bottom of the Consumer Concern choices.

SoundSmart is built on one page with bookmarks for lightning-fast navigation during an incoming call. Don't answer your inspection business phone without the SoundSmart page loaded and ready to help you... sound smart! Learn more at www.nachi.org/soundsmartintro

On Hold

It is now fairly inexpensive to adopt a phone system with custom "on-hold" advertising for your company. You can even do the voice work yourself using the microphone on your laptop. Your message could tell your caller about your company and the services you offer. An on-hold message can greatly increase a caller's patience by answering routine questions in advance of their actual conversation with you so they won't feel that their time is being wasted while being on hold.

Logos and Taglines for Inspectors

Good design is about quick and clear communication. There's a science behind how people judge beauty, which can be applied to how information is visually organized. This information can be used to your benefit or your detriment. Especially in professions such as inspection, you must stand out from your competition and demonstrate—in an instant—that you have an appealing visual aesthetic. Good marketing materials and especially a good logo do this, and more.

Design is, first and foremost, a method of communication. Everyone has heard the phrase: "A picture is worth a thousand words." Good marketing design works on a subconscious level. For the consumer, the quality of your logo subconsciously translates into the quality of your service. The advent of innovative design software that's available in most retail stores has raised the bar on the quality of visual design.

Download InterNACHI logos, webseals & taglines for your brochures & website at <u>www.nachi.org/logos</u>

Leave Your Logo Design to a Pro

Unless you're a mechanic yourself, you wouldn't take your vehicle to a mechanic and tell him/her exactly what's wrong with it and exactly how to fix it. You take your vehicle to him/her because you need the help of someone with professional training. The same goes for being an inspector. And the same goes for marketing designers. A designer is not merely a decorative artist, but a professional who understands how to visually organize elements in a way that is both engaging and visually appealing. Designers are trained to understand the ins and outs of visual structure. Everyone can recognize a good or bad design subconsciously, which leads to the false assumption that anyone can create a good design. However, a good designer can tell you why something is effective, as well as why it fails, in precisely the same way that a mechanic can tell you the same things about your car.

You may have the software, but you still need the training and skills to come up with the marketing design and logo that will sell your services. Don't spend valuable time trying to teach yourself what others have been educated and trained to do for you. Every business worldwide is paying more attention to how they market. The businesses and people you compete with directly are paying attention to your marketing design, so you should, too. Even if you have plenty of experience, a poor design for your business will make you appear amateurish and, fairly or not, it will reflect on the quality of your services.

Save yourself time and money in the long run and have your logo designed by a professional. If you're just starting out, a good design will make your company look established immediately. On the flip side, even if you have 20 years' experience, a poor design will make you appear unprofessional and out of touch. A good design will give you the appearance of both credibility and experience no matter how long you've been in business.

Remember: You are not a marketing designer. That's the only argument you need to convince yourself to have your marketing professionally done, including your logo. Don't worry—a good designer will ask you what's important to you and will find a way to incorporate those principles into your design.

Logo Design Tips

Here are some more important tips to remember to effectively market your inspection business using a great logo:

- Your logo should cause your prospective customers to immediately associate it with the products and services you offer.

- If you're planning to alter or expand your business, products or services down the road, you can make your logo a little more flexible and generic by adding a tagline under it that you can later change as your company changes.

- Make sure that your design isn't so similar to a competitor's that it infringes on their trademark. Your logo should be distinctive, and you want to avoid legal hassles.

- If your logo is in color, it should also work in black and white so that it is legible when photocopied.

- Your logo should be available in vector format so that it can be scaled to any size without pixelating or losing its sharpness.

- When you have your logo designed by a professional, make sure that you obtain all the file formats necessary for use in your various marketing channels. Also, make sure you retain all copyrights to your design so that you can use it freely, and so that if someone else's design looks too similar to yours, you will have legal recourse to make them change theirs.

Taglines

Taglines are the written equivalent of logos. The main role of a tagline is to quickly communicate what you do. It shouldn't be cute or fancy. It's the sign over your storefront. It should be placed under your logo. A tagline is especially important for inspection companies that don't have the word "inspection" in their company's name.

For example:

ABC Enterprises

[Your Company] is [Your City]'s Premier [Your Service] Company

Tips for Taglines

- Your tagline should be punctuated properly, meaning that if it's not a complete sentence (following the standard rules of grammar), it shouldn't have a period at the end of it. It's okay that a phrase has no punctuation mark at the end of it. On the other hand, exclamation points can serve where a period would be improper because text that is specifically for marketing can bend the rules of proper grammar and punctuation. However, you must break the rules discreetly; people may notice a misplaced period or comma, so, as the saying goes, "When in doubt, leave it out."

- Never put your tagline inside quotation marks. Quotation marks are reserved for quoted words that have actually been spoken by someone, such as testimonials by past clients. Quotation marks are never to be used for general emphasis. This is one punctuation rule you cannot break. Unfortunately, you will often see quotation marks misused in marketing text—in brochures, in window signage, on work vehicles, etc. It's always wrong, and it's the telltale sign of amateurish marketing. Don't fall for it. The pros will know, and these pros may be your future high-end customers.

- Instead of misusing quotation marks, always italicize your tagline. Not only does this lend your tagline the emphasis that you desire, but it also highlights its proprietary nature, topped off by the trademark symbol at the end.

- Trademark your tagline by adding the superscript "TM" after it. This is the equivalent of copyrighting your original work by adding your name, the copyright symbol (©) and the year. It's not necessary to "officially" copyright something in order to own that copyright and be legally protected. By the same token, you don't necessarily need to register your trademarked tagline with the federal government, although you will be afforded greater protections if you do. (For one thing, it will allow you to use the registered trademark symbol, which is ®.) Whichever path you choose— self-trademarking or filing for a federally registered trademark—be sure you use the superscript "TM" symbol immediately upon disseminating your tagline on your website and in marketing materials. Also, create a Google Alert for that phrase to track down those who may infringe on your rights by using your tagline. Threaten legal action in all cases; your trademark is as precious to you as your logo, so protect it.

- Visit InterNACHI's page of trademarked Logos, Webseals & Taglines at www.nachi.org/logos to find the right items for your website and marketing materials.

Bringing Clean Air to Life® is one such tagline that you can use to promote your indoor air quality inspection services. It's a registered trademark for use by InterNACHI and IAC2 members.

The Right Inspector, Right Away® is a great multi-inspector tagline. It's a registered trademark for free use by InterNACHI members.

Anyone else is just looking around® is another great tagline to promote your inspection business. It's a registered trademark for free use by InterNACHI members.

Have a Tagline for Each Service

Don't limit yourself to just one tagline if you offer more than one service. There is some wisdom in using one tagline for brand recognition, but if you offer different services, you can stick with the same logo and swap out your taglines instead. Remember that people are visual creatures, so your logo should be the same across the board.

Business Cards

Business cards are so inexpensive that it's affordable to have different business cards for the different inspection services you specialize in. If you're going on an appointment for a particular service, bring your corresponding business card.

Tips for Business Cards

- Use the back of your different business cards to emphasize each different service you offer.
- Make sure that your full-color logo is on the front.
- Make sure that your full contact information is on them, including your website address and "red phone" number for new business.

You should also consider getting a business card holder for the outside of your work vehicle. Some manufacturers sell card holders with suction cups so that you can attach one to your truck. At an inspection appointment, place it on the exterior of your truck on the side that faces foot traffic.

Brochures

You only get one chance to make a good first impression.

The home inspection business is different than any other business in that you don't get to meet your client until *after* s/he hires you. This means that the home inspection business is almost all marketing, and very little sales. A key part of successful marketing is your home inspection brochure, and many consumers will decide whether or not to call you based on it. Since your client won't get to meet you until after you're hired, your home inspection brochure—not you—defines your image. You might only get this one shot, so make it a good one.

We all have strengths and weaknesses. Being able to identify your own may be difficult, but it can be very beneficial. Some weaknesses can be improved quickly, but others may require so much time that it may not be worth the effort. If design is not one of your natural talents, you need to recognize that and hire a professional for your marketing materials. But if you intend to create your own business brochure, start by collecting good brochures and make note of the design details that make them outstanding.

The Goal of a Brochure

The main purpose of an inspector's brochure is to:

- generate leads;
- provide documentation to justify higher prices; and
- sell additional services.

In short, a brochure's goal is to sell more inspection services to more people, more often, for more money.

Synergy

A good brochure is one of the three critical parts of successful home inspection marketing, those being:

1. its quality and design;
2. the proliferation of your contact information on the Internet, where all the home buyers are nowadays; and
3. your certification by a prominent industry organization, such as the International Association of Certified Home Inspectors.

These three critical parts are intertwined. When a home buyer types "certified home inspectors" into Google, they are lead to one of many InterNACHI-owned websites. There they will find your contact information and can request your information (a brochure), which states that you are certified… and so on… with each part reinforcing the others.

Bad Brochures Un-Sell

A quality brochure implies that you are a veteran inspector, and a cheap brochure implies that you are new to the business. If you are a veteran inspector with a home-printed, cheap brochure, you will look new to the business. By the same token, a high-quality brochure makes the statement that you're a pro, even if you're just starting out. A brochure can sell or un-sell. It's up to you.

Manufacturers' Brochures

Many inspection product manufacturers offer brochures that you can adapt for your company's use. Some even offer to help you pay to have them printed. But they aren't helping you by paying to print your brochure—you're helping them pay for theirs. They're promoting themselves and their product, not you. So, don't use them. You can have your own brochure that is equally professional-looking and that works solely for your business, and not someone else's.

Delivering the Message

If your brochure design is just a hodgepodge of material without a well-planned, focused message, don't even print it. What is the message you want to convey?

Answer: *I am the quality inspector you want to hire.*

Headlines

Headlines are often all that people read. If you can say the same thing using fewer words, do it. The reader is scanning your brochure, so your headlines should read like that of a news story. Brochures are nothing more than garbage on the way to the trash can. Your job is to get a message delivered on the way to the trash, so keep your headlines short. If you must break a long headline by continuing on to a second line so that it fits on a tri-fold brochure, try to find a natural break, with the second line being longer than the first, if possible. But breaking at the natural pause takes precedence.

Worst:

*ABC Inspections Is Num-
ber One in Kentucky*

Better:

*ABC Inspections Is
Number One in Kentucky*

Best:

*ABC Inspections
Is Number One in Kentucky*

Another mistake is to put a period at the end of a headline. Periods stop the reader from going further. Their use may also be wrong in terms of the rules of punctuation. In headlines in marketing materials, just skip them.

Nothing to Brag About

Avoid "minimum expectation" taglines or slogans.

For example:

*ABC Inspections
Thorough and friendly service is our motto.*

Your service had better be thorough and friendly! There is general overuse of the words "thorough," "professional" and "quality" within the inspection industry. Avoid such cliché adjectives.

Here's a better slogan:

*ABC Inspections
Done once, done right!*

Words That Sell

The overall impression your brochure conveys is more important than the actual information. There are certain words that sell inspection services.

- "You" and "Your": Talk directly to your reader. Instead of writing, "*Our clients receive the service...*" try, "*You will receive the service...*"

- "I": If you're a one-man operation, say so. Customers seek personal service. Instead of writing, "*Our company's goal is...* or "*We at ABC Inspections seek to...*" try, "*I will perform...*"

- "Easy": Home buyers don't want their lives made more difficult at this time.
  So, write: "*Your report will be easy to read and understand.*"

- "Benefit": Most home inspection brochures do state the benefit of a home inspection. However, they neglect to actually include the word "*benefit.*" So, perhaps write, "*As an added benefit, ABC Inspections...*"

- "Certified": Anyone can say whatever they want about themselves. The word "certified" is the ultimate testimonial (more on this later). Use this word.

Your Photo

A picture of you is a must. You're not selling a product… you're selling yourself. You are the product. However, while you can't judge a book by its cover, many people do, so reconsider using a photo of yourself if you look:

- very overweight. It implies that you can't do the work yourself;

- very young. It implies that you are inexperienced; and/or

- like a mass-murderer.

If you're male and have a ponytail, hide it in the photo. You want the reader to identify with you. Keep your picture as simple as possible. Consider using digital air-brushing to touch up your photo. Don't wear a tie, except for maybe in "My Promise to You" (explained below). This is too professional-looking and implies that you are so dressed up that you won't inspect a crawlspace. Also, don't wear a t-shirt. This is too unprofessional. You are a step above that; you inspect the work done by men in t-shirts. Try to find a middle ground, such as a collared shirt with the top button undone. Read InterNACHI's article on inspector attire at www.nachi.org/attire

Other Photos & Images

Make sure each picture earns its keep. Each image should help sell your service. Perhaps the photo could show you working at a job. Each picture should help sell your service. Perhaps the picture could be of you using a SureTest® meter. Sell yourself. You cannot bore people into hiring you. See www.nachi.org/images

Don't Be Silly

Avoid cartoons. Cartoon graphics do not present a professional image. Would a professional engineer use cartoons? And don't use puns or clever plays on words. Strike the right tone.

Captions

Make sure every photo and illustration has a caption below it. Each caption must be an ad within itself. Each caption must promise the reader a benefit. If you include a picture or illustration of your report, don't have the caption read: "*Our reporting system.*" Instead, have it read: "*Detailed yet easy-to-read report!*" Also, a picture of a sample report is smart. Cookbook recipes always show a picture of the finished dish.

Testimonials

Add a few quotes from satisfied agents and clients. The use of short references works, but you should always get permission first.

Don't include anonymous quotes, which can be dismissed as fake. Testimonials must include a name and a city. Only credible testimonials work. Do clean them up to make them error-free, but don't change their content.

"ABC Inspections did a great job, finding defects even the seller wasn't aware of. I highly recommend ABC Inspections."
—Mrs. Jane Smith, Toledo, Ohio

Tip: To assure even greater believability, ask your clients for permission to display their pictures next to their testimonials.

Don't Preach to the Choir

Don't waste your time and advertising budget on helping the entire home inspection industry. Including "Reasons to Have a Home Inspection" is a waste of prime advertising space. Anyone reading a home inspection brochure is past the stage where they need to be sold on getting an inspection. Instead of telling the reader why they should want a home inspection in general, tell them why they should want your home inspection services.

For instance, instead of stating merely that you are a member of InterNACHI, state something like this:

My Qualifications:

- *I am a member in good standing of the International Association of Certified Home Inspectors (InterNACHI).*
- *I have passed InterNACHI's Online Inspector Examination.*
- *I abide by InterNACHI's strict Code of Ethics.*
- *I follow InterNACHI's Standards of Practice.*
- *I fulfill 24 hours of Continuing Education and inspection-related training every year.*

Additionally:

- *I own and use state-of-the-art inspection equipment, including a gas leak detector and an infrared camera.*
- *I am available evenings and Saturdays.*
- *Your easy-to-read report will be emailed to you within 24 hours.*

Make Them Want You

Make your list of qualifications as long as possible. List your direct work experience, your licenses, your special training and qualifications, and any higher education you've acquired (including the name of the school), even if your degree is not directly related to your business.

Breathing Room

White space is a tool to use sparingly. Make lists of related items compact. Then use white or blank space around them to clarify and set off those groupings of related items. Be consistent with the spacing and margins throughout the brochure, but don't overdo it. Give your readers enough information to hire you. Direct-mail advertisers use long body copy because it works (and they know it). Your list of qualifications can practically run right off the bottom of the brochure, as if you didn't have enough room to list them all.

Insurance

List the fact that you carry general liability and E&O insurance. Always offset your premium costs by exploiting your policy for marketing purposes.

"My Promise"

The following is text you could adapt to add to your brochure. It's a promise. Include a headshot of yourself looking straight into the camera, positioned above the promise. Add your signature on a slight angle below it. Few people will actually read the promise word for word, but the message will be conveyed nonetheless.

My Promise to You

Choosing the right home inspector can be difficult. Unlike most professionals you hire, you probably won't meet me until our appointment. Furthermore, different inspectors have varying qualifications, equipment, experience, reporting methods, and pricing.

Ultimately, a thorough home inspection depends heavily on the individual inspector's own effort. If you honor me by permitting me to inspect your new home, I guarantee that I will give you my very best effort.

This, I promise you.

Ben Gromicko

Ben Gromicko
ABC Home Inspections

Inspected Once, Inspected Right!®

Certifications & Affiliations

Include logos in your brochure that demonstrate third-party certifications and qualifications, and other relevant affiliations. They should be visible on the outside of your brochure. Download InterNACHI logos, webseals and taglines at www.nachi.org/logos

Contact Information

Your contact information should be one local phone number and one professional email address. Avoid toll-free numbers. Avoid filler words, such as "Call today!" Every unnecessary thing you include diminishes the important points you are trying to convey. And put your contact information at the bottom of your brochure. Readers will first look for the phone number near the bottom.

Placement of Your Company Name

Make sure that your company name is at the top of the front of your brochure and not the bottom. Brochure holders used for display on countertops at businesses are designed such that they obscure the text that may be at the bottom of the brochures.

Help Them Read

People are accustomed to reading words that appear in lower case. Using all capital letters is a mistake in that it makes it harder for the reader to recognize the words. All caps tend to be read letter by letter. When in doubt, avoid ALL CAPS.

Fonts

Avoid using many different font types, sizes and colors. It diminishes the continuity of your brochure. Stick to two fonts: one for headlines and one for the body text. "Impact" fonts are best reserved for headings. Impact fonts command attention, and they help the reader determine what's important. Choose a serif font for the body text. Serif fonts exist for a purpose: they help the reader's eye pick up the shape of the letter. Bolding and italicizing do not necessarily count as separate fonts. However, only use them to add emphasis and clarity. And never use comic fonts… you are a professional, not an entertainer.

Spelling

Check your spelling and grammar. By the way, it's "peace of mind" and not "piece of mind," and your automatic spellchecker won't catch that one!

Size Matters

Size your brochure to fit in a #10 envelope. You'll want to be able to mail it, so make sure it fits in a standard business-size envelope. Furthermore, most brochure display holders are made to accommodate this size.

Paper

Use glossy, premium brochure paper. Brochures printed on your home printer using 20-pound paper look cheap and flop over in a display holder. Gloss paper with bold colors creates an upscale image. Plain copier paper creates a poor image.

Ink

Avoid light-colored ink. It's simply too hard to read. Light-colored ink is also difficult to copy and fax. If your brochure has light-colored ink, try test-copying and faxing it to yourself to make sure it comes through. Also, avoid reverse copy (white or light-colored text on a dark background) unless it's professionally designed and this design aspect is integrated with the brochure's overall look.

More Than One Weapon

Consumer: *"I'm buying a 100-year old home and I'm looking to have it inspected."*
Inspector: *"I specialize in older homes. Let me email you my brochure."*

Consider having a separate brochure for every target audience. Target specific brochures to:

- home buyers, who are your most frequent customers. Their brochure should emphasize your:
  - thoroughness;
  - the ease of understanding your report; and
  - ancillary services you offer.
- real estate agents, who are less frequent customers. Their brochure should emphasize your:
  - schedule availability;
  - risk-reduction (such as E&O insurance or your contract's hold-harmless clause); and
  - the speed at which you generate the report.
- home sellers, who are your least frequent clients. Their brochure should emphasize your:
  - price;
  - the marketing advantage of a seller's inspection; and
  - disclosure liability reduction.

Remember that your brochure is not likely to be read by the public at large; rather, it's intended for a targeted clientele. If you create more than one version of your brochure, keep them all consistent in their overall look so that your brand isn't obscured by a new design. Just as you may have different business cards for your different services and specialties, they still readily identify one brand—yours.

Tip: It costs the same to print a good brochure as it does to print a bad one. The only difference is in their results.

How Many?

A home inspection brochure should be:

- provided to real estate agents to give to their clients;
- direct-mailed to home sellers (who are likely also local buyers);
- left behind after each home inspection;
- displayed in banks; and
- delivered to attorneys.

If you're planning to have only 1,000 brochures printed, you're planning to fail.

So Sad

An inspector's brochure, like all marketing, is a catalyst or a magnifier. If you offer a poor service, marketing will lead you to your demise quicker. If you do good work, marketing will magnify it. Your brochure is second only to yourself as the key ingredient in achieving success. If you are a good inspector, you have an ethical duty to market so that more of your fellow citizens can learn about and benefit from your good work. It is so sad to see a good inspector with a bad brochure.

You Don't Have to DIY

The easiest way to tackle your business brochure is to have InterNACHI's Member Marketing Department design it for you. From logo to layout to text, your brochure will be professionally designed so that you can compete at your optimum level. It's one of InterNACHI's most popular member benefits, and it's free. You pay only for printing. Visit www.marketing.nachi.org to see what our professional design team can do for you.

Marketing to Professional Marketers

Unlike other professionals, marketing is especially important for inspectors for two important reasons.

First of all, real estate agents have difficulty distinguishing a good inspector from a bad one, but they can instantly recognize great marketing. They respect it. After all, marketing is the business they're in!

Secondly, an inspector's finished product—the report—is essentially a document, an orderly and well thought-out document. And an inspector's brochure is a preview of that finished product. If your brochure looks like something your kid came up with and printed out on your home printer, prospective clients are going to infer that the inspection reports you generate are similarly unprofessional. You simply have to have a professionally designed and printed brochure to compete on a professional level.

Tip: Email InterNACHI's Member Marketing Department at marketing@internachi.org to see what we can do for you. Command the respect of clients and professionals, and keep your inspection calendar booked solid. To view examples of logos and marketing that we have designed for InterNACHI members, visit www.marketing.nachi.org

What Makes You So Special?

What distinguishes you from your competition?

For InterNACHI's Marketing Team (at nachi.org/marketing) to create the most effective marketing materials for you, we'd like you to take some time to think carefully about how your business differs from your competitors'.

Read all of the following questions. It's possible that you've come to take for granted even the most basic tools and services in your arsenal, but they may be the very things that your competitors don't offer. So, think in as much detail as possible about the different things you believe distinguish you from your competition, including tools, inspection services, report features, customer service conveniences, ancillary services, etc.

For example, do you have a work background and/or formal education or training in a field related to home inspections, such as construction, engineering, code compliance, etc.? Do you have multiple certifications and/or licenses? Do you provide thermal imaging as part of your standard home inspection?

Do you carry special tools and equipment, such as an extra-tall ladder or a Spectoscope for inspecting roofs? Do you perform inspections on green/alternative housing? Does your company employ more than one inspector? Do you use certain technology while performing your inspections, such as an iPad? Try to think outside the box!

- Your contractor background and experience make you special to your potential clients. Get the contractor logo at www.nachi.org/logos.htm#contractor (free to members).

- After you become a certified member by successfully completing InterNACHI's core Continuing Education curriculum, take advantage of the **Certified Professional Inspector (CPI)**® designation. Use it in all of your marketing, and download the web seal. It's free to members: www.nachi.org/logos.htm#cpi

- Thermal imaging is a great tool to use for inspections and an impressive skill to market to your prospects. If you're looking for free training, become **Infrared Certified**® at www.nachi.org/ir

- Roof inspections can be made easier, faster and safer by using a **Spectoscope**. Visit www.InspectorOutlet.com to learn more about it.

How many years have you been in business as a home inspector?

- Order your free gold 5-Year Pin (at www.nachi.org/5yearpin) or 10-Year Pin (at www.nachi.org/10yearpin) and wear it on your work clothing for that extra prestige that will impress your clients.

What is your business philosophy? For example, do you pride yourself in running a green business (low carbon footprint, energy offsets, etc.)? Do you employ people from your community? Do you consider yourself First-Time Home Buyer-Friendly? Again, think of things that your competitors cannot claim, and then download the relevant logos and web seals to add to your website and other marketing.

- Become **IAC2-Certified** for Mold and Radon Inspections for free. Visit iac2.org to learn how.

- Become a **Home Energy Inspector** at www.nachi.org/home-energy-inspection. All the training, tools and logos are free to members.

- Advertise yourself as **First-Time Home Buyer-Friendly** at www.nachi.org/first-time. The logo is free to members.

- Find Green Resources, including a free **Green Inspection Checklist**, at www.nachi.org/green

What training and certifications have you attained?

- Find over 30 free certifications, programs, and logos from which to choose at www.nachi.org/logos.htm#services

- Remember that all of InterNACHI's online training and certifications at www.nachi.org/education are free to members.

List your individual inspection services for which you may charge extra, and write a brief description for your clients if the service is not self-explanatory. These inspections may include mold, radon, deck, garage, commercial property, pool & spa, WDO/pests, thermal imaging, child safety, aging-in-place, green building/features, private wells, septic systems, outbuildings, historic homes, mobile/manufactured homes, new-home construction and/or draw-down inspections, multi-unit housing, rural properties, Move-In Certified™ Seller Inspections, etc.

- Read about our ancillary inspection marketing campaign at www.nachi.org/ancillary

- Read about why you should offer **Move-In Certified™ Seller Inspections** at www.moveincertified.com. We offer many free items to help you market this service to home sellers.

List your customer service conveniences. For example, do you have staff that answers phones during regular business hours while you're out on inspections? Do you offer evening and/or weekend appointments? Do you take payments by credit card? Do you encourage clients to attend your inspections so that you can answer their questions? Do you provide a free copy of *Now That You've Had a Home Inspection* home maintenance book with your report? It's also available in Spanish. Are you pet-friendly? Do you include a $10,000 Honor Guarantee™?

- Sound smart on the phone by using **SoundSmart** for incoming customer calls. Keep track of important details for the appointment, and maximize your time on the phone. Learn more about this free tool at www.nachi.org/soundsmartintro

- Accept credit card payments from clients by getting free **merchant accounts** at www.nachi.org/free-merchant-account

- Get InterNACHI's *Now That You've Had a Home Inspection*, the ultimate home maintenance book for clients, at www.nachi.org/now. It's available in Spanish, too!

- Advertise that you're a **Pet-Friendly** inspector by downloading our logo at www.nachi.org/logos.htm#pet and our Pet Safety Checklist at www.InspectorOutlet.com This is another free benefit for members.

- Provide your clients added security with our **$10,000 Honor Guarantee™**. Read more about it at www.nachi.org/honor. It's free for use by members.

List the unique and special aspects of your inspection reports and/or features of your report delivery. For example, do you deliver on-site or same-day reports? Do you offer electronic reports that can be emailed or downloaded from your website? Do your reports include narratives in addition to checklists? Do your reports include digital photos and/or thermal images for comparison? Do you provide online videos or DVDs of your inspections?

- Using special **inspection report software** will help you create professional-looking reports quickly, and you can market this fact to your prospective clients. Find discounted report software at www.InspectorOutlet.com

- Offering convenient online reports is a great way to keep your business green and your report turnaround time fast. Market these desirable features of your services when you use **FetchReport**. Upload your reports for your clients to download at www.nachi.org/fetchreportfriendlyseal

- Get InterNACHI's free **Home Energy Report™** software at www.nachi.org/home-energy-inspection (free to members).

List the other specialties and features of your business not stated previously that make you unique or unusual compared to other inspectors in your service area. For example, do you have a wraparound on your truck that readily identifies you? Do you offer 11th-Month Builder's Warranty Inspections on new builds? Do you inspect built-in and/or portable appliances (if not required by your state)? Do you offer referrals to green contractors who can perform energy upgrades? Do you offer consultations for EEMs or HUD/203Ks? If you're a Florida inspector, do you perform Wind Mitigation or 4-Point Inspections? Do you offer fast turnaround of lab testing results for mold sampling? Do you inspect for special types of events, such as earthquake preparedness or post-disaster inspections (floods, storms, etc.)? Do you offer Home Energy Reports™, Home Energy Inspections, Green Building Inspections, or Log Home Inspections?

List some of the personal details relevant to your business that you think may be of benefit for your marketing. For example, are you a veteran? Have you been a resident of your community for many years? Do you give back to your community by volunteering for or donating to local nonprofits, sports teams, youth organizations, etc.? (This may also be considered part of your business philosophy.)

- Do you have or use a **tagline**, your own or one of InterNACHI's?
    - *The Right Inspector, Right Away*® Use this great multi-inspector tagline. It's a registered trademark for use only by InterNACHI members.
    - *Anyone else is just looking around.*® Use this tagline to promote your inspection business. It's a registered trademark for use only by InterNACHI members.
    - *Bringing Clean Air to Life*® Use this tagline to promote your inspection services related to indoor air quality. It's a registered trademark for use only by InterNACHI and IAC2 members.

What are your most profitable or popular services? Do you offer any specific services that you're especially interested in aggressively promoting?

Are you (or anyone on your staff) fluent in any language(s) besides English? Did you know that many of InterNACHI's inspection-related articles at www.nachi.org/articles are also in Spanish and French? And InterNACHI's home maintenance book, *Now That You've Had a Home Inspection*, is available in English and Spanish at www.nachi.org/now.

Websites

The home inspection business is different than most other businesses in that you (the home inspector) never meet your client until after you are hired. That's right—when you get out of your truck at the inspection site and introduce yourself to your client, s/he has already hired you. There is almost no salesmanship involved in the home inspection business. Success relies almost solely on marketing. But where should an inspector market? Well, a home inspector's clients are nearly always home buyers. And many of these home buyers are conveniently located all in one place… online. They are online touring new homes, researching schools, emailing their real estate agents, shopping for mortgages, and looking for home inspectors. And since you will not have an opportunity to sell your inspection services in person, it's important that your website be capable of doing your selling for you. To a potential client, your website is a sample of what you and your report are going to be like.

Your website is the flagship of your company. It makes little sense to drive traffic to a website that doesn't represent you well. It's a wise investment to have your website professionally designed and maintained so that its overall look is attractive and its navigation is problem-free.

The door to your website is your homepage. It's the most important page of your website. Most of your visitors will never even click through to your other pages if your homepage doesn't make them want more. As an inspector, you might work on some of the most expensive real estate in the world, but no property is as valuable, per square foot, as your own website's homepage. The right homepage can generate you many thousands of dollars in inspecting business if it's designed properly. You only get one chance to make a good first impression. Make sure your site doesn't un-sell your inspection services.

Tip: Webmasters don't have the skill sets to design websites that sell any more than auto mechanics have the skill sets to create car ads. Webmasters are mechanics, not marketers. Don't leave your website design in the hands of an HTML programmer.

Don't Be Shy

If you're a good inspector, you have an ethical duty to market yourself and stay in business so as many of your fellow citizens as possible can use your services. If you feel your clients who are about to make the purchase of their lives are served well by hiring you… you shouldn't pull any punches. Marketing is no place for humility. You're serving your clients by allowing them to learn of, and benefit from, your good work.

Nailing Down Your Website Name

If you have yet to create your website, do an online search for a business name that's as close as possible to your actual business name. Purchase all the registrations for your domain name, including all the variations you can think of so that they will re-direct searchers to your site. You can do a generic search or use a registration vendor site, such as GoDaddy.com, which sifts through the various searches for you. The searches are typically free; it's the registrations that will cost you. As an extra precaution, ask family and friends to test for natural typos for your business name so that you can buy those, too, before the typo-squatters get to them. This may seem like a large and unnecessary investment, but the downside is that you can lose control of your brand, which can create endless hassles not only for you, but for those trying to find you online. It's much better to pay an annual fee and be assured that you will remain the registered owner than to worry about legal delays and possible litigation later. This will rob you of valuable time you need for work. Website management and all its tangential considerations shouldn't be a full-time job.

If someone else has registered your most desirable website name (and/or its variations), find out who the registered owner is. If this information isn't provided on the website itself, there are websites that specialize in helping you search, such as DomainTools.com (which charges a fee), or the "whois" query-and-response protocol at whois.domaintools.com. When you find out who the registered owner is, it's best to contact him/her using a non-business email account. Writing from an email account that reflects a variation of the online business name that you're interested in purchasing will tip your hand and demonstrate that the domain you want to buy is valuable to you, which may automatically inflate the price. Since it's difficult to predict how much you'll need to spend, it's best to keep your opening gambit low. When you've made successful contact, ask whether the name is for sale, rather than immediately extend an offer to purchase it. Again, you want to keep the transaction as low-key as possible. The purchase price can be anywhere from a few hundred dollars to a few thousand; you will have to decide what it's worth to you. (Remember that you'll have to pay this fee only once; re-registering it every year is similar to registering your vehicle annually, and you'll be dealing with the site's registrar.) The downside for the domain owner is that if s/he gouges you on the price and you tell him/her you don't want to purchase it, s/he may realize that s/he won't get the opportunity again to sell it, which is the only reason s/he purchased it in the first place. It can be an unpleasant negotiation, but remember that it's still a negotiation, so try not to get emotional.

If you're determined to acquire the name but you can't do so at an affordable or fair price, it may be time to call in the big guns. Disputes with bad-faith registrants over domain names can be resolved using the Uniform Domain Name Resolution Policy process developed by the Internet Corporation for Assigned Names and Numbers (ICANN).

When you have acquired the right to purchase your domain name (and all its variants), purchase the longest registration period available, and make sure you know the date your registration expires so that you don't accidentally allow it to lapse.

Tip: Use InterNACHI's Inspection Business Name Search Tool and search for a company name for your inspection business at www.nachi.org/namesearch

Your Website Isn't About You

Your website should be all about your prospects. Toward that end, its text should address your visitors directly. That means that you should refer to your visitors as "you," just like you're reading here.

Your Website Is Not a Brochure

A company brochure is nothing more than a pompous business card. Brochures are widely accepted as corporate propaganda. Readers don't expect to find much real information in them, so brochures are not really something a potential client is going to study with any seriousness. You should consider yourself lucky to have a potential client even open your brochure. However, Internet users are much more goal-driven. They have clicked on your website for a specific reason—not to just flip through the pages. Therefore, your web developer has to predict what information these visitors are seeking and then quickly give it to them, or at least make the visitor believe they are just a click away from finding it. A website is far more important to an inspector than a brochure.

Your Website Is Not a TV

There are still some web developers out there who forget that the real purpose of an inspector's website is to generate business for the inspector. Some common designs include slow-loading graphics, a happy couple standing in front of their new home, virtual tours, and, of course, the obligatory tie-wearing, clipboard-holding, hardhat-wearing, grinning inspector. These sites may look great, but they generate very little inspecting work for their owners. Visitors are seeking information. Your website's job is to quickly make visitors believe that the information they're seeking is just a click away (at most), and then shape the delivery of that information such that it leads each visitor toward a decision to hire you. That's it. This isn't art—it's science. There's a big difference between a professional-looking website and a pretty one. Pretty websites only sell their developer's services. However, there is some correlation between clean, visual design and quality.

Your Website Is Not a Magazine

Your website is not a magazine, and your homepage is not a magazine cover. The purpose of a magazine cover is to grab your attention so you pick up (or visit) the magazine. However, there's no sense in trying to make your homepage grab attention, since no one can see it until after they choose to visit it anyway. It's the links on your homepage leading the visitor toward a decision to hire you that must be the attention-grabbers. A homepage cannot attract or send visitors to itself.

Your Website Is Not a Building

Your website is not a building, and your homepage is not a true "lobby." Most websites have a homepage that acts as a lobby, directing traffic in different directions. However, an inspector's homepage should be a "trick lobby." The signage (links) should appear to offer visitors directions to different departments. But, in reality, they should merely take visitors through sales pitches that all lead back to the goal of making the visitor decide to hire you. These departments (pages) are not destinations in and of themselves, but, rather, routes which you allow the visitor to pass through on his/her way to hiring you. Typical link titles that lead to these sales routes include: *"Reasons to Hire Me," "My Qualifications"* and *"My Promise to You."*

Your Website Is Not a Newspaper

Your website is not a newspaper, and your homepage is not the newspaper's daily headline. A newspaper should have fresh news every day because readers who visit the same newspaper every day rightly expect to read something new. However, your homepage is not going to be visited daily by the same people. Very likely, you'll get only one chance to say anything to a potential client with your homepage. Forget about freshness. Throw your same old—but best—pitch every time.

Furthermore, a newspaper's basic format is largely universal. Most readers know that the sports scores and weather forecast are on other pages deep within the newspaper. This advantage permits newspaper publishers to dedicate their front pages to big headlines. However, your visitors are not as convinced that what they seek exists within other pages of your website, so you'll have to use part of your homepage to assure them. For instance, if you specialize in certain inspection services, you'll need to say so on your homepage. Little details make all the difference.

An Inspector's Website Should Have Only One Lone Goal

An inspector's website is not a brochure, not a TV, not a magazine, not a building, and not a newspaper. Unlike many websites, it should not serve multiple purposes. Don't give your visitor any freedom to find anything but reasons to hire you. You must have an understanding of who your visitors are and who among them are important—in other words, who is likely to hire you. An inspector's website has only one purpose: to cause visitors to contact you to hire you (or, at the very least, to contact you for a free estimate, if you offer them).

Because most people only use an inspector every several years, nearly all visitors to an inspector's website are first-time visitors and will likely never return. This is the main reason your homepage must use universally-adopted conventions, which you must finely tweak and customize to suit your inspection business.

Your Website Is a Series of Billboards

No visitors read your entire website's content. They glance at your homepage, scan it, and make a crucial decision—especially crucial to you, the inspector. The decision they make is whether or not to click on anything on your homepage, or to exit and head for a competitor's website.

There are only two ways to get them to choose to stay: **Give them what they want quickly.** Unlike other industries that have to worry about fulfilling many visitors' multiple needs, your visitors have one basic need that you need to meet. Immediately let them know that you have what they want, and that it is, at most, a click away. This should be easy because inspectors already know what their visitors want: to hire a good inspector. So, just give it to them.

OR

Give them something they weren't originally seeking, but something that appears so enticing that they can't help but click on it. An irresistible link titled "3 Mistakes Every Consumer Makes When Hiring an Inspector" is an example of this strategy.

Omit needless words on your homepage. This will make the pertinent words more prominent. Your homepage is like a billboard that your visitors are whizzing by. Give them only those words that will cause them to hit their brakes. Stickiness begins with one click on the homepage. This may sound obvious, but your homepage must compel visitors to make that first click.

Your Visitors Arrive with Baggage

By the time most visitors arrive at your website, they will likely have experienced thousands of other sites on the Internet in general, so they'll expect yours to follow the same standards. Visitors will expect your site design to follow common conventions.

To the extent that your web design veers from these conventions, your visitors will find it uncomfortable, assume your report will be similarly difficult to navigate, and, with a click of their mouse, leave. Most visitors won't drill down into your site if they don't immediately find what they want and find it where they expect it to be.

So, your site has to be smooth—smooth in terms of meeting your visitors' expectations. Forget about being creative. Play the odds and appeal to the masses. Let your competitors' web developers be creative. If you want to be an artist, go be one. Many web developers should be on stage doing interpretive dances or pounding lumps of sculpture clay. They have no business screwing up our website designs. Some inspectors' websites use clickable links placed on different parts of a picture of a house. That may be cute, but it's confusing for a first-time visitor to navigate. Conventions only become conventions under the force of natural selection. In other words, they're conventions because they work. Visitors get a reassuring sense of familiarity from a website that doesn't veer from accepted conventions. This sense of comfort earned by your website then transfers to their sense of you, the inspector. Remember: This is a science—*and your business!*—not an art.

You Must Deny Your Visitors Their Freedom

Within a second or two, some websites permit visitors to find what they're looking for. They are everything to all visitors—they grant visitors the freedom to seek and—more importantly—find anything they might want.

Conversely, an inspector's website must deny this freedom. Every link on your homepage should lead to a page that starts with something relating to that link's title, or the "lead-in." Then, every link from that page should link to a sales pitch for your services. Then, every link from that page should lead to a sales closing—the reasons to contact you now. Finally, every link from that page should lead to your contact information. These pages should have the one-way title of "Continue," as visitors have no business navigating themselves around. Your site should covertly chauffeur your visitors.

Tip: Your visitors won't ever figure out that they aren't behind the wheel unless you give them a site map. So, don't.

Your website should have only one goal: to cause your visitor to hire you. Like the former Soviet Union's elections, where every candidate was a Communist, your visitors should also be free to choose any link that leads them toward the same end. Your website is a funnel, with visitors "freely" and unconsciously choosing to spiral down it. You cannot afford to grant your visitors any real freedom.

Let your competitor build a website that provides visitors with real freedoms and lots of information. You build a website that provides food for your family—one that will pry the hard-earned money from your visitors' hands. Visitor freedom and sales are inversely related. Grant your visitors the complete freedom to never choose incorrectly.

How to Treat Visitors Seeking Something You Don't Sell

If your visitor wants something else—something that you don't sell—treat that visitor like a window-shopper instead of a potential customer. Don't let him/her cost you anything. Let your competitors waste precious homepage real estate with stuff like "Search the Web" functions. Design your site as if every visitor is there to actually hire you.

Distinguishing Your Homepage

Unlike monster sites, where many millions of visitors arrive through pages other than the homepage, almost all of your visitors will arrive at your website through your homepage. Nevertheless, it should still be apparent to your visitors that they are on your homepage. The best way to distinguish your homepage from the other pages on your site is with the word "Welcome." It's a universal signpost for homepages. This signpost will help ensure that visitors recognize their starting point, should they return to your homepage after exploring other pages of your website.

Don't be compelled to offer a lengthy welcome message or *happy talk* that eats up prime homepage space. The simple and lone word "Welcome" at the start of your homepage text is sufficient.

However, don't make "Welcome" the first word in your window title, determined by the title tag of each HTML document. Titles play a critical role in search-engine bookmarking. Use "inspector," or, better yet, use your city name to exploit differentiating site information. A good window title might be: *Boston's best inspector.*

The whole purpose of your website is to get your phone to ring, so if you have both an email address and you answer your phone regularly, you might want to also turn "*Contact Me*" into a category titled "*Contact Me Now*" and put the actual contact information under it. Also, if you are willing to answer your phone in the evening, say so in parentheses after your phone number. This removes a visitor's hesitation to call you late.

A small percentage of visitors (mostly real estate agents) who visit a home inspector's website do so for the sole purpose of looking up a familiar inspector's contact information. Therefore, repeating your contact information again on the right side of your homepage, near the top, seems reasonable. Furthermore, some clients referred to you only by company name may be visiting your site solely to retrieve your contact information to schedule a home inspection.

Don't Use Too Many Images on Your Homepage

People are naturally drawn to photos, pictures and images, so if a picture doesn't tell a story that sells your inspection services, don't use it. An example of an image that sells would be a photo of yourself (the inspector) standing next to your truck with your company name and logo on it, or in action during a home inspection. This action shot of you is a strong visual sales pitch that you might consider building your homepage around.

Look in the Mirror

You can't judge a book by its cover, but many visitors will, so, as previously mentioned, reconsider using a photo of yourself on your website if you look:

- very overweight. It implies that you can't do the work yourself;

- very young. It implies that you're inexperienced; and/or

- like a mass-murderer.

Follow the same rules for photos of yourself that apply to those you might include in your marketing brochures. These rules are outlined in the previous section (i.e., if you are male and have a ponytail, hide it in the photo, etc.). You want your site's visitor to identify with you. Keep your look as simple as possible. Don't wear a tie, except perhaps in your "My Promise" photo (discussed earlier). This look is generally too professional and implies that you're so dressed up that you won't take some jobs. Also, don't wear a t-shirt. This is too unprofessional. You're a step above that—you're inspecting the work done by men in t-shirts. Try to find a middle ground, such as a polo shirt.

Tip: Inspector Outlet (at www.InspectorOutlet.com) offers high-quality polo shirts with InterNACHI's logo embroidered on them.

On Your Homepage, Less Is More

There is another picture that may serve to increase sales. That's one of something that conveys that you're locally owned and operated. Use an image depicting the local sports team, a familiar town monument, or a recognizable local geographical feature. Visitors like to contact local inspectors.

Fight the temptation to include other images on the homepage. Other photos, such as those of defects, can be placed deeper on different internal links and pages, but not on the homepage. They'll dilute your visitor's attentiveness, which is so critical to sales. Photos and images also slow loading time. Photos distract visitors from critical, interactive sales text. This is an unfortunate fact, so go for the goal—acquiring new clients—and avoid what merely "looks nice."

Tip: Your search-engine ranking is decreased by visitors coming to your homepage and simply leaving (bouncing). Search engines such as Google and Bing will think they provided the wrong website because your visitor left without clicking on anything. So, make sure something on your homepage causes your visitors to click somewhere.

Use High-Contrast Colors for Legibility

Dark-colored text on a light-colored background works best, especially since convention dictates the use of blue for links.

Scroll

Avoid adding blank space between bodies of text or inserting blank lines between paragraphs if it looks like the text might fall on the "fold" of the homepage. Otherwise, a blank space might happen to land at the bottom of the visitor's screen, making it appear that they're at the end of the text. Continuous blocks of text help visitors realize that they should keep scrolling to reach the end.

InterNACHI's Certification Verification Seal

Put your InterNACHI certification verification seal somewhere above the fold of your homepage, with the other logos at the bottom of every page (where a visitor wouldn't need to scroll to notice). The seal is an InterNACHI member's most powerful sales tool, designed to be interactive with your visitor. Use it. Find it online at: www.nachi.org/webseal

Add Logos to the Very Bottom of Every Page

Use logos demonstrating third-party certifications and qualifications, if you've earned them. They should go at the very bottom of every page.

Licensed: The word "licensed," along with your state license number, should be included, and its inclusion may, in fact, be required in some jurisdictions. However, consumers will give you little credit for being licensed, as they know licensing is a minimum standard, and they assume that you are operating legally, even in states without licensing. Nevertheless, make it easy for a consumer to verify your licenses.

Training Institute: Unfortunately, the schools or training institutes you attended can work against you a bit. Schooling is sometimes associated with being a novice. Use only their logo (if permitted). Don't write out "graduated from..." Your qualifications list (discussed later) is the better location for detailing your educational background.

Your Company Logo

Put your logo in the upper left-hand corner of your homepage. It should be bigger than anything else on the homepage, except maybe one main photo (described later).

Also, avoid cartoons. Cartoon graphics do not present a professional image. Don't include any silly characters standing on a roof. Again, would a professional engineer use cartoons?

Tip: Link your logo to your homepage, if you wish, but not in place of having a text link to your homepage on every page.

Your Tagline

This is the most important part of your homepage. The main role of a tagline, as discussed previously, is to communicate what you do, and quickly. It's the sign over your store, and it should be placed to the right of your logo. A tagline is especially important for inspection companies that don't have the word "inspector" in their company name.

For example:

A & B Enterprises, LLC

This company name doesn't clearly convey what business the company is in. Imagine seeing a sign for a store without knowing what it is they sell. A tagline solves this problem. See how much better the company name looks with a tagline under it:

A & B Enterprises, LLC
Denver's Best Property Inspector

Remember to italicize your taglines.

Fonts

Avoid using many different fonts. That will diminish the visual continuity of your website. Stick to two fonts: one for headlines and one for the body text. As with the design for your brochures, reserve the use of "impact" fonts for headings. Impact fonts command attention, and they help the reader identify the text that's really important.

For the body text, choose a sans serif font, such as Verdana, Arial or Helvetica. Bolding and italicizing do not count as separate fonts. The same reasoning goes for using different colors. Use a different color to emphasize a word or set of words, but don't overdo it. Use these techniques only to add emphasis and clarity.

Tip: Never use comic fonts.

Your Homepage's Links Are Stand-Alone Advertisements

Because a homepage serves as the portal to the different areas of a website, homepages tend to have more links than the site's other pages. A wide border of links makes them easy to see. However, be mindful that easy navigation is a secondary purpose of your homepage. The primary purpose is to sell your services.

Therefore, the links on your homepage should be mini-ads for your inspection company, in and of themselves, even if your visitor never clicks any of them. Compose your links as if they weren't live links, but, rather, ad copy (the advertising industry's term for the text within an ad).

Tip: Remove unnecessary words from your link titles and make them as short as possible while still retaining their purpose and meaning.

Left-Border Navigation vs. Top-Horizontal Navigation

Most tests that have been conducted on this subject declare that navigational links are best placed vertically in the homepage's left border for left-to-right reading languages, such as English. Visitors often suffer from "banner blindness," so they tend to ignore anything placed horizontally at the top of a webpage. Furthermore, vertical lists imply hierarchy, whereas horizontal tabs do not. This hierarchy can be effectively exploited on inspectors' websites to compose a sort of ad made up of link titles. Think of your navigation links as ad copy.

Border Links to Include

The following list includes the internal links that your website should have. They should probably be placed in a left border underneath your logo in this general order. However, this is not meant to be a boilerplate. Toward that end, the following is an example of the development of your navigation composition. Remember: Your links comprise an ad in and of themselves, even if your visitor doesn't click on any of them.

Homepage:

- Full Home Inspections
- Additional Inspections
- Why Hire Me
- My Qualifications
- Certification Verification (Add your **Education Transcript** to your website at www.nachi.org/my-transcript)
- Standards of Practice
- Code of Ethics
- My Promise to You
- Watch My One-Minute Video
- Contact Me

If you offer more than two additional inspections, you can list them separately under the category of "Additional Inspections" so that visitors know you provide these services without having to click. "Additional Inspections" would then become a category title, and not a link that is blue or underlined, like so:

- Homepage
  - Full Home Inspections
  - Additional Inspections
    - Radon Gas
    - Wood-Destroying Organisms (termites)
    - Mold
  - Why Hire Me
  - My Qualifications
  - InterNACHI Certification Verification
  - Standards of Practice
  - Code of Ethics
  - My Promise to You
- Contact Me Now

Put the word "Gas" after "Radon" to help those who are unfamiliar with radon. Also, put the word "(termites)" in parentheses after "Wood-Destroying Organisms." Don't use "WDO," since few visitors are familiar with that abbreviation.

If you can offer a sample report online that is downloadable, put it as link at the bottom of the *Full Home Inspections*" page, as well as a sub-line underneath it. It is frustrating to be thrust into a new medium, so, if the sample report link goes to another site, or is a PDF file, warn your visitor in parentheses, like so:

- Homepage
  - Full Home Inspections
    - Download a Sample Report (PDF)
  - Additional Inspections
    - Radon Gas
    - Wood-Destroying Organisms (termites)
    - Mold
- Why Hire Me
  - My Qualifications
  - InterNACHI Certification Verification
  - Standards of Practice
  - Code of Ethics
  - My Promise to You
- Contact Me Now
  andy@abenterprisesllc-dot-com
  (123) 456-7890 (8 a.m. to 10:30 p.m.)

Tip: Add a *Call Me Now* button to your website. When a potential client clicks on it and submits his/her call-back number, the InterNACHI member is instantly called by an automated office assistant and given the client's call-back number. There are no phone tolls, lead-generation fees, or other charges for this service. Learn more at www.nachi.org/call_button

Where Are You Taking Them?

Your "Homepage" link takes your visitors to your homepage, of course. Many web developers add extra code to prevent the homepage link from being live on the homepage itself. Some even remove the homepage link from the border on the homepage, since there's no reason to try to go to a page that you're already on. This is unnecessary code and may even cause rather than eliminate confusion. Nowadays, Internet users are well aware that navigational links often include links to the very page they're on.

Your "Services Offered" link should take your visitor to a page that describes what you offer.

Your "Standard" or "Full Home Inspection" should outline the items that you inspect, and should reflect the Standards of Practice (at www.nachi.org/sop), such as:

> I will inspect the following, when visible and accessible:
> - Roof (including all penetrations, flashing & drainage system)
> - Exterior Cladding & Structure (including deck, patio & porches)
> - Attic, Insulation & Ventilation
> - Electrical System
> - Plumbing System
> - Heating System
> - Cooling System
> - Interior Structure (including doors & windows)
> - Built-In Appliances
> - Fireplaces & Wood Stoves
> - Basement/Crawlspace
> - Attached Garage

Tip: There are sound legal reasons to include a live link to InterNACHI's Standards of Practice at the bottom of this list. Find it at www.nachi.org/sop

Each of the links under "Additional Inspections" should take the visitor to a page that offers information about that issue, a short description of how you inspect that issue, and the additional fee you charge for that inspection (so that no one accidentally assumes that it's included with your full home inspection).

Your "My Qualifications" link should take your visitor to a page that lists every qualification you can come up with. Make your list of qualifications as long as possible. Your list of qualifications can be broadened to include information such as your schedule of availability. If you make the list long enough, no one will read it. Your visitors will be impressed enough by its sheer length.

Only competitors read your webpage content; everyone else just scans it.

Each qualification you have should be broken down and expanded as much as possible. Deliver the message: *I am the quality inspector you want to hire.*

If you use subcontractors to perform any portion of your work, include their qualifications. For instance: "Wood-infestation management is performed by a licensed pest-control subcontractor." Again, make this list as long as possible. Even list the number of years you've worked with a particular subcontractor.

Tip: Don't list the actual names of your subcontractors. You don't want your clients or competitors contacting them directly.

Your "Why Hire Me" link should take visitors to a page that is similar to your "My Qualifications" page, only backwards. First, list the reasons to hire you, and then follow up with your formal qualifications.

Your "My Qualifications" page list and your "Why Hire Me" page list are really just the same list in reverse order.

Your "InterNACHI Certification Verification" link points to InterNACHI's online certification verification seal system. When making a purchase online, most consumers will look for a seal of approval from a company such as Thawte® or VeriSign™. You can give your clients the same kind of confidence by letting them know you are certified by the world's largest home inspection organization. The HTML code for this link can be found at www.nachi.org/webseal

Your "Code of Ethics" link should point to www.nachi.org/code_of_ethics

Your "My Promise to You" link should take visitors to a page that has a promise and a photo of you. Similar to what you have in your brochure, include a headshot of yourself looking straight into the camera, and position it above the promise. Also, add your signature on a slight angle below it. Few will actually read the promise word for word, but the message will be conveyed nonetheless.

My Promise to You

Choosing the right home inspector can be difficult. Unlike most professionals you hire, you probably won't meet me until our appointment. Furthermore, different inspectors have varying qualifications, equipment, experience, reporting methods, and pricing.

Ultimately, a thorough home inspection depends heavily on the individual inspector's own effort. If you honor me by permitting me to inspect your new home, I guarantee that I will give you my very best effort.

This, I promise you.

Ben Gromicko
ABC Home Inspections

To recap:

Your "Contact Me Now" information should be straightforward. None of this *debbieandbobgonefishin4321@aol.com* stuff, though. Make your email professional-looking, professional-sounding, and easy to spell. And don't use online forms, of course. No one wants to fill out a form requiring that they give out their personal information (which they would reasonably suspect may put them on a marketing spam list) just to contact you. They want to email or call you.

Your "Click Here for a Free Estimate" button (if you provide them) should link to a page that instructs visitors to contact you for a free estimate. The bottom of that page should include your contact information in the manner that you want potential customers to contact you, such as your "red phone" number and email address. If you get busy and can't handle all the requests coming in for free estimates, you can stop making it so easy for visitors to request one by temporarily hiding the button so that only potential clients who really want an estimate have to go to your contact page for your contact information.

Most potential clients don't spend much time researching before choosing their home inspector. And a visitor, if you're savvy enough to get him/her to your website at all, is likely going to grant you three or four clicks, at most. This leads us to what the length of the text should be on the pages that the navigational links point to. The answer is: short. Even if you have a lot to say, don't say it without offering the visitor a chance to shut you up with cash.

For example, let's say you have a link titled "Radon Testing." It may be tempting to put all sorts of scientific definitions of radon, the history of radon, graphs illustrating the cancer risks that high radon levels pose, etc., but refrain from doing this. Instead, have the link go to a short "Radon Testing" page that briefly describes why testing for radon is important, why your form of testing is the best, and how to contact you. If you're concerned that your sales pitch on this short radon page doesn't satisfy overly inquisitive visitors, simply add a link that says "More About Radon" at the bottom of your short radon page, and include on this secondary page everything anyone would ever want to know about radon, and then some. Make it one long page, and feel free to make it as long as you like, with pictures. However, make sure that you periodically offer to bring the visitor back to your shorter main radon page with "Back" links. Let your visitors decide for themselves when they've been sold.

Pricing: You're Not Fooling Anyone

Don't offer a downloadable discount coupon. Such built-in coupons are a silly way of simply charging less, and everyone knows it. Something available to everyone is worthless. You might get away with it if you announce that it's an exclusive online offer and "available till the end of the month," or something similar.

For basic services, avoid complicated and ambiguous pricing formulas and charts. Instead, keep your price structure straightforward and respectably high.

Use InterNACHI's Home Inspection Fee Calculator at www.nachi.org/fee-calculator to determine the fee for the inspection.

Nothing Says "Quality" Louder

If your pricing is much higher than your competitors', flaunt it. High pricing is the surefire way to convince a customer that you are one of the best. Americans believe in the axiom that you get what you pay for. If your website is making the contention that you are the best inspector in town, your pricing has to support this contention. Charging too little contradicts this claim and instead cries out: "*I am the town's worst inspector and I charge less to prove it.*"

Avoid Naming Links "Click Here"

Never title a link "Click Here." Instead, tell your visitors what they get when they click the link. For example, rather than a link that says: "Click Here for My Code of Ethics," just title the link "Code of Ethics" or "My Code of Ethics."

Avoid Naming Links "More"

Rather than having a link titled "More" at the end of a list, tell the visitor what there is more of, such as: "More references and testimonials from my past clients."

Don't Change Your Links' Colors Once They're Visited

Most websites have links that change colors once they're visited to keep a visitor from revisiting a page. However, assuming every page of your website is designed to sell your services, there's no reason to stop a potential customer from reading something twice. Therefore, if possible, remove the code that provides this courtesy to your visitors so that all of your links remain underlined and blue, even after being visited.

Tip: Font and color changes for link hovering are fine, as they encourage your visitor to click on the link.

Don't Choose Icons or Buttons Over Simple Text Links

Nearly all visitors to an inspector's website are first-time visitors. First-time visitors can read a word faster than they can discern what an icon means. Don't make them interpret icons (other than a universal icon, such as a printer icon). Use text-only links.

Don't Let Them Off the Ranch

Keep the number of links to outside websites to an absolute minimum. External links to other websites may move or disappear. It's better to rebuild content on a page on your own website and link to that page. If you simply must link to an outside website, have the link open in a new browser window so that your visitor never really leaves your site.

Don't Live-Link Any Graphics

If a visitor's pointer changes while hovering over a graphic, which indicates a live link, the visitor will often check every other graphic for live links. This is a distraction, so skip it.

Noise

Don't use watermarks, background images or wallpaper. They add clutter, decrease visibility, slow loading time, and are merely decorative. Some tasteful exceptions exist, but those are few.

Don't Offer a Search Feature

Don't grant your visitor any real freedom to search your site, or, worse, the entire Web from your website. Don't let them wander to weather forecasts or stock quotes. The goal of your website is to lead the visitor toward a decision to hire you. Your website does not exist to provide your visitors with any distracting conveniences or information other than that which you want them to have, in the order that you want them to get it.

Don't Offer to Ship Visitors Anything They Didn't Purchase

You shouldn't offer some trinket or costly book to your visitors in the hope that they'll give you their address, in the hope that you can ship them something, in the hope that it will arrive before they hire an inspector, or in the hope that, upon receipt, they'll hire you. Forget about it. It's better to ask for their email address. Besides, all visitors are justifiably hesitant to give up their home addresses, but they'll have no problem giving you their email addresses. So, if you get their email address, use it! Email them something every day, forever, or until they scream Stop! Work every lead to death or until that lead turns into a scheduled inspection. Top real estate agents will often work leads for years until those leads produce. We can learn something from these agents.

Tip: It's fine to offer a free e-publication in order to capture your visitor's email address.

Help Wanted = Poor Service

Never use your website to advertise employment opportunities. It gives the impression that you are short-handed, or that you might send an inexperienced employee to your client's job. Reserve your inspection website for only one thing: to convince visitors to hire you.

Don't Turn Your Site into Craigslist

Never use your website to sell tools or equipment. It gives the impression that you're going out of business. Reserve your inspection website for only one thing: to convince visitors to hire you.

Forget About Online Booking

Any hint of online booking, even posting your schedule on an online calendar, will deter sales. It may be cute, but there's a reason real salespeople are employed all over the world. Answer your phone!

Don't Yell!

There's no reason to use exclamation points on your website. Never yell at your visitors!!!

Act Like You've Been in the End Zone Before

Avoid giving the impression that you're new to the business… even if you are. Don't put anything on your website that would reveal your inexperience. Kiss-of-death terms include: "Just-licensed," "Grand Opening," "recent graduate," "Introductory Offer," and the mother of all kiss-of-death terms: "New to the Business."

Don't Misppel

Because inspectors are in the "perfection" business, it's important to check and double-check for typos, as well as broken links.

Don't Pollute

Your site should not contain any slow-loading introductory text, ads, pop-up windows, rollovers, pull-down menus, music, Flash animation, banners, things that move content, things that blink, things that make sounds, and instructions. Yes, even instructions. If you have to include long instructions, even for downloading a document, you're doing something wrong. Don't make your visitors think.

Add How-To Articles

Such articles are great for search-engine optimization and demonstrate to consumers how much work is involved in their inspection. Don't use articles that make your job look simple. Add enough specialized articles to let a prospective client know that you have the training, expertise and equipment in an area that your competition lacks.

For Clients: Ten Tips to Speed Up Your Home Inspection

Giving your clients and their realtors some tips to prepare for their home inspection will give them a better idea of what to expect. Their active cooperation will help the process goes smoother, since they will be aiding in their home sale via your professional approach.

Sellers can speed up their home sale by preparing their home for the inspection ahead of time using the following tips. The inspection will go smoother, with fewer concerns to delay closing.

1. Confirm that the water, electrical and gas services are turned on, and that gas pilot lights are lit.

2. Make sure your pets won't hinder the inspection. Ideally, they should be removed from the premises or secured outside. Tell your agent about any pets at home.

3. Replace burned-out light bulbs to avoid a "light is inoperable" report that may suggest an electrical problem.

4. Test smoke and carbon-monoxide detectors, and replace dead batteries.

5. Clean or replace dirty HVAC air filters. They should fit securely.

6. Move stored items, debris and wood away from the foundation. These may be cited as conducive conditions for termites.

7. Remove items blocking access to HVAC equipment, electrical service panels, water heaters, the attic and the crawlspace.

8. Unlock any locked areas that your home inspector must access, such as the attic door or hatch, electrical service panel, the door to the basement, and any exterior gates.

9. Trim tree limbs so that they're at least 10 feet from the roof. Trim any shrubs that are too close to the house and can hide pests or hold moisture against the exterior. If necessary, hire a professional.

10. Repair or replace any broken or missing items, such as doorknobs, locks and latches, windowpanes and screens, gutters and downspouts, and chimney caps.

Checking these areas before your home inspection is an investment in selling your property. Better yet, have your InterNACHI inspector ensure that your home is Move-In Certified™. Your real estate agent will thank you!

Find this article online at www.nachi.org/tentips

Add Your Inspection Contract

Many inspectors agree that displaying your standard agreement or client contract on your website can be useful in defending the charge that your client "didn't have time to read it" on-site. You can use a link titled "Please Read Our Standard Contract" for this purpose.

Add Testimonials

Ask every client for a letter of reference. After the inspection is completed, send them a postage-paid envelope and a letter asking them to jot down a brief letter of reference. After you accumulate at least 20, you can put them on a page on your website with a link to it. No visitor will really read that many, but they might just check to see how many you have, so wait until you collect a bunch. See InterNACHI's example at www.nachi.org/thankyou

Tip: To assure believability, ask your clients for permission to display their picture next to their testimonial. And if you can get them, include videos of your clients praising your company.

Add Photos of Yourself Working in Your Clients' Homes

Consider asking for permission to take and use photos of your clients at their homes showing you performing your inspection. You can place these images on your website above their testimonials. This will give the testimonials credence. You can also add these "action shots" to your marketing materials to show prospective clients what you look like and a flavor of what you do.

My Trick for Building Inspection Websites That Convert Visitors into Clients

Inspectors focus on the words they write in their reports and often continue this habit when they build their websites. The images they use on their websites are typically stock photos, and they're often little more than background or filler between the written words of their text-heavy websites.

However, images are the best and fastest way to convey a message. That's why the images on your inspection business website should tell a story—the right story about your inspection service.

InterNACHI's own proprietary online inspection agreement is signable and legally binding. It allows the client to read and sign your agreement before you do the inspection, or, at least before they view their report online. Visit www.nachi.org/onlineagreement

The most memorable movie scenes made by the greatest filmmakers are based on images and little or no dialogue. The best writers and reporters live by the axiom "Show, don't tell." You can make the same powerful impact with your website.

Here are some images inspectors should use on their websites:

- The inspector is lying on his back in a crawlspace with his flashlight aiming upward. What message does that image convey? *I look carefully in places that most people don't.*
- The inspector is wearing eye protection and gloves while opening an electrical panel. What message does that image convey? *My work is dangerous, but I'm careful.*
- The inspector is holding an IR camera or a gas leak detector. What message does that image convey? *I bring specialized tools to the inspection.*
- The inspection report pages are fanned out on a table, and some have annotated color photos. What message does that image convey? *My report is detailed, yet easy to understand.*
- The inspector is being presented with the Certified Master Inspector® award. What message does that image convey? *I am the best and proud of it.*
- A wall is shown covered with inspection course Certificates of Completion. What message does that image convey? *I value training and Continuing Education.*
- The inspector is standing next to the sign on his dedicated inspection vehicle and wearing a shirt with his business logo. What message does that image convey? *I'm a full-time inspector.*

Remember: A picture is worth a thousand words.

Try this experiment when you start building your inspection website: Do the entire thing using only images and no text. Imagine that the images you use are chapters in a book, and that each image has to tell part of your story. Don't use any text at all—just build your entire website using images that convey a series of messages, and together tell a story... your story.

If you can do that, you're really only one small step away from having an awesome website. Your last step is to add supporting text.

A Goal Other Than Direct Sales

If you market heavily to real estate agents, you might want to put something on your website that causes them to refer clients to it. Links pointing to www.nachi.org/what_really_matters and www.nachi.org/3mistakes are examples of links that generate referrals.

Website Design Is Only One-Third of the Equation

For example, if your website is getting 500 hits a month, and of those hits, 3% contact you (attributable to website design), and of those that contact you, one-third schedule inspections, then you are getting five jobs a month from your website, which can be translated mathematically as 500 x 0.03 x 0.33 = 5. However, if you can double all three factors in the equation so that you're getting 1,000 hits a month, 6% are contacting you, and you're converting two-thirds of those contacts into scheduled inspections, then you've far more than doubled your results as 1,000 x 0.06 x 0.67 = 40 extra jobs a month! Each factor counts. Do the math and make sure your website is not the weak link in your formula for success.

Take It for a Test Drive

Have someone test-drive your website. Tell them to talk out loud as they move around your site, describing what they're looking at, what they're noticing, and what they're having trouble finding.

Brutal Truth

The total number of inspections to be performed in the world is a constant; you aren't going to single-handedly change your local economy. So, every job counts. Furthermore, every job you get is one that your competitor doesn't. The total number of inspections is a constant. Make sure you're doing everything you can to get your share of the pie.

----- Original Message -----

From: John Cordeiro

To: Nick Gromicko

Sent: Wednesday, May 03, 2006 8:23 AM

Subject: Brutality Online Works!!!!!!!!!!!!!!

Nick:

Wanted to let you know I followed your advice in the IQ called "Brutality Online" www.nachi.org/brutal and designed my web site, www.hdetectives.com, around that advice. Today, two days after posting it and two weeks after joining InterNACHI, I got my first call for an inspection from the site and booked it easily.

1. They never asked, "How much do you charge?"

2. They never asked for qualifications.

3. I did no selling, just order-taking.

When I asked how they heard of us, he stated he searched online and I was second from the list and my site looked better than the others, so he picked me.

Thanks for the advice,

John Cordeiro
House Detectives, Inc.

Custom Online Video Ad

InterNACHI can produce an awesome video ad that will generate lots of business for you.

We'll search engine-optimize your video to promote your inspection business in your local markets.

We'll add translated custom captions to your video. Because Google owns YouTube, captions are an important tool for video SEO and YouTube visibility for businesses. Custom captions are indexed by Google, making your video searchable by a larger audience.

We'll upload your custom video to InterNACHI's YouTube channel for an additional SEO boost. You do not need your own YouTube channel.

We'll upload your custom video to Facebook for an additional SEO boost. You do not need your own Facebook page.

We'll send you a simple YouTube link with your video already uploaded. You can then:

- email your video to your potential and past clients;
- download your custom video as an FLV or MP4 video file;
- embed your video on your website;
- add the video to your Facebook page;
- add your custom video link to your InterNACHI message board signature for an additional SEO boost; and/or
- simply use the YouTube link we give you.

Visit www.InspectorOutlet.com to order your own Custom Online Video Ad.

Your Livelihood Online

Legal Issues Regarding Your Website & Emails

The Internet has created tremendous opportunities for marketing your business, but it has also created new legal traps for the unwary. Here are five considerations inspectors should bear in mind when building and adding to their business websites:

1. **Jurisdiction:** This is important if you live close to a state line and routinely offer or provide services across state lines. Generally, a court cannot exercise jurisdiction over a resident or company in another state unless that person or entity does business in that state. If your website attracts potential customers from another state, you want to make sure that if an out-of-state customer sues you, s/he must do it in your state—not in his/hers. In other words, you want the home-field advantage.

   For this reason, you should consider posting something like this on your homepage:

   This site provides general information about our services and qualifications. By using this site, you agree that our maintenance of this site does not constitute the transaction of business in any state other than [Inspector's State].

2. **Protecting Copyrights and Trademarks:** Many people don't realize that in order to legally copyright something, all you must do is put the public on notice of your claim by including your name, the year, and the copyright symbol © on your published work. There are more complicated and expensive ways to secure greater copyright protections, but this is effective (and enforceable) for most people's legal needs.

   Similarly, to trademark something, all you must do is put the public on notice by using your trademarked name or tagline followed by the ™ symbol. You don't have to file any documents with the government; you only have to do that if you want to register your copyright or if you want to apply for a registered trademark so that you can use the ® symbol with your trademark. Registration does offer some advantages if you end up in litigation, but it's not mandatory. Your website may include photos, drawings, and/or wording that you worked hard to create.

   You should protect these things by placing a notice on your homepage, such as this:

   This website and its entire contents are copyrighted [Year] by [Your Company].

   Or something even simpler:

   © [Year] [Name]

   Note that three elements must be included in your copyright notation in order to make it legally enforceable:

   - your name or your company name;
   - the copyright symbol or the word "copyright"; and
   - the year of copyright.

3. **Other People's Copyrights and Trademarks**

   - Do not use any copyrighted photos, drawings or language from other websites or sources on your site without permission. This is known as copyright infringement. Most copyrighted works on the Web now have embedded code to track the IP addresses of downloads and re-posts of the protected work. If you get caught doing this, you will pay thousands of dollars to defend and/or settle a lawsuit.

- Do not create a trademark that is so similar to a competitor's trademark that it is likely to cause confusion to the public; this is known as trademark infringement.

- Do not use the ® symbol unless the U.S. Patent and Trademark Office (USPTO) has issued you a Certificate of Registration for your trademark.

4. **Your Website as Evidence Against You:** One of the first things attorneys do when deciding whether to sue on behalf of a client is to visit the defendant's website. They often find language that they'll be able to use against the defendant if they file a lawsuit. So, avoid this possibility by reviewing your website with a critical eye. Does your website make promises that you can't keep or claims you can't prove? For instance, if your website states that you're "The Most Experienced Inspector in Nevada," you'd better have some data to back up that claim; if you don't, some plaintiff's attorney may make you eat those words in court someday.

5. **Privacy Issues:** Websites are useful to business owners because they allow you to collect the email addresses of visitors, and that information becomes more valuable as the list grows. However, if you use that list to send commercial emails to others, you must comply with the federal CAN-SPAM Act.

A "commercial email" is defined as "any electronic mail message, the primary purpose of which is the commercial advertisement or promotion of a commercial product or service."

All commercial emails must include:

- a legitimate return email address and a physical address;

- a clear and conspicuous notice of the recipient's opportunity to "opt out" or "unsubscribe";

- a mechanism that must be provided or an email address to which a recipient may send a message to opt out; and

- a clear and conspicuous notice that the message is an advertisement or solicitation.

The "existing business relationship" exception under the federal anti-fax law does not apply to commercial emails, so even if you have a prior relationship with the recipient, you must still comply with the Act.

Defending Your Online Brand

Your brand—which includes your business name, logo, and other identifying features—should be well-guarded. It's unique. It's an extension of your physical business and services. And it's likely to be the first and perhaps only advertising about you that your prospective clients will see. The Internet presents almost overwhelming challenges to policing one's commercial identity both online and off, so part of your regular marketing duties must include monitoring your brand and reputation. Litigation after the fact may be necessary in the long run, but it's costly and time-intensive, and the violations worth suing over are largely preventable, if you keep tabs on yourself.

Website Domain Defense

Anything that can be sold or monetized online can be unfairly—and often illegally—exploited. Just because you have a registered business name and are willing to pay an annual fee to a site-hosting vendor doesn't mean that you're legally entitled to use that name. Someone else may have claimed your unique name—and even variations of its proper spelling. A simple search of your business name may reveal that a site for it already exists. What's more, it's likely that it's a site that has no other reason for taking up cyberspace than because the registered owner is waiting for you to contact him/her to offer to buy the domain name, which is really genuinely valuable only to you. However, the only way for you to legally use the site name is to purchase it from the registered owner—typically, for an exorbitant fee. This is known as domain-squatting or cybersquatting. It's technically defined as bad-faith registration because the registered owner purchases domain names for the express purpose of selling them at a profit to those who have a legitimate professional or commercial interest in them.

Laws prohibiting this practice went on the books as early as 1999 with the enactment of the Anti-Cybersquatting Consumer Protection Act. But because it can't be enforced on a global scale (as well as arguments of First Amendment protections of free speech), its legal effectiveness is limited. However, the Federal Trademark Dilution Act of 1995 protects against trademark violations and those whose intent is to profit by registering or using an identical or confusingly similar name.

A variation of cybersquatting is typo-squatting. Bad-faith registrants anticipate that users who look online for website names often get the names wrong, so they buy up domain names with similar but slightly altered spellings to account for users looking for the proper domain name but who then misspell or mistype the name in their browser bar or into a search engine.

Still another notorious practice of unscrupulous cyber trolls is known as renewal-snatching or alert-angling. Most domain owners must re-file and pay for their site registration annually. Trolls and cybersquatters may use software tools that automatically register a popular site's domain name the moment the registration expires. A lapsed registration is fair game, regardless that you may have paid for it and legally owned it for the past five or ten years. This can be devastating to your online brand and your ability to conduct your daily business.

Search Engine Optimization Tips for Inspectors

Here are some simple SEO tips that inspectors should understand and use every day. From ads and brochures to blog posts and contributions to message boards, most of these suggestions will work for you with very little effort on your part. It's the kind of marketing that you don't really have to think about, once you start doing it.

"If a tree falls in a forest and no one is around to hear it, does it make a sound?"

—George Berkeley, philosopher (1685-1753)

Try these:

- Put your location in your text. Say "Cheyenne, Wyoming" instead of just "our location."

- Add your local market region to every page. By tracking IP addresses, Google knows where their users are searching from and customizes their search results accordingly. Therefore, it is important that Google knows where your service area is. Put your address, market suburbs, market subregions, satellite cities, and metro areas on every page of your website. If you serve more than one town or city, include them all. Even better, add geographically-specific phrases about your market area within your website text.

- Build keywords, such as your local city, into your page URLs (web page addresses).

- Ensure that your name, address and phone number (NAP) are consistent, and that these citations appear at the bottom of every page of your website and your Message Board signature.

- Use InterNACHI's free local SEO tool found at http://www.nachi.org/local-seo-intro

- Take advantage of InterNACHI's free search engine submission service found at www.nachi.org/seotracker

- Title your navigation links with optimization in mind. For example: "Contact the Inspector" instead of "Contact Us."

- Add new content to your pages on a regular basis. Content freshness counts for much as search engines cycle through their search algorithms. InterNACHI offers free inspection-related articles for this purpose.

- Contrary to what you may have learned, don't try to stuff your text with keywords. It won't work. Search engines know if your use of a term is abnormally high because people have tried to game the system, and this practice is a red flag. They prefer natural language content.

- Get your inspection-related vendors and suppliers to link to your site. InterNACHI already does this on behalf of its members.

- If you have a client who owns a big company with a popular website, ask if s/he will to link to your site. One single, authoritative and high-traffic site (like InterNACHI) can do a lot more for you than a dozen poor-quality links.

- Be sure links to your site and within your site use your keyword phrases. In other words, if your target is Cheyenne home buyers, then your link title should be "Cheyenne home buyers" instead of "Click here."

- Title your images using relevant phrases, such as "Photo of inspector inspecting a roof in Cheyenne" instead of "Picture of me."

- Mention the specific ancillary inspection services you offer in your first few paragraphs of text, and then try to work them into a few other paragraphs (at least).

- Place keyword-rich captions under your images (and as screentips), just like newspapers do.

- Be aware that private domain-name ownership may increase a search engine's belief that you are a spammer.

- Renew your domain name a few years into the future. It shows search engines that you are keeping your domain name.

- Post frequently on InterNACHI's Message Board. At over a million posts, InterNACHI's Message Board is the largest accumulation of inspection-related material on the Internet.

- Make inspection-related posts in the open forums of InterNACHI's Message Board so that they're accessible to everyone, including search engines.

- Make sure your Message Board signature contains a live link to your inspection business website and NAP. This instantly gives you a lot of link juice (proportional to how many posts you've written).

- Create an online video. Google owns YouTube. And think about your script from a search engine optimization standpoint. According to Google, their new audio indexing system uses speech-recognition technology to transform speech into text and then ranks videos by spoken keyword relevance, YouTube metadata, and freshness.

- Make sure the privacy settings of your website allow it to be visible to everyone.

- If you are a Certified Master Inspector (CMI)®, make sure you exploit the custom ebook that has your contact information embedded throughout.

Google AdWords

Google AdWord campaigns can be an inexpensive and effective customer-acquisition strategy. The concept behind AdWords is that you bid on keywords in an effort to have your ad appear. The goal is not to generate traffic to your website, but to generate traffic from visitors who are likely to want your inspection services.

Here's a list of suggested keywords:

- your name (to help searchers who know your name find you);

- your company name (to help searchers who know your company name find you);

- the name of your town/city;

- the regional areas within your market; and

- all your services (or, at least the ones you want to sell the most).

Google Analytics

Sign up for Google Analytics. It's free. Google Analytics provides you with statistics about your visitors, including which sites referred them, what city they're in, what search phrases they used to find you, and much more.

"The winner is the chef who takes the same ingredients as everyone else and produces the best result."

—Edward de Bono

Common Mistakes in Print Ads

An effective ad is actually not designed to tell the world about your greatness. An ad isn't about you; it's about your prospective customers. Your ad should deliver a compelling message that causes the reader to call you. Don't un-sell your services with the wrong kind of ad.

Here are some common mistakes typically found in print ads that inspectors have made (or have paid an advertising rep to make for them):

- a poor logo created by the inspector or an enthusiastic amateur;

- the company name hogs precious ad space (name recognition without sales = bankruptcy);

- an unappealing color scheme;

- a mix of several different fonts;

- a silly pun in the ad copy (as if consumers demand witty inspectors);

- a picture of your service fleet (which will give the automatic visual impression that you sell work vans instead of inspection services);

- technical buzzwords (which the average person will not understand or care about);

- manufacturers' logos (you're paying to promote yourself, not someone else);

- the phrase "Discount Prices" (consumers who want quality will call someone else);

- the phrase "Best Prices" (doesn't everyone claim this?);

- the phrase "No Home Too Small" (which will send your big-ticket clients looking for someone who can handle their 3,000-square-foot home);

- a weak premise, such as "Here's a great deal!";

- the lack of an attention-grabbing, compelling headline;

- no list of features or benefits of your services;

- no sense of urgency (Why not just say "Please call us sometime"?);

- no call to action; and

- the phrase "Satisfaction Guaranteed" (as if you're bragging that you won't make the customer unhappy).

Reminder: It costs just as much to run a good ad as a bad one.

Newspaper Ads

Do tell the rep that you want the "stand-by" rate. The newspaper will run your ad when and where they want to, depending on whether they need to fill empty space on a page.

Don't let the rep sell you on a "re-run" contract until you run your ad first for a week to test its response.

Yellow Pages Ads

Don't work.

Card Deck Advertising

Don't waste your money.

Cold-Calling

Don't waste your time.

Dissect Your Competitors' Ads

After WWII, the Japanese bought several U.S.-made cars and tore them apart. Each part was scrutinized. They learned to build high-quality cars from paying attention to what their competitors were doing. Inspectors can learn a lot by emulating what the Japanese did. The more you know about your competitors, the better you'll be able to compete with them.

When a Competitor Goes Under

Try to acquire that competitor's old phone number and domain name to have calls and website searches forward to you.

Off-Peak Marketing & Creative Marketing

It's easier to get the attention of prospects when no one else is bombarding them. There are fewer customers to be had at certain times of the year, but also fewer inspectors competing for them.

Tip: Be straight up and admit to prospects that "It's the slow time of year for us and that's why I'm able to offer..."

Movie Theater Previews

Although this requires you to have a commercial professionally produced, it's worth every penny. You get your message in front of a local and captive audience.

Profitable Home & Garden Shows

Inspectors who find themselves between jobs should consider investing some time in manning a table at a trade show. The opportunities to do so are frequent—they include luxury home tours, garden shows, building and home supply events, and real estate functions. Prospective homeowners who are considering a new build generally take the time to gather ideas for architectural choices, housing plans and layouts, and interior and exterior materials, especially features that are newer, innovative, and save energy. Essentially, these potential clients are pre-house shopping for concepts that reflect their dream for creating a unique home that meets their space and comfort needs, as well as their desire to save energy and have a lower impact on the environment. Inspectors should take advantage of these events for their built-in marketing opportunities because a trade show provides the chance to do live advertising, where you sell yourself and your business ethic as much as you sell your services.

Do:

- **Prepare:** It goes without saying that your **website** and hard-copy **marketing materials** should be professionally designed, as well as regularly maintained and updated. This is the source material that you will be directing your booth visitors to and the product that you're giving them now. If you've successfully engaged these people, they're going to pore over your brochure and visit your website once they get home, so make sure everything is in top condition beforehand. That includes testing your website's links and navigation to make sure there aren't any glitches that need intervention. Whether you have an event lined up or are considering participating in one for the first time, always have a **trade show kit** that is ready to go. Preparing ahead of time will virtually guarantee a productive experience, even if you don't nail any new clients.

- **Pre-Promote:** Always let your former clients and prospects know that you'll have a booth at an upcoming event. An event is the perfect excuse for a local press release.

- **Remember Quality:** Invest in high-quality images for your booth. Don't be cheap. "Go big or go home"—this conventional wisdom cannot be denied. Especially if you've reached the midpoint in your career, you want to meet your market's needs by offering quality instead of merely economy. This means providing services that are more expensive than that of your usual competitors. Your sales pitch and your trade show display should reflect that. Invest in durable, high-quality signage and displays. For outdoor events, have a sturdy table, a chair for yourself and a "booth buddy" or employee, and two chairs for visitors who will be glad to take a load off and, consequently, will be more receptive to your message.

  Also, for primarily outdoor use, invest in a customized tent that provides shade and a bit of quiet and privacy, especially at events that are noisy and get a lot of foot traffic. Put your name and logo on everything.

- Use a **headline on your booth's sign** that attracts attention.
- Wear **attire** appropriate for the event. Your shirt should display your company logo.
- Try to get **booth space near the food court.**
- **Open the conversation** with visitors by asking, "What attracted you to our booth?"
- **Get out in the aisle** and engage people with your giveaways.
- Use a **prepared script** to get the conversation started with prospects that stop by. Be enthusiastic when speaking to everyone.
- Schedule an **initial meeting** with a prospect at the show.
- Have **two people** man the booth at all times.
- Have free **snacks and bottled water** available for booth visitors.
- Send **follow-up** marketing pieces to everyone who gives you their contact information.
- Use large flat-screen monitors to display interesting **videos and slide shows.**

Don't:

- Don't agree to sponsor an event (for a fee) unless you can man the table or have someone man it for you. You'd essentially be paying rent for table space for a stack of your brochures, and that's not the wisest investment of your marketing budget.
- Don't use your company name as the headline for your booth unless it clearly reflects what you do.
- Don't display old or outdated images, or use old brochures or other dated marketing materials.
- Don't ask, "Can I help you?" You should be directing the conversation.
- Don't sit.
- Don't act bored.
- Don't eat food at your booth.
- Don't limit your event choices. Think of other events where your direct competition will not be in attendance. Consider events that your desired prospects are likely to attend, including those that may exist slightly outside the traditional market. Affluent prospects visit boat shows, auto shows, and other events and exhibits that feature high-ticket purchases and luxury goods. They'll be at energy symposiums, sustainable-living fairs, alternative building fairs, and community events—rather than only home shows.

After each event—even before you've replenished your supply of brochures and business cards—do a post-game decompression. Take some time to reflect and write down what went well and what didn't. This is especially essential if you had a representative at the show in your place. Figure out what you (and/or your rep) can do better next time, whether it's being better prepared with information for certain questions, deciding to offer some new or different freebies (which, of course, should have your logo and contact information on them), whether you should have had refreshments (or different ones) available for your visitors (and your staff or yourself), or whether you had any issues with the venue's facilities or staff that will inform your future requests for other shows. An indispensable skill of being a good marketer for your business is to ask for and process feedback, so make a thorough self-assessment after each event in preparation for the next one. Make your time and effort count. This will boost your confidence, as well as keep you realistic about how effectively you're marketing your business live.

Customized Articles

Articles that are informational and educational are a great way to promote your company and generate leads. They're useful for homeowners and others with an interest in issues related to the services you offer.

Common uses for customized articles for inspectors include:

- your website (improves search-engine optimization);
- your newsletters (great to email to real estate agents and past clients);
- your special reports (include appropriate articles for particular issues); and
- trade show handouts (make copies with your contact information on them).

You should also offer them to local newspapers and trade magazines for publication.

Tip: You may also want to have your articles translated into other languages appropriate for your market.

Special Reports

Special reports are similar to articles but they're particularly timely or relevant to potential customers in a certain geographical area. For example, if your local building department adopts a code change, you might want to inform potential clients about it using a special report that also promotes your inspection company or announces a new service you offer.

Tip: You should also offer special reports on your website for free (in exchange for the visitor's contact information, of course).

Marketing Yourself on Message Boards & Online Forums

Are you taking advantage of message boards and online forums to help market your inspection business? Consumers and real estate agents searching online for specific inspection topics often find their answers in message board threads and, subsequently, the inspectors who are contributing to those threads. Some inspectors report that they receive a substantial influx of work from online message boards.

Here are some tips for getting the most marketing value out of posting online:

- Contribute often. The more posts you author, the more likely you will be found.
- Make real, substantive posts that search engines can find and that potential clients will find useful.
- If you are an expert in a particular area of inspection, make very detailed, helpful posts regarding your expertise, and start new threads about those issues.
- Be conscious about what you say online. Search engines, such as Google, will see and index your comments. So, your strategy should be to keep non-inspection-related discussions (especially religious and political discussions) in non-public areas of online forums, and post technical discussions in appropriate and open forums.
- Add a link for your inspection business website to the signature of your posts.
- Add your business phone number to your signature.
- Add your city to your signature, such as *Serving Columbus, Ohio*, or, even better: *Providing inspection services throughout Columbus, Ohio*. It helps search engines index your inspection business website.

Tips:

- Visit InterNACHI's interactive message board at www.nachi.org/forum The board allows inspectors to interact, post pictures, and discuss inspection topics.

- Contribute an article to InterNACHI's Inspector Blog at www.nachi.org/blog The blog contains information and news for both inspectors and consumers.

Online Videos

"Once a new technology rolls over you, if you're not part of the steamroller, you're part of the road."

—Stewart Brand

Inspectors who are marketing-savvy should maintain their websites by occasionally adding consumer-targeted videos. As technology becomes cheaper and more dummy-proof, it's easy for an inspector to shoot a short video at a jobsite and upload it to his/her website. Such a video should give consumers some basic home maintenance tips or even a brief tutorial about a step in the inspection process that imparts some interesting information. Short videos on your website can serve several purposes.

Videos can show your prospective clients:

- what you look like, as well as a flavor of your personality;

- an indication of how you conduct yourself on the job;

- that you're knowledgeable about the subject matter of the video, even if it's brief, and even if it's strictly informational regarding the inspection process;

- that you're busy with work and not sitting around waiting for the phone to ring;

- that you're comfortable with technology; and

- that you're confident engaging your prospective clients by putting yourself out there on the Internet.

Consumers will naturally feel more comfortable with an inspector they can see in action before hiring him/her, which is actually a rare opportunity. Think of your video as an audition that you're offering your website visitors. At the very least, it's a visual advertisement, which consumers are used to watching for the products and services they want to buy. All things being equal—including licensing, experience, and overall pricing—the inspector who offers a video of him/herself on the job will surge ahead of the competition. Creating familiarity ahead of your actual appointment is something that will stick in your prospective clients' minds. As the saying goes, "A picture is worth a thousand words."

Some Do's & Don'ts for Website Videos

Do:

- Write a basic script beforehand so you have a general idea of what you want to say during your commercial. The more comfortable you are with the material, the better it will sound when recorded.

- Appear in your own videos. Unless you look like a serial killer, you should be the star of your own website videos.

- Rehearse. If you have a camcorder (or even a cell phone with video capabilities), take some time to practice being on camera. When the camera turns on, even a confident inspector can lose his or her composure and come off as uncomfortable, unsure, and maybe even unqualified. We typically look and sound different when recorded, and getting comfortable with those differences before your shoot will translate into a better commercial. If you don't have a camcorder, practicing in front of a mirror can be helpful.

- If you're shooting in a studio, wear crisp-looking attire, which translates well on camera. Consider having your clothes professionally dry-cleaned and pressed. You want to look as professional as possible.

- If you're a man, considering getting a haircut a few days before the shoot and shave as late as possible before shooting (you might even want to consider bringing your razor to the shoot and shaving there).

- Dress appropriately for both the job and the image you want to present to your viewers. Save your on-the-job videotaping for a day when you won't be covered in mud or dirt, which will make verbal and visual communication more difficult.

- Do vocal warm-ups before the shoot. As silly as this may feel, having a confident and commanding voice can really help you connect with your commercial's viewers. It doesn't need to be much: clear your throat, open and close your mouth a few times, and maybe try a few tongue twisters that you remember from childhood. What's most important is that you prepare yourself to speak clearly and confidently.

- Look into the lens of the camera, which translates on video as making eye contact. Look directly at the camera to show that you are engaged and ready to demonstrate your prowess as an inspector. Try not to look down between sentences (unless you're referring to your script), as this can convey shyness and a lack of confidence.

- Smile! Remember, your clients want to feel like they can trust you and be comfortable asking you questions about their inspection. If you appear relaxed, comfortable and happy, your potential clients will be relaxed, comfortable and happy while watching your commercial.

- Introduce yourself on camera. Don't assume the viewer knows who you are.

- Introduce everyone else appearing in the video with you. This is simply demonstrating common courtesy and respect for your staff and colleagues.

- Mention your website address throughout the video.

- Get permission from your current clients if you're shooting a video during their inspection on their property. It demonstrates your professionalism.

- Engage in some inspection activity. Walking and talking is okay, but your video should show you doing something.

- End your video with a brief sales pitch, such as "Be sure to contact ABC Inspections if you're thinking about buying a new home."

- Provide your business name, logo and contact information, including your service area, as a super-imposed image before your video ends. In case it gets uploaded to other sites, such as YouTube, your contact information should be a part of the video that cannot be edited out.

- Copyright your video using your business name, the copyright symbol and the year. Again, super-imposing your copyright notation at the bottom of the last few frames of video makes it difficult to edit out.

- Catalog your videos using titles and brief descriptions that will be of interest to consumers so that they can find them easily, both while they're searching the Web and searching your site.

- Take advantage of social networking sites. Do you have a Twitter account or Facebook page? Be sure to post a link to your latest videos there to drive traffic to your website.

Don't:

- Don't wear green. You may want to use a green screen to superimpose your video onto a different background. If you're wearing clothes that are similar to the color of a green screen, it will be hard for the editor to remove the screen without also removing part of your body. You should also avoid wearing stripes (particularly tight ones), bright red, or all white or all black, as these generally look bad or visually distort in the video. Also, avoid using an all-black background, as this tends to darken the overall look of the video.

- Don't make your video a straight-ahead sales pitch. You should be (mostly) providing a service rather than annoying your website visitors with an infomercial. While this approach has some limited value, it will be far more interesting for your visitors to watch you in consumer-targeted videos rather than commercials, and they will be less likely to be put off and click off.

- Don't stand in front of the camera reading a script word for word. This is boring video. You should be engaged in an activity and speaking at a natural pace. Pretend that the camera is a person who's accompanying you on part of an inspection.

- Don't act lethargic. Be confident in your stance to reflect your confidence in your professional abilities. The camera will tend to cloak subtle movements and weak posture. You'll have to go a little bit over the top for things to look natural on film. Be sure to stand tall with your shoulders back. Plant both feet solidly on the ground, and avoid rocking from side to side. If you don't know what to do with your hands, try holding a tool or item that you normally use during the job (such as a clipboard or some safety gear), or stand with your hands behind your back (similar to the military parade rest position). Don't lean on anything. Be expressive in your movements when they're intentional, and avoid nervous movements, such as tapping your feet or fussing with a tool.

- Don't make off-color jokes or engage in non-professional behavior (even if it's scripted) during your spot. While you may want to show that you're an upbeat, funny and relaxed person, you may not want to have such moments preserved for time immemorial on the Web if they misfire. Remember who you're creating your videos for and how you want your business represented.

- Don't go crazy with post-production. Loud or fast music, and special effects and quick or flashy edits will do more to distract the viewer than add something worth watching.

- Don't make your video longer than two or three minutes. Keep the topic brief.

- Don't post your videos in multiple locations. They belong on your website and, ideally, also on You Tube (which is owned by Google). If you use Twitter, Facebook, or some other social networking tool, post a link for the video that drives traffic to your website—that's your ultimate goal.

In the end, the most important thing is to be yourself. These tips should help you prepare, but if you over-think things, you might start second-guessing every word and every movement you make on camera. Before your shoot, take a moment to remind yourself that you're a great professional inspector and that people ought to hire you. Take a deep breath, smile, and say, "Take one."

Tip: Create a video showing you on the job during an inspection.

"Watch My One-Minute Video" — Why does this sentence work?

It works because people don't want to commit the time to watch a 45-minute video. Alerting visitors to the fact that the video on your website is only a minute or two long actually entices them to watch it.

(And the argument for including a short video on your website in the first place is compelling. Many people are visual learners, and the ability to remember information, faces and impressions is also primarily visually-based.)

The theory for specifically advertising a short video comes from years ago when grocery stores used to place popular items at the end of long aisles, which forced consumers to commit to walking down them—and past lots of other potential purchases, of course. The strategy eventually backfired as consumers who saw long aisles began carefully reading the aisle signs at the front of the store before committing to heading down a long aisle, thereby making their shopping trips much more efficient and shorter in duration. Consumers basically stopped consenting to having their time engineered for them through the store's bald attempt to separate them from their cash through impulse purchases.

So, grocery stores resolved this silent consumer revolt by opening up aisles to other aisles—creating a more divergent traffic pattern—so that consumers could see that, halfway down the aisle, they could jump sideways to another aisle. Grocery stores gave up precious shelf space to create these intersections between aisles, and consumers regained some of their freedom while offering up more shopping time.

The compromise worked.

The same strategy works for inspectors who have online promotional videos on their websites, too. Keep your visitors on your site for as long as possible by giving them useful information, but let them know that you respect their time by presenting that information sensibly and in a user-friendly format, which includes videos. Advertising that your video is short lets them know that their valuable time will be well spent.

InterNACHI produces Custom Online Video Ads for its members. See what we can do for you by visiting www.InspectorOutlet.com

YouTube

Google owns YouTube, so it gives YouTube clear preference in its organic search results. It's not unusual to see a new YouTube video outrank a website that has been up for years. And think about your script from the standpoint of search-engine optimization. According to Google, their new audio-indexing system uses speech-recognition technology to transform speech into text and then ranks videos by spoken-keyword relevance, YouTube metadata, and freshness.

Radio Ads

Many local radio stations are constantly short on new or live content. Offer yourself to them for interviews. Shows that are of interest to the general public are the best forums for what you offer.

Tip: If you're interviewed on a call-in show, you don't want the host to beg for callers, so have your employees or friends call in with some pre-written, generic questions that are helpful to a wide variety of listeners.

Leads

Whenever you meet someone new, always try to find a point in the conversation where you can tell him/ her what you do for a living, and always have your business cards handy to give out.

Deputizing Your Employees, Family & Friends

You should supply your employees, family members and friends with your brochures and business cards to hand out. If your employees have their own names on your company's business cards, perhaps it should include only the company's contact information. You might even prepare a box for each of them that contain a sample of all of your company's different marketing materials.

Instruct Your Employees to Keep Their Eyes Open

Your employees should always be looking around for other services that your clients might need. If you provide more than one service, your employees should be noticing if your clients need something else that you sell, and they should report such discoveries back to you.

"Hey, boss, while we were at Mrs. Smith's, I noticed that she also needs...."

How to Turn Your Field Employee into a Salesperson

You can't. You can turn a salesperson into a field employee with training, but it's almost impossible to do the reverse. So, instead, turn your field employee into walking marketers. Do this by providing them with brochures that list all the additional services that your company offers. Instruct them to hand out the brochures to every client they come in contact with. The only thing your employees need to learn to do is to say something simple, such as, "Here's a list of other services we offer."

Tip: You might want to get your field employees to upsell annual home maintenance inspections. You can perhaps offer them a modest commission for their successful sales.

Ask Your Former Clients for Leads

This is a sample letter that you can mail to your database of former clients. It's designed to get you more work in several ways. If you haven't created a database of the names and contact information of all of your past clients, you should, and you should work it regularly. By now, your client has probably forgotten your name and has misplaced your contact information. Building a word-of-mouth business requires a little bit of work.

[Your Logo or Letterhead]

[Date]

Dear [Former Client],

I hope you and your family are well. It's been a while since we last talked, and I wanted to touch base with you to let you know about some services I'm offering that you (or someone you know) could probably use. [Insert info on your latest news, new services and/or return services.]

If you have any questions about the services I've already rendered for you, or if you have any questions about any of my other services that you may be interested in, please give me a call anytime at [Your Phone Number].

Thank you in advance for the opportunity to serve you or someone you know.

Sincerely,

[Your Name]

[Your Company Name]

[Your Phone Number]

[Your Email Address]

[Your Website Address]

Remember, your former clients are most likely to hire you again and least likely to "shop" for you.

Tip: Don't forget to include several of your brochures and business cards with each letter.

Advanced Tip: InterNACHI members can download this other sample letter to mail to former clients: www.nachi.org/former-client-letter

Ask Your Vendors for Leads

This is best done by phone. Referrals from real estate professionals are also a good source of leads.

Start a Referral Program

If you don't have a referral program for the clients you get, you're missing out on potential work. Create an incentive for employees, family members, friends, former clients, vendors, subcontractors, and even your barber to recommend you. Try offering something like a $50 gift card to any homeowner who refers you to someone whose inspection you schedule. Email the details of your referral program to everyone in your database.

Jobsite Yard Signs

These signs should display your company name, logo, phone number and website address. Also, if your company name doesn't explain what kind of work you do, add a tagline that lists the services you offer, such as:

ABC Pros at Work
Specializing in Rural Home, Outbuilding & Pool Inspections

(123) 456-7890
wwwABCPros-dot-com

Also, add a brochure holder or tube box to the sign (the type real estate agents use) to offer your brochures.

Tip: If your jurisdiction prohibits commercial yard signs, make them "caution signs" instead (that include your contact information), as the city probably won't complain about a caution sign. Or, you can park your work truck on the street for maximum truck signage visibility.

Vacant Lot Signs

Look for vacant lots that are visible from high-traffic roads. Call the owner and see if you can rent the lot for the purpose of placing a sign. To be legible from the road, the sign will likely have to be much bigger than you imagine.

Tip: First check with your local jurisdiction to see if signs in vacant lots are prohibited.

Jobsite Door Hangers

Doorknob hangers are marketing pieces that are hung on the doorknobs of homes in the immediate vicinity of your inspection. The headline could say something like: "Your neighbor is a genius!" The hanger should include an explanation that you are currently working in the neighborhood, as well as your logo, a list of services you offer, and a call-to-action, such as:

"Call me on my cell phone while I'm in the neighborhood and I'll give you a free consultation."

Whoever hangs the doorknob hangers should be well-groomed and wearing a collared shirt with the company logo, and perhaps even a photo ID badge hanging from a lanyard around their neck. Check with the municipality first before sending someone out; some cities prohibit this practice.

InterNACHI's Member Marketing Department can design these for you. Visit nachi.org/marketing

Marketing Tip for Inspectors:
Hit Up the Neighbors with Your Annual Inspections

Many inspectors recommend that their clients have an annual inspection performed every fall. Seasonal maintenance is extremely important to a home's top condition, and the best time to have an annual inspection is before the weather turns cold.

In addition to recurring business from repeat customers, inspectors can capitalize on the annual inspection by alerting the client's neighbors. The neighborhood is really a built-in local market, so inspectors should take advantage of this kind of close-proximity marketing opportunity.

Upon completing an annual inspection, it's a good idea to mail a letter to all the neighbors asking them if they would like a pre-winter inspection. Include a copy of the testimonial from the client whose inspection you just completed (but be sure to first ask your client for permission to do this).

You can look up the neighboring homes' addresses on the county assessor's website, and by matching up the owners' addresses to the homes' addresses, you can personalize each letter. (And if some of the homes are rentals, you can still send a letter to the owners and offer an inspection, and suggest that it will minimize and/or pinpoint their own landlord maintenance tasks.)

Here's a sample letter:

YOUR NEIGHBOR IS A GENIUS!

Dear [Prospect's Name],

I'm writing to let you know that we performed an annual home inspection for [Client's Name] on [Client's Street]. [Client's Name] has given us permission to send you their enclosed testimonial.

As an InterNACHI member trained and certified in providing top-quality home inspections, I offer my extensive experience to help you keep your home in optimum condition. Before the onset of winter, let me evaluate your home and help you discover any deferred maintenance and other potential issues before they become problems. Winter is the most inconvenient time of year for daily disruptions and costly repairs, which is why I strongly recommend that you have me perform your first annual inspection now.

I'd like to talk to you about our annual inspection service. Please call me on my cell phone at [Your Phone Number] for a free consultation. I look forward to hearing from you soon.

Sincerely,

[Your Name]

[Your Inspection Company Name]

[Your Phone Number]

[Your Email Address]

[Your Website Address]

Encl. 3: Testimonial, brochure, business card

Annual inspections clustered in the same neighborhoods during the fall can mean big business at a time when new-home builds and purchases are slowing down for the year. Just a little bit of research (and some stamps) can mean the difference between a dip and a drop in revenue.

Always Include a P.S.

People read their mail over a wastebasket. To speed up the process of determining what mail is important and what should get tossed, many people skip to the end of the letter to get to the punch line. Inspectors should provide an extra incentive to recipients to respond to a call to action, such as including:

"Call me now while you're thinking about it."

P.S. At a minimum, your P.S. should quickly re-state your reason for writing.

Every Door Direct Mail® Service

Using the Every Door Direct Mail® (EDDM®) service provided by the U.S. Postal Service, you can reach homeowners in the area you want to work. You don't even need to know names or street addresses. You simply identify the neighborhoods you want to target, and your printed piece is delivered with the day's mail to every address.

Teaser Copy

"One-hundred percent of the shots you don't take don't go in."

—Wayne Gretzky

Teaser copy is a message pre-printed on the envelope that attempts to cause the recipient to open it. Don't use teaser copy. It just makes your envelope appear to contain junk mail before it's even opened.

Post-Inspection Letter with Neighbor Testimonial

Upon completing an inspection, it's a good idea to mail a letter to all the neighbors asking them for work. Include a copy of the testimonial you ask for from the client whose inspection you just completed.

Here's a sample letter:

Dear [Prospect's Name],

I'm writing to let you know that I performed a home inspection in your neighborhood for [Client's Name] on [Client's Street]. [Client's Name] has given me permission to send you the enclosed testimonial.

I offer extensive experience in [Your Services].I'd like to talk to you about my inspection services. Call me on my cell phone at [Your Phone Number] for a free consultation. I look forward to hearing from you soon.

Sincerely,

[Your Name]

[Your Company Name]

[Your Phone Number]

[Your Email Address]

[Your Website Address]

eNewsletters

Inspectors who want to connect with prospective clients, as well as stay in the forefront of the minds of former clients and other home professionals, should consider creating an e-newsletter to email to subscribers every month.

The advantages of doing this are many. Newsletters are a great way to improve client retention. Similar to website videos, the purpose of your e-newsletters should be to provide a public service, but the marketing value to you is built in. Inspectors can acquire a free customizable template from specialist vendors, such as MailChimp or Constant Contact.

Many e-newsletters are designed to be smartphone-compatible. Subscribers can scan a QR code that you can have printed on your brochures and business cards, and this allows them to read your latest news on their mobile devices so that they don't need to be glued to their laptops.

Emailing the newsletter is free if you have less than a couple of thousand subscribers (terms vary by vendor). In exchange, you'll receive reports and updates detailing who reads your newsletter, which can alert you to do some friendly and timely follow-up.

Tip: Check out InterNACHI's Homeowner eNewsletter at www.nachi.org/home-maintanence-newsletter and read about how you can get your clients to sign up for it. You can customize every monthly issue for each client based on their specific type of home and issues revealed during your inspection. In return, you'll receive all kinds of user data that will help you target repeat business (and new clients) more efficiently.

How to Acquire (and Not Acquire) Subscribers

Inspectors should always save contact information and sort their email contacts in their online address book for business purposes. Take advantage of the fields in your address book that allow you to fill in reminders and details about who each contact is, be they real estate professionals you've worked with (or ones you're trying to get to know), vendors, past clients, and those who have expressed an interest in your work. This makes inviting clients and industry colleagues to subscribe to your e-newsletter easy.

You can also trade and/or pay a fee for email lists from service vendors, home builders, building suppliers, and real estate professionals. You can troll for prospective subscribers in the public domain. Don't forget that those who lead you to prospective clients are themselves good candidates to become regular newsletter subscribers. Don't discount the long term in any marketing endeavor.

Start by emailing these lists of prospective subscribers a sample of what your newsletters include by way of an announcement, along with a link to your website, and a few headlines or the first sentence or two of an informational article that hooks your readers.

You must be careful not to send these contacts your entire e-newsletter unsolicited; they must opt in by actively subscribing, using a link that you provide them that you get from your newsletter service. Otherwise, you will be in violation of federal spam laws. It's also a good way to alienate potential clients and strain current business relationships; busy people don't like to have their time disrespected by being sent spam from business contacts who flout both federal regulations and commonsense 'netiquette.

Keep It Simple

Once you've worked out the terms of your e-newsletter with your service of choice, take some time to develop your template. Keep the name of your e-newsletter uncomplicated and easy to recognize so that recipients will instantly associate it with your business.

Keep the design simple and the layout easy to read; too many visuals, including colors and animation, may detract from your content, which should be your newsletter's focus. Also, most email services won't automatically display images. Your newsletter should be designed with that in mind and not rely heavily on images in order to be understood.

There are some elements that all online newsletters must have, including:

- a brief description or logline of what your newsletter is, such as "A Monthly Newsletter from ABC Inspections";

- an "unsubscribe" link for recipients who want to opt out of receiving your newsletter;

- a contact link to notify you (or your newsletter vendor/manager) of any technical glitches;

- your business contact information; and

- a copyright notation for each issue.

What to Include in Your eNewsletters

Give careful thought to the order of each item you include in each issue, and its general theme and flow. For a small fee or barter, you can include ads from contacts and vendors; however, remember that the thrust of your newsletter is informational, and not a sneaky way to monetize and purvey third-party advertising, so any ads you include should be lower in the presentation lineup.

Readers scan newsletters. You want to make it easy to find something of interest to them. The more content your e-newsletter contains, the more important it is to include an eye-catching table of contents. The items in your table of contents should link to their corresponding areas of the newsletter for easy navigation.

Other items you can incorporate:

- a "Here's what ABC Inspections is up to this month"-type of article to maintain a sense of timeliness;

- consumer-related articles that you or someone you commission can write. Keep these topical and seasonal;

- informational articles that are relevant to most of your subscribers;

- informational articles that are of interest to the real estate profession, such as local housing trends;

- a link to your website;

- direct links to your website's videos;

- images of an inspection in progress (after acquiring any necessary permissions, which you can forgo by providing prior notice in your client contract);

- images of your staff in action;

- information and links for community events, especially those sponsored by you or that you'll be participating in;

- links to sites that are important to you (although you should be careful that these are not so politicized that you will alienate any prospective clients); and

- informational articles and links in the public domain that are relevant to your business activities. Material sourced from the public domain means that you aren't required to get anyone's permission to use it. Reproducing copyrighted material on your website or in your e-newsletters requires prior permission, and possibly a fee, to avoid copyright infringement.

InterNACHI has hundreds of original articles for free use by members. Visit InterNACHI's Inspection Articles Library at www.nachi.org/articles

What Not to Include

With the exception of ads and static information that your readers will expect to see every month, each of your newsletters should contain fresh content, and this rotating content should be prominently featured. Keep the static items lower in the presentation lineup. Remember that the purpose of your newsletter is to cultivate new business.

So, don't include:

- personal information, such as family vacation photos or details about activities not related to your business;

- gossip or criticism about anyone or their business. Rumor-mongering or trashing colleagues and fellow members of the community will do more damage to your image than your target's, and it's a surefire way to turn off both old clients and new ones. Furthermore, you could be sued for defamation or libel;

- political, religious and other hot-button topics. A business newsletter is not an appropriate forum for such opinions;

- sounds, music, large images or animation that may take a while to load, which can cause your readers to close your newsletter without reading it;

- any content or links to content that may be considered adult in nature; or

- copyrighted information or images. Do not plagiarize content and pass it off as your own. If there's something online that you really want to include in your newsletter, you must first ask for permission from the copyright holder (the creator or license holder) in order to link to it. However, remember that your ultimate goal is to drive traffic to your website, so make sure the content has some unique or undeniable value before going to that trouble. Including content and links that send your readers away from your newsletter should be a rare option that you provide (with the exception of ad providers).

eNewsletter Data and What to Do with It

The data collected by your newsletter manager is essential information that will help you methodically design your subsequent newsletters. Also, it will help you conduct personal follow-up, based on your individual subscriber's reading trends. You should take advantage of these user metrics, as generating leads is the main reason for launching a newsletter in the first place. Good marketing is anticipating what your clients want, and the algorithms involved in collecting user data make your users' interests and habits very easy for you to track.

The data you can get from your newsletter manager includes:

- how many people click on or open your emailed newsletter;

- who these people are;

- when they open your newsletter. Special alerts can prompt you to follow up with subscribers personally, which they will really appreciate;

- how much time users spend reading your newsletter;

- how often particular users read your newsletter by monthly trends;

- which links within the e-newsletter get clicked on the most and which get clicked on the least, including those of vendors;

- the geographical location of your subscribers; and

- interactive features, such as auto-respond messages and online polls. These can add a personal touch for each user's experience, which can ignite their anticipation for future issues.

Once you have acquired data, you can make marketing decisions based on it, such as what content is popular and what's unpopular (including ad providers), how much time users can realistically devote to reading your newsletter (which may lead you to shorten it, if it's especially long), and what they'd like to see in your issues that you don't yet provide.

As well as demonstrating that you're comfortable with online technology, e-newsletters can arguably gather more information for you than you actually provide in them. By committing a few evenings or weekends each month, you can use interesting articles and information that you run across and save for yourself anyway and insert them in your newsletters. You'll also become more motivated to research industry trends on a regular basis, and you can parlay your discoveries into fresh newsletter content. A newsletter lets you to compile this information and package it attractively, and rewards you by automatically filtering through all the users' details to provide you with the solid information you need to help you focus your marketing efforts for acquiring new business. It's easier than you think, so start exploring this low- to no-cost opportunity now.

Tip: Send your former clients a newsletter that makes them feel like an "insider" who's connected to you while you're subliminally marketing to them. As an example, mention the importance of getting an Annual Home Maintenance Inspection performed every year.

Creating Customer Profiles for Marketing Purposes

From a marketing standpoint, there is nothing like delivering the right message to the right prospect, at the right time. There is little sense in wasting money on advertising that reaches prospects that have no use for your products or services. To customize messages for your potential clients, you need to have information about them—information that you intentionally gather and store. This information can also be used to create loyal customer relationships, whether those clients are repeat customers or whether they refer you to other new customers.

As an example of how customer profiling works, it's been proven that online purchasing is enhanced when buyers are shown other choices similar to ones they've already made, or from vendors they've already purchased from, or even those whose sites they've simply browsed. These "recommendations," such as those shown while you're shopping on Amazon.com, or the scrolling ads that appear in your free email account window, are the result of mining stored data using cookies and analytics. But just because you may be a one-person operation doesn't mean that you can't do some of this valuable data-mining yourself, old-school.

Here are some examples of things you should consider trying to capture when "profiling" your inspection clients:

- the customer's age
- income level
- profession/employer (or retired?)
- gender
- education level
- personality (i.e., Were they pleasant to interact with?)
- Is the customer a do-it-yourselfer?
- How long has the family been in the home?
- personal interests and hobbies (as evidenced by items around the home)
- Do they have pets?

- household size and composition:
  - single?
  - single parent with small children?
  - single parent with school-age children?
  - single parent with teenage children?
  - couple?
  - couple with small children?
  - couple with school-age children?
  - couple with teenage children?
  - couple with children living away from home?
  - extended family in the home (such as elderly parents/grandparents)?
  - any special-needs family members?

You should also compile data about the home itself, such as:

- location
- the age of the home
- the size of the home
- the last sale price of the home (and last assessed taxes)
- any outbuildings, such as garages or barns?
- Does the home have a swimming pool?
- What type of roof?
- What major repairs are evident?
- What upgrades have been made (and when) according to any permits that were required to be drawn? (This information is often available through the property's tax assessment records.)

Don't forget to track and update information having to do with your own interaction and transaction(s) with your clients, such as:

- products and services you have previously sold them
- What did they buy?
- reasons for buying?
- How often do they buy?
- How did they hear about you?
  - website?
  - review site?
  - friends or family?
  - colleagues?
  - real estate professional?
  - trade show?
  - brochure?

- ◦ e-newsletter?
- ◦ print ad?
- products and services you have previously marketed to them
- How did they prefer to communicate with you (phone or email)?
- What were the results of the Client Satisfaction Survey you asked them to fill out the last time you worked for them?

You can gather all this information from a number of sources, including on the jobsite, from your own client paperwork, and from public records (such as those found in person or online through the county tax assessor's department, and other public sources). Each time you interact with your customer, his/her profile should evolve.

By entering this data into a basic spreadsheet program, you can not only keep track of client data in an organized way, but you can use certain information for occasional targeted campaigns that focus only on certain clients in certain areas or those having specific identifiers or demographics.

If you send out monthly e-newsletters to your past clients, you can use some of this information to customize them for your subscribers. This personalized touch will make your marketing memorable.

It's not necessary (and not very smart time- or money-wise) to launch only single-note, generic advertising campaigns and then cross your fingers and hope they reach someone who needs what you're offering. These days, it's easier than you think to actually target clients who want your services.

There is a surprising amount of easy-to-access customer information that you can plug into your own marketing plan, and some of it you simply have to observe or ask for; the rest you can find online, and without paying for it, like the big dogs do. So, make the most of your marketing by customizing the right message to "hyper-target" the right customer at the right time.

Working the Public Records

Public records are exactly what their name implies: they're records that are available to the public. While increasingly more institutions that accept, record and store records have put many of their documents online for convenient remote access (depending on the type, size and location), there exist offices that still require an in-person visit (and perhaps a small photocopying fee). Depending on the type of record you're after, you may be able to view it only on the premises.

Becoming familiar with your local government offices and agencies, as well as the documents they maintain that are available to you as a citizen, can guide you to leads that you may not have considered before. With some curiosity and preparation, you'll find records that are perfect—and perfectly legal—for you to exploit for your marketing.

Mining Building Permits

Head down to your local building and zoning department and mine their database of new building permits. Sending these residents a letter telling them about the services you offer and that you're available to help them could be very fruitful. You can get a head start on your search by going online and reading the meeting minutes and upcoming agendas for your local planning and zoning commission or department so that you know about new projects going up. This information can also give you some clues about otherwise attractive projects that are experiencing problems getting approved, zoned or funded, as these may not be worth investing a lot of time in trying to sell your inspection services to until they're green-lit by The Powers That Be.

Mining Real Estate Transactions

Your local newspaper likely publishes a list of recent real estate transfers. New owners are often looking to renovate, and sellers are often new owners, too. It's a great idea to send these folks a letter listing your services and telling them that you're available to help them with inspections for any projects they're contemplating, especially because many new homeowners may have their home-improvement projects on their to-do list, but not the inspector for the work. Your well-timed marketing letter may be more welcomed than you think.

Mining Public Tax Records

Your local county tax assessor's office maintains a list of all real properties under its jurisdiction. In these records, you'll find a wealth of comprehensive details about the property, such as: the year it was built; its architectural style or type (including foundation); its legal description; the type and date of any renovations that required a permit; the number of rooms it has and its overall square footage; whether there are any attached or ancillary structures on the property; and the type of utilities it uses.

Additionally, the record includes: a history of its transfers (including refinancing); the type of document used to transfer or refinance ownership; the assessed value of the real estate; the amount of the most recent taxes assessed; the name of the owner of record; and the address that the property tax bill is mailed to. The information in these records can help you target the affluent or other type of ideal prospect and craft your letter to include important, specific details.

Tip: Remember that mailing your marketing letter to the property address doesn't guarantee that it will reach the property owner, especially if it's a commercial property or a rental. However, mailing your marketing letter to the address noted in the public record (where the property's tax assessments are sent) probably does.

Associations

You should also consider mining housing-related associations, such as neighborhood homeowners associations (HOAs), local investor groups, the Better Business Bureau, and your Chamber of Commerce. Gear your letter specifically to your recipient so that it has a better chance of not going straight into the trash.

For instance, for a member of a real estate investors group, start your letter with:

"As a real estate investor, you're probably interested in…"

Use some creativity to anticipate the types of services that you offer that may be most attractive to your targeted group. If you have a close friend or colleague who belongs to any of these kinds of associations, conduct an informal interview with him or her to find out what's currently on their radar so that you can tailor your marketing to be timely and effective.

List-Sharing

List-sharing is another efficient way to market because it's simple and complementary. It works like this: You give your mailing list to a company that doesn't directly compete with you, and they give you theirs.

Cross-Mailing

Offer to include a flyer from a non-competing business in one of your mailings in exchange for your flyer going out in theirs.

Tip: Make sure the extra weight of the flyer doesn't require an increase in the cost of postage for either party.

Be Careful

Don't accidentally send a discount offer to a client you recently charged full price.

Maintaining a basic database of the dates of mailings, the types of marketing pieces you send out, and the recipients you target can prevent you from duplicating efforts and annoying potential clients, as well as help you pinpoint which campaigns are the most (and least) effective. Your marketing should evolve based on its response, or lack thereof.

Getting in Front of Your Prospects

Offer to provide all the hot cup sleeves your local coffee shop can use. You can buy these for pennies apiece. Have them printed to say something along the lines of:

> *This cup sleeve is brought to you by*
> *ABC Inspections,*
> *Hoboken's Premier Home Inspector.*

These sleeves act just like a business card, so don't forget to include your business name, logo, phone number, website address, and list of services you offer (if there's room). Get your company right in the face of prospects every morning. The best part of this low-cost marketing piece is that someone else is handing them out for you. Talk about repeat impressions!

Tip: Most of these sleeves are made of compostable cardboard. So, while you're having them printed anyway, you might as well tout that they are "biodegradable" or made from "75% post-consumer waste," or whatever applies. Remember that being green sells.

Press Releases

Inspectors should use the format of the standard press release to make announcements on their websites and inspector blogs. This lends an official quality to any announcements that deserve particular attention or that are time-sensitive.

This will help the website visitor distinguish between sales-type information and general news announcements about the inspector's business.

Press releases can also be emailed to business contacts to help spread the word, as well as increase essential SEO hits—a huge advantage of having your press releases searchable online. Since they are considered soft marketing, press releases are more likely to be widely distributed by the recipients while having the same impact as paid advertising.

Some good uses of press releases include announcing the following:

- introducing new staff;
- the formation of new partnerships with consulting experts or other industry-related personnel;
- the inspector's having earned new training accreditations and/or certifications;
- offering new types of services;
- the business's relocation or expansion;
- a change in the business's name or contact information;
- the inspector joining industry-related associations, such as InterNACHI; and
- the formation of a new InterNACHI chapter, with the sender of the press release as its president or spokesperson.

Here's a sample press release:

CONTACT: John Smith, President
(720) 555-1212
john.smith@abcinspections-dot-com
wwwabcinspections-dot-com

FOR IMMEDIATE RELEASE

BOULDER, Colo. (August 22, 2015)—ABC Inspections is pleased to announce that John Smith is now credentialed as a Certified Master Inspector (CMI)®, which is the inspection industry's top professional designation.

The Master Inspector Certification Board has awarded the Certified Master Inspector (CMI)® designation to Mr. Smith for demonstrating the highest level of competency by completing 1,000 fee-paid inspections and/or Continuing Education credit hours, for having been in the inspection business for at least three years, and for abiding by the industry's toughest Code of Ethics.

Mr. Smith wishes to thank his clients and colleagues for their continued support of ABC Inspections. Homeowners may schedule their inspection by calling him at 720-555-1212 or by visiting ABC's website at wwwabcinspections-dot-com.

ABC Inspections has been serving Boulder County for the past 20 years, specializing in historic home and new-construction inspections, with an emphasis on energy savings.

Note the various conventions, elements and formatting in the sample press release, from top to bottom, which should be used for all press releases (as they will lend your press release legitimacy and a better chance of being published):

1. Your name, title, and contact information (but not mailing address), as well as website address, should be included following the capped and (optionally) bolded word "CONTACT." This will give the staffer who receives your press release an easy way to instantly contact you without having to hunt for your information. The press release doesn't have to be issued by the company president, however. But the person who can field questions about it (should any arise) should be the one noted as the contact person. (The company's full name and snail-mail address are already included in your letterhead on which you'll include your press release, so it's unnecessary to include them in the line for your contact information.)

2. The header of a press release is "FOR IMMEDIATE RELEASE," which should be centered and bolded, and optionally italicized. Some organizations send out their press releases before they want them actually released; this gives the recipient extra time to organize multiple press releases from different entities, etc. In this case, the press release should read "EMBARGOED UNTIL AUGUST 1, 2013." The option of embargoing a press release also allows the writer to make any changes and send a revised press release before the actual release date. An embargoed press release should be sent out only as needed. Typically, most press releases are for immediate publication.

3. The city is spelled out using all capital letters.

4. The state or province is abbreviated in the style originated by the Associated Press, which is the style guide used by newspapers. Because press releases, as a form, fall somewhere between advertisements and actual news, the AP Style guidelines are followed for press releases.

5. The date is enclosed in parentheses. Except for month names that are short (including March, April, May, June and July), they are also abbreviated using AP Style, such as "Jan.," "Aug.," Sept.," and so forth.

6. Following the date in parentheses is the em-dash or double-dash, without any spaces between the date and the body of the press release.

7. The body of the text follows; it can be more than one paragraph, with the main announcement in the first sentence, followed by additional supporting information. The press release in its entirety should not exceed one page. Make the news timely and focused; save your "kitchen-sink" marketing for other types of mailings.

8. The end of the press release is indicated by a triple hash mark that is centered on the page. This is another AP Style convention that indicates to both newspaper editors and radio announcers where the press release actually ends.

9. The italicized information below the hash marks identifies the person or organization supplying the press release. This information is straightforward and factual but may have a mild marketing tone to it.

When emailing your press release to other parties, such as past clients, real estate professionals, and industry associations and organizations, be sure to put your press release on your letterhead and convert it into a PDF, and email that as an attachment, indicating in your email's subject line that it is a press release, so that its timeliness will be readily understood. This will give your recipients the option of posting the entire document on their own website (which will display your business letterhead), or they can simply copy and paste the text. Your press release should be no longer than one page and should contain no photos, graphics or pictures, except those that may already appear in your company letterhead.

Press releases should be used sparingly so that your company's legitimate news doesn't get ignored because you've attempted to disguise routine marketing as something newsworthy. Marketing doesn't rate the same level of attention, especially when you are sending out your press release to third parties.

Some reasons that press releases should not be used include announcing the following:

- special sales or discounts;

- non-business-related news, including news of a personal nature;

- endorsements of other businesses, entities or products; or

- news or information (such as a press release, white paper or news article) that is plagiarized from another source and repackaged as your own. Your press release should be specifically relevant to your business, rather than to your industry at large.

Press releases are a great way to announce news affecting your business that lends legitimacy to its importance. Used with discretion, they are a meaningful way to cultivate your connections with people and organizations that can help indirectly market your business and services.

Tip: Be sure to check out www.CertifiedMasterInspector.org to see how you can become a CMI.

Tracking Results

"What gets measured gets done."

—Tom Peters

You must track where your leads are coming from, how much those leads cost, how many of those leads convert to inspections, and the profit margin on those appointments. The success of any lead-generation program is determined by its cost-per-dollar of profit generated, as represented by a percentage.

For example, let's say you put together a multi-piece mailing that includes a cover letter, a testimonial from a local client, a brochure, and a business card. Now, let's assume that you mail it to 100 people who live near an inspection you recently completed for another client. If the piece costs $2 with postage, your cost would be $200. Now, let's say that you get 50 leads from that mailing, and 15 scheduled appointments for an inspection. It cost you $200 to generate 15 inspections, for which you'd charge between $350 and $500 each, on average. Not a bad marketing investment.

Inspector Outlet's Report Presentation Kit

Many inspectors rely on the same marketing techniques as their competitors. They don't understand the competitive edge they will gain if they put just a little more thought and money into their presentation.

InterNACHI's Home Inspection Kit, available to InterNACHI members at www.InspectorOutlet.com, includes everything that a Realtor wants to see in a presentation kit:

- a place for an inspection report;
- a pre-closing checklist;
- a copy of InterNACHI's Standards of Practice for Performing a General Home Inspection;
- a copy of the International Standards of Practice for Inspecting Residential Properties;
- a copy of InterNACHI's Code of Ethics;
- a copy of InterNACHI's Glossary of Terms; and
- a copy of *Now That You've Had a Home Inspection*.

… all in one attractive package.

Follow these instructions to learn what to do with the kits once you receive them:

1. Call all of your existing Realtor contacts to tell them you have just updated your entire inspection package, and that you would like to stop by to show it to them and leave them a sample. You can tell them that you need only five minutes to show them your new system. They may be hesitant to give up their time, but it's important that you see them in person. You most likely get most of your inspection referrals from about 20% of the Realtors you know (following the "80/20 Rule"). Even though you get referrals from them often, you probably do not actually see them all that often in person. This is a great opportunity to have a little face-time with them. Just calling them up to say "Hi!" is great, but you really should have a reason to see them and take up their valuable time. To the 80% of the Realtors who give you 20% of your inspection referrals, it is even more important to see them, and this gives you a great reason.

2. Now that you have confirmed some appointments, you need something to say when you get there. If they are pressed for time, get right to the point and keep it to about five minutes. The longer you are there, the better your relationship will be. The better you know someone, the higher the likelihood that they will recommend you. What you need to show them is that you have upgraded your entire presentation package. You now use a printed binder that includes easy-to-read tabs, a glossary of terms to help their clients better understand their new house, and a pre-closing walk-through checklist for them to use after the inspection and just before they go to the closing. Of course, your new report presentation package also includes *Now That You've Had a Home Inspection*, the home-maintenance guide about how to preserve the value of their home (a gift for them to keep). Ask for some business cards and offer to put one in the binder so their client will always have it on hand.

Point out that, unlike other inspectors who just staple their reports or put them in a 10-cent folder, your new inspection kit is way too nice for someone to discard, and because it has "The Homeowner's Handbook" inside, they will probably keep it on their bookshelf.

1. You should offer to leave the Realtor a copy as a tool for him to show the different inspector options that are available to their customers. Most likely, you will be the only inspector with enough forethought to have given a sample report with a full presentation kit.

2. You should point out that one of the main reasons you upgraded to this new package is your belief that whatever the inspector does reflects back on the Realtor, and you want to bring your image up to the highest level possible so that everything you do makes the Realtor look even better.

3. Ask if there is one other Realtor in the office whom s/he respects, is a professional like himself, and who might like to see the benefits of your professional presentation kit. Ask if that Realtor is available and if you could you be introduced right now. If that is impossible, just leave an entire kit with the front office and then follow up with a phone call. When you call back, you have a reason to call; it's to see if he got the package that you left him and to tell him that the reason you left it was because, of all the people in the organization, your Realtor friend thought that he was the ONE person in the organization who might appreciate this upgraded professional package the most.

4. Also ask if you could leave a copy in the lobby so that the public can compare the different inspectors in the area. If you are given permission, write "Lobby Copy—Do Not Remove" across the binder with a magic marker so it will stay there and not walk off with someone. For this one, glue your business card inside so that it stays there permanently. Always be sure to leave plenty of your brochures and business cards in the front and back pockets of the binder. Stop by on a regular basis to replenish the brochures and cards. That also gives you another opportunity to interact with agents in the office.

The Marketing Tool That Keeps on Marketing

Make sure your local real estate office has at least one.

What are real estate agents reading while waiting for you to finish the home inspection? Make sure it isn't the sports page! Give them something interesting to read.

Fill this 3-ring binder with some of the following:

- some local articles about real estate (from the local newspaper or the Internet);
- multiple copies of the rack card for InterNACHI's Buy-Back Guarantee Program;
- multiple copies of the handout for InterNACHI's Negligent Referral Program;
- multiple copies of the state-specific Continuing Education for Real Estate Professionals postcards;
- multiple copies of the article "What Really Matters";
- multiple copies of the article "Pre-Listing Inspections";
- a copy of InterNACHI's Code of Ethics;
- a copy of InterNACHI's Standards of Practice for Performing a General Home Inspection;
- a copy of InterNACHI's Continuing Education Policy;
- copies of your educational Certificates of Completion;
- your marketing literature, flyers or brochures;
- household tips, maintenance advice, etc., found in various articles at InterNACHI's Inspection Articles Library (www.nachi.org/articles);

- a copy of your InterNACHI Membership Certificate (www.nachi.org/mycertificate);

- a copy of your E&O insurance certificate (if you carry insurance);

- a copy of your state license (if your state issues them);

- copies of a few reference or thank-you letters from past clients (examples to follow);

- a copy of "Is Your Inspector Blind?" (www.nachi.org/blind);

- a copy of InterNACHI's home inspection Glossary of Terms;

- the seller inspections sample letters;

- a copy of a sample home inspection report;

- a copy of *Now That You've Had a Home Inspection*; and

- a copy of "My Promise to You." (www.nachi.org/promise)

Make sure one of your flyers or business cards is actually taped to the inside cover. Do not include anything that indicates that you are a "Candidate" or "Associate" member of any other inspection association. These derogatory terms will work against you (especially on the Internet). Many agents blacklist associates and candidates.

The words "International Association of Certified Home Inspectors" alone have a strong marketing value. This is especially true with agents who are unfamiliar with you or sellers' (listing) agents. The binder itself says a lot about you and your inspection service.

Some members have created labels on their own color printers that say "Please Read" or include their contact info. It is not difficult to match the label's color to the blue of this professional 3-ring binder. However, don't personalize the outside too much. You want the outside to appear to be a general reference manual from a national association.

If you notice the real estate agent sitting down, offer this binder to read. If you notice the real estate agent taking an interest in it or if s/he asks to take some of the literature in it, offer the entire binder to them to take and keep.

Permit sellers to read through them, too. Most sellers are also buyers and you may get another inspection.

You can find many of these products (postcards, rack cards, etc.) at www.InspectorOutlet.com

Nick's Tip

The time, energy and cost of producing nicely packed binders makes them too expensive (unless you form a family assembly line) to give out to sellers in hopes that they'll use your services on the buying end. Sellers can potentially give you only one inspection, at most. However, real estate agents will give you many inspections. Let them have the binder to keep. It is too nice for them to throw away and appears to be an office reference manual because it is from a national association, not a specific inspector. It will likely be kept on their office book shelf or in their real estate office library surrounded by other real estate agents. So, make sure at least one of your business cards or flyers is taped to the inside cover.

Tip: If you're leaving the binder at a real estate office, take a marker and write "DO NOT THROW OUT" over the back cover's white check mark. Write it a little sloppy and at an angle over the check mark. I won't explain why... Just trust me on this one.

If you have questions or suggestions, please email Nick at FastReply@nachi.org

To order, visit www.InspectorOutlet.com

----- **Original Message** -----

From: Steve Henderson

To: Nick Gromicko

Sent: Tuesday, August 01, 2006 1:31 PM

Subject: InterNACHI binders

Dear Nick,

My name is Steve Henderson. I am the owner of 1st Choice Home Inspections. I have been an inspector in Texas only a short time. I have 12 years' prior experience as a home builder.

I have been following all the marketing info that I can find on your website. And I want to thank you for such a great job. I recently got a case of InterNACHI binders. I copied all the suggested documents, added a few of my own, and had Kinko's print it all on card stock with their high-end laser printer. I began passing these out to the most successful Realtors, when one lady phoned me and said that there were three other ladies in their office wanting a notebook. Wow—people asking me to market to them! Amazing. I went and met two of the ladies at this office, which just happens to be one of the largest in my city. I spoke with them about doing pre-listing inspections and offered to do one complimentary for them. They loved the notebook so much, they asked if they could show it to their broker. Of course, I told them, sure.

Well, long story short, I have now been invited to give a presentation to all, around 30 Realtors in this firm. I wanted to ask if you have any specific info that I should use. Also, I was thinking of spending most of the time promoting pre-listing inspections, which, according to the Realtors in this area, no one else is doing. Yea! Any info or realtor testimonials about pre-listing inspections would be greatly appreciated.

Steve Henderson

How to Get Real Estate Agents to Hand Out Your Card

by Nick Gromicko

As a REALTOR for many years, I dreaded the thought of having to listen to a local home inspector's presentation at the mandatory Tuesday morning sales meeting. Home inspectors are so boring and never offer any information that is useful to my real estate business: *"Hi, I'm Bob from ABC Inspections. I'm thorough, I arrive on time, uh… did I say I was thorough?"* Uggghhh!

So, when I became a home inspector, I knew I needed to do something better, something interesting, and something that would actually be useful to real estate agents.

I came up with this:

I asked the broker/owner/manager of the real estate office if I could bring in a truckload of insulated concrete forms (ICFs) and demonstrate how a corner of a foundation is constructed using ICFs. I also explained that I was going to bring in a stack of 3.5x8-inch cards with all the sales talking points for ICFs printed on them. The cards would help a listing agent highlight a home with an ICF foundation, and they'd help a buyer's agent talk intelligently about ICF foundations when showing a home built with them. The cards were sized to fit in the glove compartment of the real estate agent's car. I said that I would provide enough cards for agents who wanted to give them out to their clients who were buying a home with an ICF foundation.

The presentation was very dramatic. Setting up the block corner gave me something to do with my hands and allowed me time to compose my thoughts between periods where I would turn to the audience of agents and tell them about the next benefit of ICF construction. I also passed around one of the insulated concrete forms, since they're light. Some agents actually stood up to watch and listen to my presentation. You know you're keeping your audience's attention when they rise to their feet.

At the end of my show-and-tell, I offered the cards. Every agent took them until I ran out. The broker/owner/manager asked if she could call the manager at one of their other offices and have me repeat my presentation at their sales meeting, too. Word got around town, and I eventually gave that same presentation at many real estate offices' sales meetings.

I was often asked to leave the ICF corner and a stack of the cards in the meeting room for an extra week so that agents who missed the presentation could see it and get some informational cards.

Agents would also call me when they ran out of cards. It was really great for my inspection business to have those talking-point cards in the glove compartments of all those agents' vehicles knowing that they were being handed out to all those consumers who were about to hire a home inspector.

You can probably guess what was on the back of those cards: my inspection company's contact information.

I accomplished so many things at once with these presentations:

1. I was able to personally introduce myself to dozens of real estate professionals gathered in the same room at the same time.

2. Rather than make an uninvited nuisance of myself, I helped take the monotony out of their typical sales meetings, which was another way I made my presence welcome and myself memorable.

3. I was able to demonstrate my competence and knowledge, and I offered them freely to the agents so that they could do the same for their clients.

4. I forged a bond with these professionals so that I'd be at the top of their list when they were recommending a home inspector.

5. I got them to market for me by passing out my cards.

You don't have to be a whiz at PowerPoint or an expert in construction to do what I did. When you know that you'll have a captive audience, you need only present an idea that they'll find useful and informative enough to pass along, even if it makes them sound like they're the expert. The relationship you create with real estate professionals is give and take, but you both have the same goals in mind: to serve your clients, and to close the sale.

Remember that you can take any type of concept to make this marketing strategy work. Find some local product or trend that may be especially popular in your area. Green homes, water features, septic systems, pools, barns, historic homes, bamboo flooring, Xeriscaping™—the ideas are endless. But it helps if you have the pulse of your service area, or at least an idea of the local listings, which are available as a matter of public record.

Once you land on an idea for a presentation, you don't need to spend weeks putting it together; just find the manufacturer's information and build on that. When I did my presentation on ICFs, the manufacturer provided facts and statistics on how strong ICFs are, their superior insulative value, etc. If you want to add some demonstration component like I did, you can look for DIY videos on YouTube, or visit a local installer. It just doesn't get any simpler.

Being innovative with your marketing doesn't mean you must be a genius researcher or gifted at oratory. It requires motivation and a little creativity. You're not likely to receive a random request from your local real estate office to give a presentation until they know its value; likewise, you can't wait for an invitation to be bold in your business.

Every Link in Your Lead-to-Profit Conversion Chain Must Be Strong

If you increase the number of leads that a mailing generates, increase the number of appointments booked, increase the number of inspections, or increase the amount of profit on each project, you earn much more profit. Always be trying to strengthen lead conversion.

Converting Calls into Appointments

What happens when your phone rings? How is your phone answered? It needs to be answered quickly and properly, every time. "Catch" the call. You should have instant access to your calendar every time your phone rings so that you can book an appointment. Your prospect will judge your business based on their interactions with you over the phone.

Remember to smile while talking on the phone; it's a fact that an upbeat facial expression can be transmitted through one's voice and speech. Regardless of how hectic or stressful your day is, do not convey this to your caller. And under no circumstances should you make disparaging remarks to your caller about anyone else you deal with, whether it's an over-billing vendor, a late office staffer, or (the kiss of death!) another client, regardless that any of your complaints about them may be justified. While you want to engage your prospect using a sense of trust, he or she is not your confidant. If you drop absentminded little tidbits about the everyday incidents on the job that are annoying or a recent source of tension for you, your caller will doubt your leadership and assume you'll add stress to their lives. Don't use negative conversation as a way to establish a business relationship. Leave the cares and concerns about your other appointments and company issues outside the realm of your interactions with your prospects. Focus only on them and what they want.

To that end, minimize workplace distractions. If you're on the road when a sales call comes in, pull over and take the call. If you're in a noisy area of your office, close the door or window, or find a quieter place to take the call. If your caller believes that they're phoning at an inconvenient time and you do nothing to mitigate it, they will feel less valued as a customer and may reconsider hiring you. They want someone who can give them the undivided attention they believe they deserve, because they do.

Ending a phone call effectively includes summarizing the call. Say, "Mrs. Smith, I have you scheduled for our appointment on Tuesday, May 5th at 11 a.m. Is that right?"

Wait for your client's acknowledgement. This recap will help reduce errors in scheduling. Before ending the phone conversation, ask your client if there is anything else that your company can do. Give your name again: "My name is Mary. If there's anything else we can do for you, or if your schedule changes, feel free to call me. Until then, Joe will see you on Tuesday."

Listen to Your Game

Using an inexpensive digital voice recorder or a phone jack and mini-recorder plugged into your landline, listen to both the way you answer the phone and the way you interact with potential customers during a sales visit. (Before you "tap" your own phone, check with your state's laws about recording your phone conversations, as it is illegal in some states.)

Listen for:

- your general tone of voice. Are you friendly and cheerful, or are you stressed and anxious?
- your enunciation and the clarity of your speech. Are you speaking too quickly or too low, or are you relaxed and articulate?
- your willingness to listen without interrupting—this is especially important in conversations that you want to end in a scheduled inspection;
- whether you respond appropriately, such as by voicing conversational cues to signal that you're actively listening, and by repeating back what your client says to you; and
- your closing. Did you actually ask for an appointment?

Tip: Ask your friends and family members to listen to some of the recordings and have them comment on what they hear.

You Can't Sell Unless You Get an Appointment

Some price shoppers don't think it's necessary for you to meet with them. They think you can give them a price over the phone. You have to get an appointment to sell these types of prospects. So, ask questions about the property, the system, or the component that the prospect probably can't answer.

Try something like this:

"I can probably help you over the phone if you can tell me…. And is it currently….?"

As soon as the prospect admits s/he doesn't know the answer to one of your questions, respond with:

"Oh, then, I'm going to have to come over and look at it before I can help you. When would be a convenient time for me to come by?"

If you get an appointment but not the scheduled inspection over the phone, be prepared to provide an estimate. But make sure your prospect knows that the cost (if not free) will be credited toward their inspection fee. Do what you can to lock up the job.

Work Every Lead to Death

A lead is a terrible thing to waste. When you leave a lead unclosed, it's like leaving money unclaimed. The lead you worked hard to acquire, which you then pursued with an appointment, could be waiting for one more nudge. Don't give up on any lead.

Tip: If you are too busy to work a lead, give it to a competitor you trust, and ask him/her to return the favor.

Before the Appointment

Before you go on an appointment to provide an estimate, first perform some basic online research about the property and potential customer. You can find out the price of the home, the location and what kind of area it is, whether your prospect is a professional or has made the news or is a philanthropist or civic activist, etc., etc. Anything you find doing ten minutes of research of the public record can help you get a feel for the prospect. If you discover that you have something in common with him/her, this information can be a great ice-breaker to help establish rapport. Plus, your prospect will realize that you've done your homework and have come to the appointment prepared to secure his/her inspection. That's what winners do, and it's a tactic that impresses other winners.

Tip: You can also do similar online research on the property address.

Call the Prospect to Confirm

Before you leave for the appointment, call the prospect and let them know you are on your way. This will reduce no-shows.

Professional Attire

*"Know first who you are,
and then adorn yourself accordingly."*

—Euripides

Should an inspector be judged by what s/he wears? We all like to think that people judge us objectively on our merits. But the reality is that strangers tend to stereotype us quickly. So, proper attire is an important part of an inspector's success. An inspector's core product is him/herself, and the product should be packaged professionally. The following are some tips for professional inspector attire, whether you're showing up to try to secure the inspection, or whether you've already scheduled it.

Clothing

- Never arrive to an appointment in dirty clothes. It's fine for clothes to get dirty during the inspection because the customer expects this to happen.

- If the inspection will require you to get dirty, consider bringing coveralls or a Tyvek® suit to wear over your clothing.

- If you have more than one inspection appointment scheduled for the day, consider bringing a change of clothes or at least a fresh shirt.

- Consider dressing up a bit (perhaps by wearing a tie) when working in more expensive neighborhoods, and dressing casually in more modest neighborhoods.

- Dress for the type of property. An inspection appointment at a horse farm may require boots. A dentist's office may require shoe covers.

- Dress for the climate. Shorts are fine in southern and beach areas but are often not adequate (or professional-looking) in cooler, northern climates.

- Cut-off jeans and gym shorts are not appropriate. Nicer shorts with pockets to carry small tools are acceptable, depending on the weather and region.

- Khakis or jeans can both be appropriate, depending on the client base.

- Tank tops and sleeveless t-shirts are never appropriate on any appointment.

- T-shirts are generally not recommended unless they sport your company logo or your company's name.

- Polo shirts and collared shirts are fine, as are sports jackets.

- T-shirts emblazoned with logos for sports teams or political or pop-culture references are never appropriate. Such messages and images can passively offend clients.

- A suit is not appropriate, as it implies that you're not a real inspector, but only a salesman.

- Shoes should be lace-up and rugged.

- In warmer climates or on summer days, it's acceptable to wear clean tennis shoes or boat shoes.

- Outside of beach towns, open-toed sandals are not appropriate, even in summer.

- Female inspectors should not, of course, wear short dresses or high heels.
- Bring an extra pair of shoes. Boots or work shoes can be swapped for a nice pair of slippers, shoe covers or sneakers before entering living areas. Never track mud, roofing tar, or pet droppings into a home. Also, some customs require the removal of shoes and hats upon entry.

Personal Hygiene

Before an appointment to provide an inspection, make sure you have:

- showered;
- brushed your teeth, flossed, and used mouthwash;
- trimmed your nails;
- shaved or trimmed your beard, if you have one;
- combed your hair; and
- applied deodorant. Also, go easy on the cologne/perfume.

Between appointments, freshen up with a travel bag that contains:

- a hand mirror (or a camping mirror);
- a comb or brush;
- mouthwash;
- deodorant;
- a spare bag for dirtied clothing;
- chewing gum (preferably a minty flavor); and
- wet-naps or waterless hand cleanser to clean and sanitize your hands before meeting with the client.

What to Bring

Bring the following to the inspection appointment:

- your business card;
- your brochure;
- testimonials from local clients (if you have them);
- copies of your licenses (if licensing is required by your state); and
- a leave-behind packet that contains the items listed here and other more detailed marketing pieces.

Dress Rehearsal

If you're out of practice or under-tested, it's a good idea to have a co-worker or friend pretend to be a new prospect in order to help you strengthen your sales skills and work on your soft skills of interpersonal communication. Instruct him or her to be as hard on you as possible as you attempt to close the sale.

"For every pass I caught in a game, I caught a thousand in practice."

—Don Hutson, legendary wide receiver for the Green Bay Packers

This is the safest kind of arena to prepare for all kinds of interactions so that, during the real thing, you can respond confidently, no matter how the meeting goes.

Meeting a Prospect/Client for the First Time

Here are a few recommendations for what you should do on the day of a meeting before your appointment:

- Make sure that your company name is prominently displayed on your vehicle.
- Wash your vehicle in the morning before your first appointment of the day.
- Schedule enough time for lunch. Avoid eating in your vehicle, but if you do, check your clothes for food stains before arriving at the appointment.
- Do not pull into your prospect's driveway with your radio or CD player blaring, whether it's music, commercials or talk radio. Anything loud is annoying and disrupts the environment, and shows a lack of respect for the neighbors.
- If you're on your cell phone when you pull up, quickly conclude your call before exiting your vehicle. You want your client to feel that s/he is your only priority.
- Don't embarrass yourself by allowing empty cans or other trash to fall out of your truck when you open the door.
- Don't arrive at the appointment smoking or chewing tobacco.
- Don't spit.
- Don't slam the door of your vehicle.
- Don't arrive carrying a cup of coffee or other beverage. Keep at least one hand free so that you can greet your client with a handshake.
- At all times, particularly when meeting a client for the first time, you ought to have a calm—rather than a rushed—demeanor, even if you're running late.
- If you're running late, call your prospect to let them know. When you arrive, acknowledge your tardiness and thank your prospect for their patience.
- Have your business card ready as you approach the property.
- Wear a nice watch. It shows that you respect your client's time.

The Handshake

People tend to unconsciously judge another person by their handshake. There are ways to shake hands properly that leave a positive impression.

"A firm, hearty handshake gives a good first impression, and you'll never be forgiven if you don't live up to it."

—P.J. O'Rourke, American writer and humorist

Grasp the other person's hand so that your palms touch. Provide a firm grip. Give an intentional shake—two or three actions, at most. Do not hold the other person's hand tightly or test his or her strength. While shaking, make eye contact to show that you're interested in the other person, and also to pick up on the other person's mood and non-verbal clues. Then release. That's it.

If you avoid shaking hands with either gender, the person may consider it a sign of disrespect. Also, a limp handshake expresses discomfort, or a lack of strength or self-confidence. These are non-verbal impressions that you may accidentally convey based on your handshake, whether or not such attributes are true.

You can greatly control the impression you give using non-verbal cues and body language, starting first with your smile, and then with your handshake.

Body Language

"I speak two languages: body and English."

—Mae West, American actress

Research says that people tend to respond less to what you say and more to your body language. Your tone of voice is the second most important factor in face-to-face communication. What you actually say ranks third. Therefore, be aware of what you are physically doing and how your clients may perceive your body language and actions.

When you're simply in the presence of another person, you are communicating. What is mostly being communicated is what you're not saying. One UCLA study suggests that 93% of our most effective communication comes through non-verbal communication.

We speak with our body—our movements, our actions, and our facial expressions. We speak with smiles, frowns, and raised eyebrows. We even communicate with the distance we put between ourselves and another person.

Some tips for conveying a positive attitude include the following:

- Maintain good posture—don't slouch.
- Keep your head up and maintain eye contact with the other person.
- Keep your hands in a natural position by placing them on your hips, by holding something (such as clipboard or a pen), or by gently clasping your hands together in front of you or behind your back.
- While engaged in face-to-face conversation, nod your head occasionally to indicate to the other person that you're listening.

Maintaining the appropriate personal space is important, too. The convention is to keep about a 3-foot space between yourself and the person you're talking to. If you are male, you should afford your female prospect greater personal space. This space should be increased even further if you are alone with her.

Also, you can sometimes convey a defensive or even hostile demeanor without even realizing it, and this can plant the subliminal message in your prospect's mind that you'll be difficult to work with. For example, facing someone with your arms crossed can project the idea that you don't believe what the other person is saying, or that you're angry. This posture can be perceived as aggressive and can create an imaginary wall between yourself and your client.

It's important that you understand that you can say the right words but send the wrong message. Always be aware of your body language.

Your First Words

If you're naturally shy or haven't had much experience interacting with prospects in person, remember to be yourself and just act natural. It's as easy as saying, "Hello, I'm Jim. It's great to meet you."

Now, start establishing rapport with your prospect by exchanging pleasantries, asking general questions, and perhaps talking about something you have in common.

Try any of the following:

- "How are you doing today?"
- "This is a really nice neighborhood!"
- "I'm looking forward to helping you out today."

Listen

A conversation is a like a tennis match, with each person having a turn. You may be more concerned with what you're going to say so that you can close the sale, but active listening is 50% of any conversation. Remember to let the other person speak. When you're actively listening, you're focusing on the other person. So, remember to pay attention. Don't allow your mind—or your eyes—to wander. When you're face to face, don't look over the speaker's shoulder to see who else is around. Try to stay interested and in the moment. Smile. Make eye contact. Nod occasionally. Say things such as, "Yes, I see," or "Hmmm." These are called "prompts" because they indicate to the speaker that you're listening and they prompt him or her to continue talking.

It's good practice to wait a second—literally—after someone has finished speaking before you begin talking. Take a moment. Allow a moment of pause or silence to exist after someone finishes his or her sentence. It will help prevent you from talking while the other person is still making their point.

One way to demonstrate that you're listening is to repeat back what your prospect says. For example, you may respond, "From what I understand, you're concerned with… Is that correct?" Summarizing your understanding of what your prospect says shows that you've been listening and are interested in helping.

Also, don't interrupt. Avoid entering the conversation while someone is speaking even if s/he has left a short pause in the conversation. Allow your prospect to pause and think about what s/he is saying. A pause in the conversation does not necessarily mean you need to jump in and say something. Filling every void of conversation demonstrates either that you're nervous or that you haven't really listened to your prospect. So, refrain from injecting something simply because there is an opportunity to do so.

Bring a Treat for the Kids If the Prospect Has Children

A low-cost option to create kid-friendly custom marketing materials is to hire an art student to create a home inspection coloring book that you can make multiple copies of for distribution. The coloring book can have an inspection theme and include pictures of your truck and you in action. Don't forget to bring the crayons! Put your name and logo on everything. You never know who will see these items besides the kids. It demonstrates to your prospect that you're family-oriented (even if you don't have kids of your own), and that you acknowledge the likelihood that your clients have a hectic lifestyle and you're prepared to help accommodate it during their inspection.

Tip: Print off and give InterNACHI's Coloring and Activity Book found at www.nachi.org/coloring-book to the children of clients who attend their inspection. (And don't forget the crayons!)

Pass

Believe it or not, there are some consumers that you don't want as clients. You don't have to accept work from everyone who wants to hire you. If a client starts off being difficult or unreasonable, it usually gets worse, not better. While it may be hard to not take a job, it's sometimes cheaper in the long run.

You can't really put a price on sanity. Money by itself is rarely adequate compensation if your client is high-stress, rude, abusive, indecisive, has a complicated story regarding your payment, or is generally drama-driven. You can't always see these kinds of prospects coming, but when you do, trust your instincts and pass. Another upside of passing on a questionable prospect is that you won't have to deal with their unhappiness or poor review after the inspection is completed.

Furthermore, an added bonus of refusing to allow these consumers to become clients is that they become your competitors' clients. Pity those competitors.

The same is true of related professions. There are bad builders and realtors out there. Avoid marketing to these people. Even if they have negative reputations, they may still have influence locally, so it's better to not deal with them at all than to have to turn down their referrals based on their response to your marketing. If you don't court them, they won't call.

No-Shows

Leave a door hanger that lets the prospect know you were there. It can read: "Sorry we missed you." Make sure it provides your contact information and asks the prospect to call you to reschedule their appointment.

All of these tips are covered in InterNACHI's free online Customer Service Course. Visit www.nachi.org/education

When You Get the Inspection

Discuss with your new client the details and schedule that you'll be allowed access to their property to perform your inspection. Call the day before to confirm the appointment.

Follow these simple, common-sense tips:

- Arrive on time and follow the same tips you should use for meeting a client for the first time.
- No offensive t-shirts or ball caps. It's ideal to wear attire that has your company logo on it so that it's promoting your brand and identity while you're working.
- Keep your tools and work area organized so that you can keep track of them, and so that hazards for others are minimized.
- Work safely. That means wearing personal protective equipment, such as gloves, kneepads, a hard hat, safety goggles, a dust mask or respirator, etc.
- Keep the site safe for others. For example, if you need to erect a ladder in an area that may get foot traffic, create a caution zone around such hazards to give people the heads-up.
- Make sure there are no unauthorized personnel in your work area, including children, pets, or curious onlookers who may have an eye on your tools and equipment.
- No smoking or using chewing tobacco.
- No spitting.
- Don't bring your dog or friends or family members to the job.

Remember that your conduct and that of any helpers or crew is its own advertising. It can make or break your reputation and brand, as well as clinch or dash recommendations and referrals.

Marketing on the Job

Check with the property owners to make sure that you can set up a promotional yard sign (with your company name, logo and contact information) in a place that will have the highest visibility to traffic. It should also be set up in an area that's safely clear of the work area(s). You don't want to create a hazard with your signage.

If there is some HOA rule or municipal ordinance that prohibits erecting your sign, park your company vehicle so that its signage is prominently displayed to passersby. Also, make sure that you have attached and/or filled your external brochure or business card holder on your truck so that those interested can just take a card or marketing piece while you're working.

Make sure that your equipment is labeled with your logo to promote your company.

Keep extra marketing materials in your truck. If you notice an interested onlooker, you can approach them and briefly chat about your business. However, remember that your clients are entitled to your time and discretion, so don't spend too much time drumming up new business while on their clock, and don't absentmindedly divulge contractually confidential details or other information that could put your clients or their property at risk. You won't necessarily know who you're talking to—whether it's a neighbor, or a prowler posing as a neighbor who is actually casing the neighborhood.

Also, don't forget your red phone, and do answer it on the job if it won't be hazardous to take the call.

Email Communication

Follow these basic rules for communicating via email. They are as legally binding as your contract, so make sure you say what you mean and mean what you say. Also, they should be as well-written as a hard-copy document. Despite email's convenience, it should not be treated less formally than a letter.

- Make sure your subject line represents the message of the email. Never leave it blank.

- Always begin an email with the person's name, such as "Dear Mrs. Smith."

- Keep your email messages short and to the point. Your client will likely not read long blocks of print. If you have something lengthy to explain, an email is not necessarily the best method for communicating it. Include as much detail as you need to, but not so much that your client will wonder why you're not asking to meet in person. Emails should be used for follow-up communication and brief notes and updates, and not as a way of avoiding in-person or more formal communication.

- Keep e-lingo, such as "LOL," "IMHO," and smiley faces and other emoticons reserved for your friends, not your clients.

- Don't use all capital letters in your email. This has the effect of shouting, even if you don't mean to.

- Be polite, and use language that denotes common courtesy, such as "please" and "thank you."

- Be sure to proofread your email for errors before clicking the "send" button.

- Read your email message out loud to hear how it sounds. Contrary to your intent, you may come across as terse or rude.

- Make sure that your email settings provide for automatically saving a copy in your "sent" folder.

- Print out emails to keep in your client's folder to maintain your paper trail.

Reminders:

- Emotions, sarcasm and humor do not transmit very well over email. Keep your communication businesslike.

- Like a letter, when you email someone, you're created a written record.

- Avoid texting your client (or relying on texts from your client). Because of the faddish nature of the specialized lingo and abbreviations used in most text messages, they can be easily misconstrued and can be used to your disadvantage in a later dispute.

Writing the Agreement and Report

"Undertake not what you cannot perform, but be careful to keep your promise."

—George Washington

Quick Tips for Your Standard Agreement/Client Contract:

- Always use a vetted contract/agreement, such as InterNACHI's Online Agreement System (www.nachi.org/onlineagreement). Have your attorney look it over to make customized amendments specifically for your business and particular concerns. (Find more links to the Agreement and other useful documents in the Legal chapter to follow.)

- Be as detailed as possible about what is and isn't included in your inspection or scope of work.

- Attach a copy of InterNACHI's Standards of Practice for Performing a General Home Inspection found at www.nachi.org/sop (or other SOP as required by your authority having jurisdiction). This will help your client understand what they can expect from their home inspection.

- Have your standard agreement proofed for spelling and grammar mistakes.

- Remember to factor travel time and mileage into your fee.

- Make it easy for the consumer to verify your licenses and qualifications.

- Triple-check your math, especially for ancillary inspection add-ons and discounts.

- For reasons of personal liability, don't sign your own agreement; just have your client sign it. If your state requires you to sign your agreement, use your DBA or business name and never only your personal name. It's important to maintain the appropriate separation and corporate veil between your personal assets and your business assets, so bear this in mind when executing contracts.

Inspection Reports: Engage Your Senses

Inspectors are "details" people. They deal in facts. They deal in what they can see. That's the very definition of the job. So, it would seem that, for most inspectors, their confidence in recognizing defects would translate just as easily into their inspection reports. But writing, in general, can be intimidating. For many inspectors, report writing constitutes the most writing they've ever done, and calls to bear their sometimes minimal skills in that area. Even for the naturally gifted or most enthusiastic writers, the act is fraught with its usual difficulties, including problems with spelling, punctuation and grammar, that often slip through the net of the average word-processing program.

Observe and Report

The point for inspectors who need to write—as well as news reporters, law enforcement, medical personnel, scientists, contractors and architects—is to communicate clearly and precisely. And details are what constitute precision. When going beyond the checklist and writing a narrative, you leave little room for misinterpretation when you describe something in sensory–based details. The rule for all writers is: "Show, don't tell." When your reports are based on having engaged your five senses—seeing, hearing, touching, smelling and tasting (although it's unlikely that you'll actually be tasting anything on an inspection!)—you provide your clients with accurate and valuable information that they can rely upon while protecting yourself against legal liability.

Many inspectors advertise that their reports are "easy to understand." That's the beauty of good writing. It is simple, but it includes observational details that are dense yet clearly written. For example, your gut may tell you that there is something seriously wrong with a roof when you first poke your head over the top of the ladder. But when you actually inspect it up close, you can see exactly why it's not in good condition.

Those are the details that you can relate in your report:

- *There was a standing puddle where the slopes intersect on the west side of the roof, but it hasn't rained in more than 48 hours.*
- *The tiles on the roof surrounding the puddle were darker, indicating that the moisture was extended.*
- *While depressing four tiles outside the perimeter of the puddle, they became detached from the roof's underlayment.*
- *There was a musty smell, indicating possible onset of mold growth.*
- *The attic vent fan operated intermittently instead of continuously; heard scraping noise of fan blades against metal.*

You're probably more adept at inspecting using your five senses than you're consciously aware of. The trick is to integrate that information into your report using language that reflects the observational details that your senses produce.

Opinion vs. Observation

One weakness of reports that lack detailed observations is that the information sounds more like an opinion. "The roof is in good condition" is arguably the opinion of the inspector, but that type of statement is all too often the sort of default language that is wide open to interpretation. And that leaves the inspector wide open to liability. Even if your client accompanied you on parts of your inspection, and even if you were confident in your findings and explanations that you verbally conveyed to him, you can't assume that he shares your perspective, knowledge or insight (or even that he remembered everything you said).

A roof that appears "in good condition" to a layperson may mean one thing to him, but another to you. The value of the adjective "good" is largely subjective. Most adjectives, unless they're based in sensory details, are left up to the individual to define, such as "good," "bad," "less," "more," and even "adequate" and "inadequate," unless the conditions are specified. That's why you should forgo the vague, value-weighted adjectives, and stick to reporting exactly what your fives senses have told you.

Furthermore, a "good" roof may still be compromised by secondary issues, which you will report, but those defects that you list may get lost in the relief of the homeowner telling himself, "At least I don't need a new roof!" While the roof may appear to be sound, your inspection may reveal underlayment problems, moisture intrusion, potential mold issues, and something that's interfering with the operation of the vent fan—all of which can compromise the roof at some point.

And if the roof is in good condition with no defects, you still need to explain what that entails in order to convey basic information to your client to prove that you performed your own due diligence as an inspector.

You don't need to overwhelm him with minutiae, but part of your job is to educate, which is especially important if you've been asked to inspect for specific concerns.

EXAMPLE:

"I saw two missing shingles, but no apparent hail damage from hailstorm two days prior. Underlayment was adequately secured to structure; saw no nail pops or missing nails; saw no visible tears. No aggregate accumulation noted in gutters; gutters were free of foliage debris. Flashing at chimney was present, with no leaks noted."

And so on.

Past vs. Present

InterNACHI recommends that all inspection contracts and agreements include language that specifically states that observations made and reported were true for the time and date of the inspection, and that there is no guarantee or implied warranty of any future condition. Some attorneys also recommend that inspectors use the past tense in all of their inspection reports. The reason is simple. It reinforces that the observation was made in the past and does not reflect a system's or component's current condition.

By reporting using the past tense, you leave a plaintiff's attorney, who may be quoting from your report, no option but to draw from past-tense statements that, again, reinforce the current obsolescence of those statements. Should a plaintiff's attorney accuse you of stating something incorrect in your report, you can respond: "I'm not stating that at all. I have no idea what the current state of the system or component is."

When an inspector writes, "The furnace is in functional condition," a customer may interpret that as a warranty of some kind. But the plaintiff's attorney will be stuck quoting what you wrote, which is written in past tense: "The furnace was in functional condition."

Your Recommendations

The observational details that you record will then inform your recommendations, which will give your client a next step, and even a roadmap to recovery:

- *Roof's condition indicated issues related to moisture intrusion, as evidenced by presence of standing water, and weakened tile adhesion to underlayment.*
  - *Recommend further investigation by a roofing contractor.*
- *Musty smell indicated possible onset of mold growth.*
  - *Recommend further investigation to include mold testing and possible mitigation.*
- *Attic vent fan operated intermittently instead of continuously; heard scraping noise of fan blades against metal.*
  - *Recommend further investigation and repair or replacement.*

How Good Is Your Product?

Your client may follow you around for parts of your inspection, and you may be able to show him many problems as you discover them. You can educate him by explaining their significance, imparting the wisdom of your experience and expertise. This is the service you provide as an inspector, and this is also part of the overall service-ethic that we encourage at InterNACHI. It's one of the things that sets InterNACHI inspectors apart. But the product of your inspection is not two hours on a Tuesday afternoon. It's your inspection report. A great inspection report is dense with relevant observational details.

Newspaper reporters are often called "the eyes and ears" of a story. They put their readers in the room, so to speak. The good ones rely on their senses because their credibility hinges on their impartial accuracy. By using observational details, inspectors can accomplish the same goals. Always keep in mind that a party who uses your inspection report may never see the property. So, be their eyes. Put them in the room. A clear and concise inspection report is a good product, and a good product leads to more business.

Digits and Hyphens

When writing contracts and reports, it's sometimes difficult for inspectors to decide whether to write numbers using numerals or as spelled-out words. The rule of thumb for grammarians is that numbers used as measurements and percentages should be rendered as digits, and numbers describing amounts and as length of time should be rendered as words, particularly when referring to single-digit numbers (amounts under 10), or where the use of double-digit numbers may cause visual confusion for the reader. Contracts frequently use both digits and words for dollar amounts as extra-legal security.

Here are some examples that illustrate the basic digits-vs.-words rules:

- *"Maintenance should be performed no less than every two years for one- and two-family dwellings."*
- *"Expect to use eight 5-pound buckets of compound."*
- *"There should be a 6-foot turnaround at each entrance, which should be at least 3 feet wide."*
- *"The slope of the grade should be at least 5 percent (or 5%)."*

But this is okay:

- *"The structure houses 24 businesses."*

  (Note the double-digit amount over 10 rendered as digits, especially because there are no other numbers to compete with it.)

- *"You will need twelve 10-inch shims."*

  (Best to spell out 12 to avoid confusion with "10-inch" right next to it.)

In addition to conforming to the basic rules of English, the numerals-versus-words distinction helps to maintain visual uniformity, and it makes information recognition easier for your readers.

Also, note the use of hyphens with numbers. In adjective phrases that modify or describe the nouns they precede, the phrases should be hyphenated, like this:

- Two-family dwelling: "two-family" describes the type of dwelling.
- 5-pound bucket: "5-pound" describes the capacity of the bucket.
- 6-foot turnaround: "6-foot" describes the space for the turnaround.

Otherwise, no hyphenation for the numbers is needed, like this:

- *"Two families live in the dwelling."*
- *"5 pounds of nails"*
- *"The cast-iron tub rests on four feet."*

"Farther" vs. "Further"

Merriam-Webster Dictionary states that "farther" and "further" are used interchangeably because their definitions have been somewhat corrupted over time. However, there are distinctions in their meanings that are useful for those in the building and home inspection trades to understand, which can help make their reports as accurate as possible, with little room for misunderstanding.

Here's the difference:

"Farther" should be used to demonstrate physical distance:

> *"The downspout should discharge farther from the house."*

A little trick to test the difference is to see if an actual distance can be used in place of the word "farther" in your sentence:

> *"The downspout should discharge <u>6 feet</u> from the house."*

If it can, you were correct in using "farther."

"Further" should be used when referring to degree, time, space, extent or depth, as in:

> *"This problem should be investigated further by a roofing contractor."*

Three Photos Every Inspector Should Include at the End of the Report

As a home inspector, you never want to be accused of failing to note a water line leak, or—worse—causing water damage because you forgot to turn off a fixture. One way you can prevent this is to take some photos of the water meter just prior to leaving the property.

Of course, in some jurisdictions, the water meter is below ground or requires a key and so is not readily accessible. Other water meters are inaccessible due to the weather, overgrown foliage, or because they aren't properly maintained by the utility company. In these cases, it will be difficult, if not impossible to obtain any photos. But you should alert your client to the fact that they are entitled to be able to read their water meter in order to reconcile its readout with their monthly water bill, so they should either rectify the problem themselves, or complain to the appropriate party to get the situation rectified.

Assuming you have safe access to the water meter, take these photos after you've:

- completed your home inspection;
- turned off all the sink and tub faucets after checking them for functional flow; and
- made sure that the washing machine, dishwasher, sprinkler system, and any other water-using systems, devices and fixtures are off.

Take three photos of the water meter that show that no water lines are leaking, assuming you didn't find any.

Here are the three photos to include sequentially at the end of your inspection report. Of course, the photos should show that the water meter is actually not running.

*This is the first photo that demonstrates that the water meter is not running.
This is your baseline photo.*

This second photo shows that the meter is still not running.

This final photo, showing that the water meter is still not running, confirms that there are no hidden and undiscovered water leaks in the house, and that the inspector didn't leave any faucets running anywhere.

It's best if the photos are actually time-stamped and show several seconds between each shot. Since some cameras don't come with this feature, take each photo from a slightly different angle to show that they are, in fact, different. But make sure that the meter's display can be viewed—the angle shouldn't distort the reading.

Of course, if these photos show that the meter is still running, you have cause to recommend to your clients that they have the plumbing system checked out by a licensed plumber, warning them in advance that the leak is apparently hidden somewhere behind a wall, ceiling or floor, and so was beyond the scope of your home inspection. But take the opportunity to remind them that by performing this extra step—which most home inspectors wouldn't even think of to do—you have been able to notify them about a problem that should be immediately addressed before it would have become an expensive disaster.

While taking these photos is an easy thing to do, this kind of customer service will give your clients some much-appreciated reassurance that you're a straightforward professional who understands his job, such as by being careful to return all fixtures and settings to their original, pre-inspected state. (So, you can also take photos of the thermostat before and after testing the furnace and air-conditioning system.) It also proves that you're the kind of pro who puts his clients' best interests first by confirming either the presence or absence of potential problems in a non-invasive but inventive way.

Providing these photos at the end of your inspection report also teaches your clients a simple home-maintenance tip. By comparing the meter readings for the first few months, they can monitor their family's average water usage, and they can be alerted to any unexpected surges that may indicate a leak in the plumbing system.

Performing this small but important step will also allay some of the anxiety that your clients may be experiencing, and this sort of empathy can translate into positive feedback that you can solicit by giving them a Customer Satisfaction Survey with your report or with a free copy of *Now That You've Had a Home Inspection*. You can then use their positive feedback in your business marketing—on your website and in your brochure. Always remember that marketing on the job is part of the job, and everything you do reflects on your business.

What Happens When Your Inspection Report Gets Recycled?

It's a sad but true fact that sometimes the product of a home inspector's labor—the inspection report will be recycled, either at the behest of an unscrupulous agent, or based on the prospect's own uneducated attempt to save some time and money. Too often, an inspection report will be presented to prospective home buyers at open houses and other events, and promoted as an accurate representation of the home's current condition.

There are all kinds of problems with this situation, including the following:

1. A home inspection—and resulting report—is a snapshot in time. It conveys the home's condition only for the date and time of the inspection. Most inspector-client agreements explicitly state as much—and if yours doesn't, it should. See item #1.1 in InterNACHI's Standards of Practice for Performing a General Home Inspection, a copy of which should accompany each of your inspection reports.

2. If the person relying on the report is not the person who hired the inspector, that person is being short-sighted indeed, as there may have been all kinds of changes in the condition of the home since the inspection that were not covered in the report, including weather events, minor defects that have progressed to become major ones, infestations, and even repairs that have been performed since then. (It's like going on a dating website and assuming that someone's profile picture is what they look like now, when it's actually their high school yearbook photo from 20 years ago—only the ramifications are much worse!) It's penny-wise but pound-foolish to try to save a few bucks by using an old report, even if that report is only a week old. The cost of an inspection is a pittance compared to the value of the home.

3. As a corollary to #1 and #2, a home inspection is not a warranty of the home's condition—not at the time of the inspection, and certainly not at some future date. And as it is not technically exhaustive, it carries no guarantee. It's difficult enough to make these points clear to the client; imagine the unmanaged expectations of someone reading the report who isn't the client.

4. An outdated report can have the effect of unfairly damaging an inspector's reputation if the home's condition has substantially changed, but the home buyer makes unfounded complaints (perhaps to a Realtor, or maybe online) based on a report that s/he never contracted for. Some bells you just can't unring.

5. Some inspectors may try to cut their losses by negotiating a halfway approach, such as by performing an abbreviated re-inspection for a new client based on an old report. Why would you sell yourself short, literally? It's all right to offer a discount to a previous client, but the house is not your client, so don't allow a new client to haggle with you about the price of your services. Nothing says "cheap inspector" like one who is willing to bargain away his livelihood, job by job.

6. Related to #5, it may actually be illegal in your state for you to recycle your own report. Check with your state's real estate laws to make sure you're not violating any statutes in a misguided attempt to ingratiate yourself with a prospective client. It's one thing for an agent or buyer to be

convinced to use you in the future based on your report's overall look, quality, and easy-to-read format. To be sure, it's terrific marketing for prospects to see what your reports look like; it's exactly why we recommend putting a sample report on your website. But you could be treading in dicey territory in terms of liability if you allow any of your reports' content to be used by those other than your paid clients.

7. Again, the report is the product of your labor, and you should be fairly compensated for it. Each inspection has only one client. Read item #3 in InterNACHI's Home Inspection Agreement.

We've come up with some simple solutions to help home inspectors reinforce these points to non-clients and other third parties who may get their hands on an inspection report, the contents of which are the property of the client and inspector, and no one else, even if permission is given by the client for others to read it.

Here's what you should do to prevent problems that can arise if someone other than your client tries to use your report:

1. Be sure to maintain adequate coverage through your Errors & Omissions and General Liability insurance, as your clients, and even some third parties in some states, do have a legal right to rely on the contents of your inspection report.

2. Number each page of your report (even using the format "Page 1 of 30") so that a page removed will be conspicuous by its absence.

3. Note in the summary of your report that any digital photos and/or video included are time- and date-stamped, and make sure they are.

4. Use the header/footer function of your report-writing software to identify the property by address, and add the time and date of the inspection.

5. Always include a disclaimer in your report and agreement stating that the inspection you performed at 123 Main Street in Anytown, USA, is valid only for the date and time of the inspection. Somewhere within the middle of the report, insert the following paragraph:

   A general home inspection is a non-invasive, visual examination of the accessible areas of a residential property, performed for a fee, which is designed to identify defects within specific systems and components that are both observed and deemed material by the inspector. It is based on the observations made on the date of the inspection, and not a prediction of future conditions. It is a snapshot in time. A general home inspection will not reveal every issue that exists or ever could exist, but only those material defects observed on the date of the inspection.

6. Since it's impossible to control who reads your report, monetize the possibility and turn things to your advantage. Include a direct message at the end of your report addressed to any unauthorized third parties, stating something along the lines of:

   If you're reading this report but did not hire me, XYZ Inspectors, to perform the original inspection, please note that it is likely that conditions related to the home have probably changed, even if the report is fairly recent. Just as you cannot rely on an outdated weather report, you should not rely on an outdated inspection report. Minor problems noted may have become worse, recent events may have created new issues, and items may even have been corrected and improved. Don't rely on old information about one of the biggest purchases you'll ever make. Remember that the cost of a home inspection is insignificant compared to the value of the home. Protect your family and your investment, and please call me directly at (000) 555-1212 to discuss the report you're reading for this property so that we can arrange for a re-inspection. Thank you!

Always look for the opportunity to turn a potential negative into a positive, and that includes being pro-active in making sure you get paid for your work. Keep your prices respectably high, maintain sound business ethics—especially those related to protecting your clients' privacy, including the contents of their reports—and let your reputation be your calling card.

More Tips for Your Report:

- Checklists are useful, but descriptive narratives add value and decrease the chance for misunderstandings. www.InspectorOutlet.com sells comprehensive narrative libraries for every system and component of a home so that the inspector doesn't have to "re-invent the wheel" with each new report.

- There are many great choices of inspection reporting software that help make report-writing easy. Also, electronic reports are convenient to store and download and allow you to deliver them to clients faster than hard copies.

- Take and include high-quality digital photos of defects. Remember that a picture is worth a thousand words.

- If you're tempted to delete or dispose of old reports, find out first if your jurisdiction has any requirements regarding mandatory length of storage.

Find more links for libraries of pre-written narratives and illustrative graphics, as well as help reviewing your report, later in this book.

Marketing at the End of the Job

There are some simple yet highly effective things you can do that will ensure that you leave your client satisfied with your work and happy to recommend your company to their family and friends. Just because their check has cleared doesn't mean that your opportunity to market your services to them is over.

Labels, Labels, Everywhere Labels

As an additional marketing piece, have bright-colored stickers created that provide your company logo and contact information. After a project is completed, place these in discreet locations on the client's hot water tank, electrical panel, attic framing, any equipment you inspected, and even under the toilet tank lid. When your client is trying to remember your name, they'll know where to look.

Tip: Create valve tags that include your contact information and put them on the water and gas shut-off valves.

Add a Personal Touch

Email is a very useful business tool, but a personal phone call or a handwritten note is always the best way to say "Thank you for allowing me to serve you."

A Leave-Behind Letter Generates More Inspection Business

Dear Home Seller:

Thank you for allowing me (and the potential buyer) to inspect your home. We realize that we are guests in your home, and we conducted ourselves with the utmost respect for your property.

Although I had to open and close windows and doors, and test systems and appliances, etc., I made every attempt to leave your property in the same condition that I found it. However, please take a moment to check the following to make sure that I have reset them for you properly:

☐ door locks	☐ thermostat(s)	☐ range settings/oven & cooktop
☐ window locks	☐ GFCIs	☐ faucets
☐ lights	☐ attic access	☐ drapes/shutters
☐ alarm codes	☐ gates	☐ other: _____

Additional comments:_____

Once again, thank you very much for allowing us into your home. If you have any questions or observations, you may reach me directly by calling 123-456-7890, or by emailing me inspector@ABCinspectionbusiness-dot-com.

Also, if you are moving locally and are in need of an inspector, please don't hesitate to contact me.

You can find a comprehensive list of my services at www.ABCInspections.com

Sincerely,

John Smith

John Smith, Owner
ABC Inspections

Download a Word.doc or PDF version at www.nachi.org/leave-behind-letter

Post-Completion Party

Your client may throw a party to show off their newly completed construction project that you've just inspected. Ask if you can have your company's literature available next to the potato chip dip.

Happy Anniversary! Best Regards from Your Inspector

For your former clients who have had their new homes built, be sure to market your **11th-Month Builder's Warranty Inspection** to re-check the home before the one-year anniversary, when the client may have to go out-of-pocket for any previously covered repairs. If you schedule this right after the initial inspection, send them a "Happy Anniversary" card and offer your services. This is just another way to remind your client that they should hire you again. This type of inspection can also be marketed to prospects in new-construction homes even if you haven't performed any inspections for them before.

Client Satisfaction Surveys

Client satisfaction surveys have clear advantages for the inspectors who conduct them. Obviously, a post-inspection client survey gives you feedback on what your client appreciated in your work, as well as what areas may need your attention and improvement. This kind of information is invaluable to your business's success.

Surveys can also increase their awareness of your other services, thereby encouraging them to purchase additional services that they hadn't considered earlier.

There is also a more subliminal effect. The very act of asking clients for their opinions can induce them to form positive judgments that might not have otherwise occurred to them to articulate, beyond paying you for your work. The implied respect of asking for someone's opinion creates positive reciprocity.

Of course, if the appointment was a disaster—caused by poor weather, lack of scheduled access to the property, etc.—your survey will force your client to recall essential and factual details, such as your professional customer service and commanding leadership, making him or her truly consider whether a problem was because of you or your staff, or was actually beyond your control. This will mitigate your review and turn a negative into a positive. In a qualified sense, it's still a testimonial that affirms your good business practices.

As added protection, a client satisfaction survey provides a factual record of the client's version of events surrounding the inspection within a reasonable and relevant timeframe, thus inhibiting their ability to change their story to fit the circumstances of a lawsuit, should you find yourself in court with the client at a later time.

InterNACHI's Client Satisfaction Survey hits seven birds with one stone:

1. **It limits your liability.** Often, a dissatisfied client will describe your services to his/her agent—or, worse, to a judge—much differently than the truth. Procuring and maintaining a copy of this survey will bring them back to Earth, so to speak. It is a nice document to have to present to a complaining agent and can often end a legal action all by itself. It is the next best thing to a deposition.

2. **It alerts you to weaknesses in your service.** Some people are too shy or embarrassed to complain to someone in person about their service, even if the complaints are justified. What they may do instead is complain only to the agent or other person who referred you—or, worse, to anyone who'll listen, especially in online forums, which are searchable using your business name. Providing a survey offers your client a way to express his/her dissatisfaction while you're still on site and can do something about it. Client feedback is vital to improving your service. You must do everything you can to ensure that your reputation doesn't suffer from a poor online review or blog rant, where the criticism remains forever and will pop up—right along with your website—in a search for your business name.

3. **It reminds your client that you don't have X-ray vision.** It's important to explain to your client that a home inspection can't reveal every defect that exists, or ever will exist, in their new home. This survey works in conjunction with InterNACHI's Agreement (between you and your client) in that it again reminds them of this fact.

4. **It suggests that your client may wish to order ancillary inspections.** Some InterNACHI members offer additional inspections, such as WDO, radon, water quality, and mold—for additional fees, of course. This survey reminds them to ask about other services that you might offer, creating repeat business.

5. **It grants you written permission to discuss the report with others.** And, even more importantly, you can point to this document when a seller's agent demands a copy of the inspection report by saying: "I'm sorry, but my client has given me written instructions not to share his/her report with anyone."

6. **It lets your client know that you care about his/her opinion.** Everyone likes being asked what they think, especially about a service they've paid for.

7. **It helps you get more work.** By sending a copy of the flattering survey back to the agent or other person who referred you, you remind that person to refer you again or recommend you to friends and family. And, if you provide your client with a copy of a book (such as the ones below), you drastically reduce your liability.

Directions: Print off copies of a blank survey. Fill out the top portion. Near the conclusion of the inspection, ask your client to fill out the rest of the survey and sign it. Send a copy to the agent who referred you. Save the original forever!

To download the surveys, go to www.nachi.org/survey

All downloads are in PDF format.

But don't stop there. Email your clients information regularly. You can send them articles that you find at www.nachi.org/articles

A Message from InterNACHI Legal Counsel Joe Ferry:

Client Satisfaction Surveys have been shown to have manifest business development advantages for the business that conducts them. Satisfaction surveys appeal to a client's desire to be coddled, and reinforce feelings that they may already have about the business conducting the survey, and make them more likely to purchase its products or services.

Surveys can also increase people's awareness of a business's products and services and thereby encourage future purchases.

There is also an effect that is quite below-the-radar. The very act of asking clients about their opinions can induce them to form judgments that otherwise might not occur to them, that, for example, they really do like your inspection services and ancillary services, and would not hesitate to recommend them to others.

In addition, the Client Satisfaction Survey also provides a factual record of the client's version of events surrounding the inspection in the relevant time frame, thus inhibiting the client's ability to change his story to fit the circumstances of a later claim.

Find this article and free downloads online at www.nachi.org/survey

At the end of the inspection, ask your client to fill out the survey and sign it. Save the survey forever!

Here are some suggestions of items and questions that you can include to help you create your own Client Satisfaction Survey:

- Client's name
- Client's phone number
- Property address
- Date(s) of inspection
- Was the inspection completed in a timely manner?
- Were the inspector and his/her staff friendly and courteous?
- Are you satisfied with the communication you had with the inspector?
- Are you satisfied with the quality of the report?
- Did the inspector explain his/her other services?
- Would you hire the company again?
- Would you recommend the inspector to a family member or friend?
- Would you like to receive future contact, including news on special promotions and e-newsletters?
- Additional comments and/or suggestions
- Client's signature
- Date of survey

Handling a Complaint

Eventually, every inspector will receive a complaint from a client, but it's not necessarily bad news. A complaint provides the opportunity to learn what your client really thinks about your service, which gives you the chance to consider making changes to how you do things in your company. Complaints are actually more valuable than compliments, in some ways. Welcome them. Clients who go to the trouble of complaining are usually interested in giving you the chance to make things right and make them happy.

The Number One rule for receiving a complaint from a former client is to listen. Remain calm and composed. A person calling with a complaint may be insulting and rude, but you must be professional throughout.

Assure the client that you will do what you can to help him or her. Have a pen and paper handy. Write down any notes that are critical to the conversation, such as dates, what happened, who discovered the problem, whether it's been corrected, etc.

Listen to what the client says. The first couple of sentences will tell you exactly what problem(s) the client is experiencing. Pay close attention to what is being said without interrupting. If the caller is upset, rambling, and not able to verbalize well, then assist them by asking questions, such as, "What happened after that?" or "Could you tell me more about that?" or "What happened next?" Finally, be sure to ask, "How can I help you?" or "What is it that you would like me to do?"

Before proceeding to a resolution, make sure that you understand the situation. Ask questions to see if there's been a simple misunderstanding that can be easily resolved. If the complaint is more than just a misunderstanding, ask specific questions so that you can understand the exact nature of the complaint and the problem your client is experiencing. Summarize what you understand the problem to be. The caller will acknowledge or correct you. Try, "So, what you're saying is…" or "Do I understand you correctly or did I miss the point?" Be patient and repeat this process until you understand exactly what the problem is.

Another important thing to do while fielding a complaint is to express empathy with the caller. Don't be patronizing, but do let the caller know that you understand their stress and unhappiness. Tell them again that you will help them.

If there is a solution, make sure that the client has no doubt as to the specifics about how the issue will be resolved. Ask the client to confirm that they agree with the proposed solution to their situation. Ask, "How do you feel about the solution I've suggested?" or "How does that sound to you?" or "Are you in agreement with that so far?"

If a staffer is fielding the complaint but the caller wants to speak to the owner of the company, s/he should try the following: "Mrs. Smith, please give me the opportunity to resolve this matter for you. I'm sure I'll be able to help. But if you're still not satisfied, I'll get the owner on the phone with you."

If the caller uses profanity, you might say, "I know you're upset, but there's no need to use profanity. Please continue to discuss your complaint with me without using that kind of language."

As a last resort, you may want to suggest that the caller call you back after he or she has had a chance to calm down, but never hang up on a caller, and don't be patronizing—always use empathy, and keep the caller on the phone with you to resolve the situation whenever possible.

You may have to schedule a face-to-face meeting with the client to defuse the situation and bring a quick resolution. The goal is to work together, to prevent their filing a lawsuit, and to come up with a resolution that is mutually agreeable.

Another tactic is to ask the client to propose a solution. Letting the client make the opening gambit lets you know exactly where you stand. Perhaps the client's solution is less costly than what you were going to propose.

Tip: If your client doesn't have a solution in mind, perhaps you can propose a discount on a future service. This way, you get an opportunity to continue to work for the client.

Remember: An unhappy, inarticulate customer is not to be dismissed out of hand just because dealing with their complaint may be unpleasant or take a while. It's up to you to decide whether you want to learn from the experience and improve your business, or wonder whether you've created ill will that will haunt your ability to secure future jobs.

Here are some statistics that can help make you a believer in practicing good customer service by obtaining feedback and resolving complaints.

According to the White House Office of Consumer Affairs:

- For every complaint you hear, there are 26 additional clients with unresolved problems, and six of these are serious. You will never hear from these 26 again, and they are the ones who could tell you how to make your business better.

- Up to 70% of the clients who complain will do business with your company again if you resolve their problem. If they feel you acted quickly and to their satisfaction, up to 96% of them will do business with you again, and they will probably refer other people to you.

- A dissatisfied client will tell nine to 15 people about their experience. And about 10% of your dissatisfied clients will tell more than 20 people about their problem. You cannot possibly afford the advertising costs it would take to overcome this negative word-of-mouth publicity. And if it goes online, it's there forever.

- It costs five to six times as much to get a new (first-time) client as it does to keep a current one.

Do you know why most clients stop using your services? The White House Office of Consumer Affairs says that:

- 1% simply die;

- 3% move out of your service area;

- 14% are dissatisfied with your services;

- 9% leave because of your competition; and, most importantly...

- 68% stop using your services because of an attitude of indifference by your company's staff. For most people, it was YOUR attitude that mattered most.

Make sure that your company is doing the right thing when it comes to satisfying clients.

The Apology Letter

"Never ruin an apology with an excuse."

—Benjamin Franklin

Sometimes, you simply have to fall on your sword. Don't quibble or qualify. If you were in the wrong, say so. You're already liable, so, contrary to popular belief, not admitting you screwed up doesn't make you less responsible—it makes you appear cowardly and lacking in integrity. So, do the right thing and apologize. In doing so, you may just avoid a lawsuit, but you will surely have done all you could and you will have upheld your own Code of Ethics. A reasonable client will see that and thank you for it, and it will likely lead to positive word-of-mouth, repeat business, and referrals.

Consider the following phrases in drafting your apology:

- *"We apologize for..."*
- *"I was troubled to discover..."*
- *"Please accept our apology for..."*
- *"We acknowledge that we..."*
- *"Can you suggest how we may resolve this?"*
- *"To ensure that something like this never happens again, we will..."*
- *"We are taking immediate steps to..."*
- *"Next time, I will..."*
- *"To make up for our error, we..."*
- *"We will not charge you for..."*
- *"We will credit you for..."*
- *"What I can offer you is..."*
- *"We are immediately shipping you..."*

Tip #1: Create a complaint-taking template for your company to use so that when your staff or you answer the phone, you won't be thrown off track and miss essential details that you need to resolve the complaint, especially if the caller is upset or rambling, or you're having a hectic day.

Tip #2: Convene a meeting to use complaints as a learning tool for the entire company, including office staff.

How to Turn a Client's Complaint into a Marketing Gain

Dear InterNACHI:

After my client moved into the home I inspected for her, she discovered a clogged sink drain and has complained to the real estate agent. This is not my fault. The agent refers a lot of inspection work my way. What should I do?

Dear Home Inspector:

Don't get upset. Handling complaints is a part of any business. Three out of every 100 people are nuts, and you can't change that. You cannot find every defect that exists or ever could exist in every home you inspect. Do not think backward—think forward. The real problem is not with the sink, it is with the damage a complaint can do to your company's reputation. Don't think plumbing—think marketing!

Many complaints are great marketing opportunities in disguise. Try to turn them around and capitalize on them. Gain marketing benefits from them that outweigh the cost of satisfying them, especially if:

1. the problem is not your fault;

2. news of the complaint could damage your image within your local market; and

3. the cost of correction is inexpensive.

Clogged drains are one of the most common post-settlement complaints directed at home inspectors. Real estate sales agreements usually require home sellers to empty and clean their home before the buyer takes possession.

A seller's final clean-up efforts often inadvertently clog the sink traps and drains with dirt and leftover refrigerator goods. Guess who gets blamed?

Here's what to do (and act fast):

1. Immediately explain to your client, the real estate agent, and anyone else aware of the complaint, that you, the inspector, are not responsible. Contact every complaint recipient personally. Be calm and talk slowly. Also:

    a. Use common sense in your explanation. Remind your client and agent that the seller did not live with a clogged sink and that the clog occurred AFTER you did your inspection.

    b. Remind your client and agent that the seller didn't disclose the clogged sink for a good reason: It wasn't clogged.

    c. Point to the InterNACHI Agreement (between you and your client). The agreement is easy for laymen to understand. InterNACHI has invested hundreds of legal man-hours into this one-page work-of-art. It explains all.

    d. Tell them that the International Association of Certified Home Inspectors is on your side and will write an official opinion in support of your contention that you are not at fault.

2. After you have made your point clear, and your client and the agent understand your position, SWITCH GEARS. Offer to correct the problem at no charge. Pay for a plumber to repair the clogged drain. Don't do the work yourself; pay a professional. Get the work done quickly. Make sure the plumber's paid receipt shows that you paid personally.

3. After the repair has been made and you have paid for it, reiterate your position to your client. Explain again that you were not responsible for this problem but that you only paid for it to make your client happy. If your client offers to reimburse you, do not accept.

4. Ask your client for a favor. Ask her to write you a brief thank-you letter—nothing fancy, just a note mentioning the problem, your quick response, your willingness to pay for correction, and her own satisfaction with your home inspection service. Offer to help her word it or offer suggested wording. It can be hand-written. Give or send her a postage-paid return envelope to get it back to you.

5. Draft and send a letter to the real estate agent. A sample letter might go something like this:

    Jane Goodagent
    ABC Realty

    Dear Jane:

    [Describe the new homeowner's problem.]

    Upon moving into her new home, our mutual client, Sally Newowner, discovered that her kitchen sink trap was clogged.

    [Then explain why you are not responsible.]

    I explained that this was not my fault, that the seller obviously didn't live with a clogged sink drain, that clogs often occur during the seller's final cleanup, and I can only inspect the condition of a home on the day of the inspection, etc.

    [Sympathize with agent's position.]

    Despite my lack of liability with regard to this problem, I nevertheless want to keep our mutual client satisfied with my inspection service and happy with the home you helped her purchase.

    [Describe your solution.]

    Therefore, I took the initiative to hire a plumber to make the necessary repairs. I paid for it out of my own pocket.

[Then describe the happy outcome.]

Sally Newowner is now very pleased. I have enclosed a copy of a thank-you note Sally wrote to me.

[Ask for repeat business!]

I hope my quick handling of this problem will earn your confidence in me and inspire you and your colleagues at ABC Realty to refer your clients to me again.

Sincerely,

Joe Home Inspector

6. Send and fax the letter to Jane Goodagent. Don't forget to attach a copy of Sally Newowner's thank-you note, the plumber's paid receipt, and a stack of your home inspection business cards.

You should never have to pay to correct a defect, especially if you are protected by the InterNACHI Agreement (between you and your client). However, if you ever feel the need to pay for a repair, make sure you offset your cost by getting a marketing benefit in return. Turn every negative into a positive.

Tip: Save all the paperwork aforementioned. When a prospective client asks you for references, explain that even the worst inspector has a few satisfied clients and that any inspector can provide references. Instead, offer your prospective client your one complaint! Then fax or send him/her a copy of your letter to Jane Goodagent, the plumber's paid receipt, and Sally Newowner's thank-you note. It works every time!

Also, include copies of thank-you notes in your binders (www.nachi.org/binder).

Dear InterNACHI is offered to provide detailed advice and possible solutions to specific questions or problems. Obviously, other solutions exist and may be better suited for you and your particular situation. Email Nick at nick@internachi.org to submit your specific problem for publication. Your name will not be used unless you give us permission.

Dear InterNACHI does not answer technical or mechanical questions or offer legal advice.

Read this article online at www.nachi.org/dear_nachi1

After the Complaint Is Resolved

There are two things you might want to procure from your client after a complaint is successfully resolved. The first is a general release. This is particularly important if you solved the issue by refunding money. The second is a testimonial.

Sample General Release

The following is a sample of a general release that you can customize to use for your company:

GENERAL RELEASE

TO ALL TO WHOM THESE PRESENTS SHALL COME OR MAY CONCERN, KNOW THAT (Your Client) as the RELEASOR, for good and valuable consideration received from (Your Company Name), as the RELEASEE, the receipt and adequacy of which is hereby acknowledged, each hereby releases and discharges the RELEASEE, each of the RELEASEE'S subsidiaries and their respective principals, affiliates, related entities, shareholders, officers, directors, agents, employees and their respective heirs, executors, administrators, successors and assigns from all actions, causes of action, suits, debts, dues, sums of money, accounts, reckonings, bonds, bills, specialties, covenants, controversies, agreements, promises, variances, trespasses, damages, judgments, extants, executions, claims and demands whatsoever, in law, admiralty or equity, which against the RELEASEE, the RELEASOR and the RELEASOR'S heirs, executors, administrators, successors and assigns ever had, now have, or hereafter can, shall or may, have for, upon or by reason of any matter, cause or thing whatsoever from the beginning of the world to the day of the date of this RELEASE, solely in connection with the inspecting services performed by (Your Company Name) arising out of that certain work performed around (Date or Month/Year Work was Performed).

Whenever the text hereof requires, the use of a singular number shall include the appropriate plural number as the text of the number within the instrument may require.

This RELEASE may not be changed orally.

IN WITNESS WHEREOF, the RELEASOR has executed this RELEASE on the _____ day of _____, ____.

(For a Corporation)

_____

By: _____

Attest/Name:

Title:

(For an individual)

_____(SEAL)

WITNESS:

_____(SEAL)

Both Releasor and Releasee will sign, in the form required (corporation or individual)

Take InterNACHI's Customer Service and Communication for Inspectors Course at nachi.org/education

Testimonial

The second item to procure after a complaint is resolved is a testimonial. This can be used in your marketing programs just like any other testimonial, even if it reveals that there was initially a complaint. These may go along the lines of: "I had a complaint about the work that was done… and ABC Inspections resolved it to my satisfaction immediately."

Most clients are generally stressed about their home-buying transaction before you've even set foot on their property, so this kind of testimonial can serve as a great reassurance to prospects that even if they're like most homeowners who deal with most inspectors, they'll be happy in the end if they use your services.

When You Don't Get the Inspection

You may not want to, but find out why. This is a link in your chain that obviously has to be strengthened. It's critical for you to do an autopsy on your unsuccessful estimates so that, as far as it is within your control, you'll succeed next time.

The following is a sample letter to use when you don't get hired. Mail it with a business-size pre-addressed, postage-paid envelope to make it easy for the person to send you their feedback.

Dear [Prospect],

Thank you for the opportunity to consult with you about your [Service Offered]. Would you please take a moment and tell us why you did not choose our company? Was our estimate lacking in some way? Was price the issue? Perhaps you decided not to proceed with the real estate transaction. Regardless of the reason, it would help us improve our service to know why.

I've enclosed a postage-paid envelope to make it easy for you to return your comments to us. Please indicate whether I may call you in the future.

Thank you in advance for your time.

Sincerely,

[Your Name]

[Your Company Name]

[Your Phone Number]

[Your Email Address]

[Your Website Address]

Your Good Name Online

What you do online regarding your business is only half the equation; those who use your services, and business names that are similar to yours, can affect your brand and reputation, too. That's why it's important to monitor your online reputation, as well as your brand.

"A brand for a company is like a reputation for a person. You earn reputation by trying to do hard things well."

—Jeff Bezos, founder of Amazon.com

Your Virtual Identity

There are online reputation-monitoring and brand-infringement services that will do this kind of tracking for you, but a quick perusal shows that a number of these services have problems with their own websites, such as their navigation, contact information, credentials, homepage appearance, and even the spelling and grammar on their site's pages. If they can't be trusted to keep their own online presence professional-looking and error-free, should you trust them with your site? More to the point is that you're paying someone else to do what you should be doing for yourself for a fee that doesn't guarantee you 100% protection. You're not a corporation that employs a gaggle of lawyers; keep your overhead low and keep on top of your own online reputation. At least in the initial stages, you should do this monitoring personally.

An easy way to monitor online activity related to your business is to do a search of your business name. You can do this weekly or daily to see what pops up. You may be surprised to discover that other businesses have mentioned you on their sites. Are these associations positive? Are they valid—do you actually have a professional relationship with them, or are they attempting to piggyback on your success or name recognition? Have they co-opted your trademarked tagline? It's important to acknowledge these positive and negative associations as soon as you discover them, to either cultivate and expand on them, or to shut them down and issue a general warning that you are monitoring your brand and are prepared to legally escalate any brand or copyright infringements, should you discover them. Never underestimate the temerity of an unscrupulous online competitor or copyright thief. By the same token, never underestimate the power of your threat to take a person to court if they infringe on your brand. Most threats work instantly, as these types of fly-by-nighters don't want to chance discovery and prosecution, which can include federal criminal charges, as well as civil penalties.

You can also be notified of instances of your business name being searched using Google Alerts. This also works for brand names, slogans and proprietary product names and services. Anyone favorably discussing your services online creates information that you can post on your website. You can do this without their permission; once it's accessible on the Internet, it's generally fair game to re-post. But if the information was written by a past client, it's good public relations to ask to re-use their comments on your site as a courtesy, as well as to get more feedback.

Perhaps a blogger has mentioned her encounter with your business; read what she's written, including any comments on her post. Online reviews can be informative and valuable. You may want to ask to link to the blogger's positive comments, or to copy them to your site. Cultivate these positive associations.

You may discover that someone has said something unfavorable about you or your business. This is always disappointing, but it can be just as valuable and informative as positive feedback—even more so. The first question you should ask yourself is whether the criticism is legitimate. If it's a comment about your office staffers, for example, don't assume that they can do no wrong; investigate the claim as fully as possible. Then, ask yourself whether you can improve your services based on the feedback.

Protect Yourself from Being Libeled Online

Some negative feedback is not instructive or constructive. It may be merely unkind commentary, or what used to be called "flaming." You may have to let certain criticisms go; the more personal or hysterical a flame is, the more it speaks to the commenter's state of mind, rather than your service, and you will have to trust that other readers can make that same judgment for themselves.

But if a business or individual has made a false claim about you or your business, you will have to take action. You can't let untrue or libelous claims go unanswered. Recycled information on the Internet has a way of becoming "fact," and you need to stop it as soon as you become aware of it and take counter-measures to protect your online reputation and brand.

If the commentary is not merely negative but defamatory, you can shut it down by emailing the offender a warning. First, find out who posted the comments. Most negative commentary is posted anonymously or by using an online username that hides the owner's email address. Can you tell who the person is by what they've written, such as a disgruntled ex-employee or a particularly unhappy client? If the person's email is not readily available based on the comment, and the comments are false and designed to injure your reputation, you should write to the site's administrator and warn them to take down the comments. Neither the owner of a website or blog nor a website that specializes in online consumer reviews is immune from legal action for allowing a false or libelous post to remain if you've lodged a formal complaint asking that they remove it. Under U.S. libel law, a website's legal liability for publishing defamatory comments is as great as the person posting it, and before things reach a litigious stage, the website administrators will likely delete the offending post. You should be aware that a deleted post can remain online through the site's own caches, but that's the nature of the Internet, rather than a fault of the site administrator—nothing posted online can ever really be "deleted."

Remember, though, that defamatory comments must be false, and they must also threaten to harm your professional reputation and damage your business. If matters were to proceed to an actual lawsuit, as the plaintiff in a libel case, you would have to prove injury based on the comment's falsehoods. Otherwise, the defendants could claim—and win—on their rights to protected speech under the First Amendment, which includes unflattering and negative reviews, even if they've resorted to childish or even profane name-calling. Pull apart these comments to discern what is merely dissatisfied bloviating, and what is opinion presented as fact. You may wish to pursue legal advice to understand these distinctions better.

The following is a sample letter you can use to try to stop defamatory comments when you know who has made them.

[Date]

RE: Defamation

Dear [Client/Blog Poster/etc.]:

You made defamatory statements about me that damaged or threaten to damage my reputation as an inspector.

Specifically, you made the following false statements:

[Describe each false statement, when it was made, what was said or written, and who heard or read the statement. Consider attaching proof of the statement and/or copies of the defamatory writings.]

The law is clear that when a person makes defamatory statements about a private person in his/her trade, business or profession, it is considered defamation per se. In such cases, the law presumes injury and the plaintiff need not prove actual damages. The U.S. Supreme Court determined that this principle is fully consistent with the U.S. Constitution. [See, New York Times Co. v. Sullivan, 376 U.S. 254 (1964).]

I demand that you immediately retract your defamatory statements. I specifically ask that you take the following actions: [State what corrective action you want the potential defendant to take].

Your willingness to take these actions immediately will play an important role in whether I decide to move forward with a defamation lawsuit against you.

If you refuse to take these steps, a judge or jury may consider your refusal as evidence of malice and may award me exemplary damages.

If you believe your statements are not defamatory, I request that you provide me with all documents that you're relying on to support your contention. I also request the name, address, phone number and email address of each person you believe can testify that the statements are not defamatory. I need this information to determine whether to move forward with a lawsuit against you.

Sincerely,

[Your Name]

[Your Company Name]

[Your Phone Number]

[Your Email Address]

Build Your Own Reputation Through Website Maintenance

In addition to monitoring the reach of your brand online, including comments and trademark usage, you can do a lot to maintain control and get regular search engine-optimization activity by maintaining a dynamic website.

You may think that since you've already posted your products, services, business hours, location, testimonials, and some great photos, that's all you really need. But you can make your site robust and interactive by adding more content. Consider adding a special section that features interesting links that are related to your business activity. For example, do you promote green building and lifestyle practices? Then post a link to some government-sponsored information that's relevant to your remarks and services.

Write an article (or hire a writer occasionally) who can add value to your website by writing relevant and topical articles or brief posts. Visitors to your site will appreciate that you don't let your website languish, but that you take an active interest in news and trends that affect your industry.

Take advantage of the power of SEO. For blog posts and articles, make sure you use keywords and track-backs as much as possible. You want your special website content to be robust and searchable. When prospective clients do a generic search online, you want them to find you first (or second, or third).

It's important to strike a balance between what you can do to pump up your online presence, and what you should leave to others. Don't get too over-invested in the typical bells and whistles found on many websites that are screaming to get noticed and make themselves obnoxious in the process. Paid ads and click-per-views are not recommended; unlike a stand-alone blog, your site is not your product—it's promoting your product. Your site is used to sell your services. If you do include paid or sponsored ads, make sure they're legitimate and that you have a sustained relationship with those vendors. Otherwise, not only will you be putting money into the pockets of counterfeit vendors, but your association with them will tarnish your own brand and reputation, and it will be nearly impossible to recover unless you change your business name and launch a whole new marketing campaign, which will be costly and time-intensive. Make these sponsorships relevant to your business and mutually beneficial. Any sites you link to your site should have link-backs, which you should verify occasionally.

It's also a good idea to occasionally search for businesses in your area to see if they're worth cultivating for an online bump in SEO and name-recognition. Or, if someone has taken a hit (such as one large engineering firm near Denver whose commercial buildings were discovered to be structurally faulty), you may want to consider removing their name or logo from your site, as well as pulling your implied endorsement from theirs. This is a delicate decision for a number of reasons. Legally speaking, any agreement or contract must be modified beforehand. But don't allow someone else's faltering reputation to indirectly compromise yours.

Remember that business reputations in a changing economy are dynamic, so monitor yours regularly, and become your own PR expert so that you can maintain control over your brand and good name.

Other Legal Issues for Home Inspectors

14 Steps That Help Inspectors Avoid Lawsuits

The following are 14 easy and inexpensive steps for inspectors to take to help prevent lawsuits.

1. Join InterNACHI, of course!

InterNACHI is the world's largest inspection trade association, and its Standards of Practice can be pointed to as definitive for the inspection industry. Substantially abiding by InterNACHI's Standards of Practice provides a strong defense against a claim that you failed to perform to a level of care or acceptable practice for the inspection profession.

Furthermore, InterNACHI's membership requirements are in addition to whatever your local, state or provincial government licensing and regulation may demand. Membership is evidence that you are the type of inspector who voluntarily goes above and beyond the minimum requirements that merely allow you to legally operate in your area.

Not a member? Visit www.nachi.org/join

2. Incorporate.

You, as a shareholder in your incorporated inspection company, enjoy limited liability for the corporation's debts and judgments against the corporation. No inspector should operate as a partner or sole proprietor... ever.

To learn how to protect your assets and prevent your corporate veil from being pierced, read "I formed a corporation or limited liability company. Now what?" at www.nachi.org/now-what

3. Take every one of InterNACHI's online courses.

We all know that many claims against inspectors are frivolous. Education and training won't prevent such suits from being filed, but education and training will help you prevail in court. Each of InterNACHI's online courses produces a Certificate of Completion. You should be prepared to produce all of your certificates as evidence of your professionalism. However, the dates of completion have to precede the date of the inspection in question, so complete our courses now.

Furthermore, education and training are key to performing high-quality inspections, which eliminates meritorious suits.

Knowledge is a powerful tool you can use to stay out of court or win if you should find yourself there.

See all of InterNACHI's online inspection courses by visiting our Educational Resources page at www.nachi.org/education

4. Never refer to yourself as an "expert" in your marketing.

Home inspectors are generalists, not experts. The word "expert" has a particular meaning in the legal profession. Experts are specialists who are held to a higher standard of care than the ordinary (non-expert) inspector.

5. If you are going to hire a helper, use a contract.

I prefer to hire helpers as independent contractors rather than employees. A good independent contractor agreement makes it difficult for a helper to:

- bind you or your inspection company into a contract;
- incur any liability on your behalf;
- claim rights associated with your publications, trade secrets, copyrights or trademarks;
- reveal your confidential information, such as marketing ideas, business plans, pricing strategies, etc.;
- steal your real estate agent database or solicit your clients;
- compel you to pay his/her expenses, insurance premiums or taxes;
- demand severance pay; or
- later claim s/he was an employee or is owed money.

Download InterNACHI'S Inspector Independent Contractor agreement at
www.nachi.org/independentcontractoragreement

6. Turn away some consumers.

You don't have to accept work from everyone who wants to retain you. If a client starts off being difficult or unreasonable, it usually gets worse, not better. While it may be hard to walk away from an inspection fee, it's sometimes cheaper in the long run. Furthermore, an added bonus of refusing to allow these consumers to become your clients is that they'll become your competitors' clients. Pity your competitors!

7. Use InterNACHI's Pre-Inspection Agreement.

It is designed to work hand-in-hand with InterNACHI's Standards of Practice and includes:

- a definition of the scope of the inspection;
- a disclaimer of warranties;
- a limitation on liability, and a liquidated-damages provision;
- a provision for payment of costs and attorney's fees;
- a "merger clause" stating that there are no promises other than those set forth in the agreement, and that all prior discussions are merged into the agreement;
- a clause stating that any modification of the agreement must be in writing;
- a forum-selection clause so that any lawsuit must be filed in the county or district where the inspector has his principal place of business; and
- a personal guaranty of payment if the client is a corporation or similar entity.

Download InterNACHI's Agreement at www.nachi.org/newagreement

8. Purchase InterNACHI's "Stay Back" stop sign.

In 2009, a home inspector opened a floor hatch to go down into a crawlspace to inspect it. While inspecting, his client fell into the opening, breaking his arm in three places. The client sued. The suit claimed that the inspector was negligent for not putting up a "caution" sign.

Also in 2009, a home inspector was on the roof of a home he was inspecting. A newer real estate agent decided to climb up the ladder to join the inspector. She slipped, fell 7 feet, and landed on top of the client who was steadying the ladder for the agent. Both suffered injuries that required them to be hospitalized. The client sued the inspector for not posting a sign to keep others off his ladder.

It gets worse. An inspector was recently blamed for an unsafe condition that already existed. During the review at the end of a home inspection, the inspector pointed out severely rotted deck planking. The client walked out onto the deck to see what the inspector was talking about when the client's foot broke through the decking, causing minor injury. The client didn't sue, but later complained to the real estate agent that the inspector should have kept everyone off the deck, once he discovered the issue.

The InterNACHI "Stay Back" stop sign does four things:

1. It shows that you care about your clients' safety.

2. It reminds everyone that there are risks, especially to children, in attending an inspection.

3. It actually keeps your clients at a safe distance.

4. It demonstrates in court that you are not reckless.

In designing these signs, our attorneys advised us to use a "stop" sign rather than a "caution" sign, as "caution" implies to proceed (to go ahead and climb the ladder, for instance), but with caution. A "stop" sign is clear and unambiguous.

Visit www.InspectorOutlet.com to order your "Stay Back" stop sign for $29.95. And save the receipt as evidence that you are a responsible inspector!

9. Take three photos of the water meter before you leave the property.

You never want to be accused of failing to note a water line leak, or—worse—causing water damage because you forgot to turn off a fixture. One way you can prevent this is to take some photos of the water meter just prior to leaving the property.

Take these photos after you've:

- completed your home inspection;
- turned off all the sink and tub faucets after checking them for functional flow; and
- made sure that the washing machine, dishwasher, sprinkler system, and any other water-using systems, devices and fixtures are off.

Take three photos of the water meter that show that no water lines are leaking, assuming you didn't find any.

Visit www.nachi.org/three-photos-inspection-report to read more about this claim-avoiding tip.

10. Write your reports properly with InterNACHI's Inspection Narratives Library.

This library is the world's largest collection of dedicated, industry-savvy home inspection narratives. These narratives were developed using a variety of sources, including the International Residential Code (IRC), technical data sheets, and systems specifications from various manufacturers' associations, installation manuals for a variety of building products, and various building science-related sites. These narratives are worded with safety in mind, and specific code is not quoted.

 In addition to reducing the amount of time you spend filling out reports, the quality of your reports will improve, and you'll enjoy greater protection from liability.

Visit www.nachi.org/narratives to order InterNACHI's DVD of inspection narratives. Can't wait? Order the digital download of InterNACHI's Inspection Narratives Library at www.InspectorOutlet.com

11. Include InterNACHI's "Estimated Life Expectancy Chart" with every report.

This chart details the predicted life expectancy of household materials, systems and components so that you don't have to.

Life expectancy varies with usage, weather, installation, maintenance, and the quality of materials. This chart provides your client with a general guideline from the world's largest inspection association—not a guarantee or warranty—and a reminder that there is no guarantee or warranty is stated at the bottom of the chart.

Visit www.nachi.org/life-expectancy to download your free Estimated Life Expectancy Chart (also featured at the end of this book).

12. Give all your clients InterNACHI's *Now That You've Had a Home Inspection* home-maintenance book.

This home-maintenance book was also written specifically to reduce your liability by reminding your clients that a home inspection does not reveal every defect that exists, that certain issues are outside the scope of a home inspection, and that a homeowner is now responsible for maintaining their home. It works well with the Client Satisfaction Survey (below).

Visit www.nachi.org/now to order a case of books.

13. Use InterNACHI's Client Satisfaction Survey.

Often, a dissatisfied client will describe their perception of your services to his/her agent, or, worse... to a judge, inaccurately. Procuring and maintaining a copy of this survey will bring them back to Earth, so to speak. It is a handy document to have to present to a complaining agent, and can often end a legal action all by itself. It is the next best thing to a deposition. The Client Satisfaction Survey creates a factual record of the client's version of events surrounding the inspection in the relevant time frame, thus inhibiting the client's ability to change his story to fit the circumstances of a later claim.

Visit www.nachi.org/survey to download a Client Satisfaction Survey, and save every copy forever.

14. If you settle a dispute with a client, get a signed release.

Right or wrong, in some cases, it makes sense to cut a deal with a complaining client to avoid a lawsuit.

Never apologize. An apology may be used to support a future claim that you were negligent. If you have to pay to have a repair done to correct a defect your client claims you "missed," always ask for a handwritten letter of reference thanking you for quickly solving the issue. Then take a stack of those letters back to the referring agent, brag about how you paid to keep your mutual client happy, and ask that the stack be passed out at the next real estate sales meeting.

Also, after you get the reference letter, get a release signed to end the issue forever.

Visit www.nachi.org/release to download a General Release for inspectors.

To Exceed or Not to Exceed: That Is the Question

by Mark Cohen, Esq. and Nick Gromicko

Inspectors sometimes ask about the potential legal consequences if their inspections go beyond what InterNACHI's Standards of Practice (SOP) require.

Of course, every inspection must, at a minimum, substantially meet the requirements of the SOP. If an inspector fails to comply with the SOP, the customer would have valid claims against the inspector for breach of contract and misrepresentation.

Therefore, when in doubt about what the SOP requires in a particular situation, the inspector should err on the side of caution and exceed the SOP. It is better to do a little more than what may be required than to do less and risk a potential claim and harm to your reputation.

A word of caution: If an inspector consistently goes far beyond what the SOP requires, a customer might successfully argue that the inspector voluntarily assumed a duty greater than the contract required. Most inspection contracts contain language stating that the inspector will perform the inspection in accordance with InterNACHI's SOP. An inspector who goes far beyond what the SOP requires may open himself up to a claim that there was an oral agreement that he was going to do a more rigorous inspection than what's required by the SOP.

If an inspector voluntarily assumes a duty greater than the duty required by the contract, the inspector has an obligation to perform those additional tasks with reasonable care.

If a Home Inspector Misses Something

Sooner or later, every home inspector is going to miss something that s/he thinks or is told s/he should have caught during a home inspection. But believe it or not, this can actually be turned into a good opportunity.

One of the measures of an inspector's ability is the gravity of the miss. Did s/he miss a structural issue that was easily visible and will cost $15,000 to correct, or was it a saturated desiccant strip in a double-pane window, which may be apparent only under certain conditions?

The best opportunity is the chance to turn a negative circumstance into a positive opportunity.

Was it Really a Miss?

Inspectors are sometimes accused of missing something clearly disclaimed in the home inspection contract, especially when they're following InterNACHI's Standards of Practice, such as air-conditioning performance. That's why it's a good idea to include the SOP in the appropriate section of the inspection report.

As inspectors, we each need to do our best to ensure that, before the inspection begins, the client has a realistic idea of what is and isn't included. We need to educate our clients.

In addition to giving a brief, verbal description of the inspection and its limitations, refer your new clients to a "New Clients" page and include web links to InterNACHI's Standards of Practice, the inspection contract (also developed by InterNACHI), and a "Systems Excluded" page detailing what's not typically included as part of the General Home Inspection. This page may also mention that you offer some of the stated exclusions as ancillary inspections, if that's the case.

You want clients to read the contract. Ask your clients to read, then fax or e-mail you signed copies of the contract and the "Systems Excluded" pages. InterNACHI's Online Agreement System includes a feature that allows clients to sign and return your contract electronically. Some contract requirements may vary by state.

The first line in InterNACHI's standard home inspection contract explains that it is not an inspector's duty to find every defect:

> INSPECTOR *agrees to perform a visual inspection of the home/building and to provide CLIENT with a written inspection report identifying the defects that INSPECTOR both observed and deemed material.*

And you should also consider providing your client a copy of InterNACHI's *Now That You've Had a Home Inspection* book. It will protect you from future claims.

Was the "Miss" Handled Well?

If you do miss something, there are times when you simply have to admit your mistake, make an apology, and get on with it. There are also times to demonstrate why you haven't made a mistake, but always graciously offer to make things right anyway, and convert the situation into a marketing opportunity. There are also times that will require you to take a position and stand fast because there are a number of situations in which others involved in the transaction may be motivated to make the inspector the fall guy.

Which approach to use involves judgment, and that's what it finally comes down to in home inspections. This is true not only for handling mistakes, but also in evaluating the limitless combinations of home systems and components, and all the grey areas in between, for which an inspector finds himself forced to make a decision that he may be called upon later to defend in court.

As an inspector, good judgment is one of your most important tools, and it's a skill that can be learned. Reading the InterNACHI Message Boards will help you sharpen this skill painlessly by allowing you to learn from the mistakes and experiences of other inspectors. In addition to providing education, the boards offer inspectors a chance to become part of the world's largest international inspection community that offers opportunities and support during the difficult times many inspectors face in breaking into the industry.

InterNACHI's Buy-Back Guarantee Program

InterNACHI now offers the "We'll Buy Back Your Home" Guarantee.

If the client's participating Certified Professional Inspector® misses anything in the inspection, InterNACHI will buy back the home. It's that simple.

There's no deductible and no "weasel" clauses.

Here are the no-frills terms of this groundbreaking Buy-Back Guarantee:

- Honored for 90 days after closing.
- Valid for home inspections performed for home buyers by participating InterNACHI members.
- We'll pay whatever price the client paid for the home.
- The guarantee excludes homes with material defects not present at the time of the inspection, or not required to be inspected per InterNACHI's Residential Standards of Practice.

Home buyers can buy a home worry-free when they have it inspected by a participating InterNACHI member.

If they're not happy within the first 90 days after buying it, InterNACHI will buy back the home at full price.

Real estate agents in North America can be assured that their clients can now buy with confidence.

Additionally, InterNACHI protects the privacy of its members' clients. It doesn't collect identifiable consumer data, so it can't sell it or release it. No names, addresses, phone numbers or email addresses are sold or released to any third party.

InterNACHI members can visit this link to sign up: www.nachi.org/buy

Proving Negligence

by Mark Cohen, InterNACHI General Counsel, and Nick Gromicko

A client asserting claims against a home inspector may rely on a variety of legal theories, including negligence, breach of contract, and misrepresentation. This article explains the four elements a plaintiff must prove to prevail in a negligence claim. Understanding these will help inspectors to better understand how to reduce their risk of being found negligent.

The four elements of a negligence claim are:

1. duty;

2. breach;

3. causation; and

4. damages.

To be successful, a plaintiff must prove all four elements by a preponderance of the evidence. Let's look at each of the elements.

Duty

The plaintiff must prove that the inspector owed a duty to him. The duty may be created and defined by a contract, a statute, or the standard of care in the industry. In common law, every person has a duty to exercise ordinary care in all activities to prevent foreseeable risks. Even if no duty would ordinarily exist, a person who voluntarily undertakes to do something must exercise ordinary care in doing it. (Even though you have no duty to provide a free inspection to a relative, if you assume that duty, you must carry it out properly.)

An inspector has a duty to comply with all applicable laws and regulations, but some state laws do not define any additional duties inspectors owe to clients. Put differently, not all states have statutes that specifically define the standard of care. Therefore, it is vital that the written contract define the additional duties assumed by the inspector. If the client and inspector both understand the scope of the duties owed, disputes are far less likely.

The best thing an inspector can do to protect himself is insist that the client sign a written contract BEFORE the inspection. The contract should explain what the inspector will and will not do. The standard InterNACHI contract explains that the inspector will perform the inspection in accordance with InterNACHI's current Standards of Practice at www.nachi.org/sop The inspector should provide a copy of the SOP to the client, or encourage the client to review them online before signing the contract.

Generally, the inspector works for the prospective buyer. A seller may sometimes threaten to sue an inspector for negligence because of statements in the inspector's report, but this threat is often hollow because the inspector's duty is to his client, not to the seller or real estate agent.

Generally, the existence of a duty is a question of law, meaning the judge—not the jury—decides whether the inspector owed a duty to the client.

Breach

Once the plaintiff proves the existence of a duty, he must prove the inspector breached that duty. In other words, the plaintiff must show that the inspector was negligent. Because it is impossible to prescribe definite rules in advance for every combination of circumstances that may arise, the question of whether the inspector breached a duty is usually a question for the trier of fact (the jury in a jury trial, or the judge in a non-jury trial).

One way the inspector can reduce the risk of being found negligent is to prepare a thorough report summarizing what he did and all his relevant observations. If the inspector identifies defects, he should list them in the report and inform the client of the possible consequences. If the inspector recommends repairs or additional inspection by a specialist, he should state that in the report. The inspector should take plenty of photos during the inspection, as they may be useful if litigation ensues.

Causation

Even if the plaintiff proves that the inspector owed a duty and breached that duty, the plaintiff must also demonstrate that the breach was the cause of the claimed damages. The test traditionally used to determine cause is the "but for" test. Under this approach, the inspector's conduct is a cause if the damages would not have taken place but for the inspector's breach of the duty owed.

Think of it this way. If an inspector breaches his duty by failing to perform a proper electrical inspection, but the client is complaining about the cost of replacing the roof, the inspector's breach of his duty was not the cause the client's damages. The "but for" test works well, but there is one situation where it fails. If two causes combine to bring about an event, either of which would have been sufficient to cause the damages, many courts ask whether the defendant's breach of duty was a "substantial factor" in bringing about the damages. If so, the inspector's negligence will be considered a cause of the claimed damages.

It is important to remember that even in situations where a home inspector has been negligent, other parties, including the buyer, may have also been negligent. For instance, suppose an inspector lists a defect in his report, fails to fully inform the buyer of the possible consequences of this defect, but advises the buyer to hire an expert to follow up on the defect. If the buyer fails to hire an expert, the buyer may be at least partly at fault for failing to heed the inspector's recommendation. When more than one party has been negligent, many states now require courts and juries to allocate a percentage of fault to each negligent party.

Damages

If the plaintiff establishes the first three elements of a negligence claim, he must still prove that he was damaged, and he must prove the amount of his damages.

Damages in a negligence suit against a home inspector will often be the costs incurred in correcting defects the inspector failed to find. However, there have been cases where an unhappy client claimed he would not have purchased a property had the inspector performed a proper inspection and, in this case, the claimed damages may be much greater.

The goal of allowing an award of damages is to make the plaintiff whole: to restore him to the situation he was in before the negligent act or omission. One issue to be alert to is claims that seek to make the plaintiff better off than he would have been but for the inspector's negligence. For example, if an inspector fails to mention defects in a roof that is 10 years old and the roof must be replaced, the plaintiff is not entitled to a brand new roof, but is entitled only to damages equal to a non-defective roof that is 10 years old.

The law recognizes direct damages and consequential damages. Direct damages include damages such as cost of repair or replacement. Consequential damages may include damages such as loss of productivity or loss of profits resulting, for example, from the inability to use a home office. In many states, an inspector can limit his liability for damages to direct damages and disclaim any responsibility for consequential damages. In some states, an inspector may be able to limit his liability to the amount paid for the inspection.

This article provides only general guidance. Always consult an attorney qualified in your jurisdiction.

Deposition Preparation

A deposition is recorded witness testimony given under oath to be used in court at a later date. Inspectors, like any other professionals whose job subjects them to a certain amount of liability, are occasionally sued and deposed. Deposed witnesses should learn testimony strategies that will make their success in court more likely.

Facts About Depositions

- They are usually held in a less formal setting than a courtroom, although the testimony provided is just as significant as that given in court. The version of events offered by a witness during a deposition essentially binds the witness to that version.
- They are designed to allow the opposing counsel to gather evidence against the defendant or plaintiff.
- Present at depositions are the defense attorney, the plaintiff's attorney, a court reporter, and the party to be deposed.
- The court reporter will record every spoken word, with the exception of "off the record" conversation, and later transcribe it into writing.
- Depositions can be long and grueling, sometimes lasting hours.
- Questions asked during a deposition may not be asked in any apparent order and may seem irrelevant. Nevertheless, it is the responsibility of the witness to answer every question unless their lawyer instructs them otherwise.

Before the Deposition

Meet with your lawyer to review all relevant documents, especially interrogatory responses. These responses are written answers to questions that were previously provided.

At the Deposition

- Do not lie. InterNACHI members should know that lying under oath is criminal perjury. If you get caught lying, your entire testimony will be discredited. President Clinton lost his license to practice law and was impeached for lying under oath.
- If you arrive at the deposition before your lawyer, do not speak about the case with anyone, especially the plaintiff's attorney.
- Dress in a professional manner. Although no photos will be taken, the opposing party's impression of you is important. If you arrive unkempt, they might think you will not appear credible to a jury, and the plaintiff will be less likely to settle out of court.

- Do not be intimidated by the opposing lawyer. Unlike in a courtroom, where a judge and/or jury is watching, lawyers may try to antagonize you so that you give up additional information. Recognize such behavior as manipulative tactics, to be brushed aside, rather than as personal attacks.

- Similarly, do not be put at ease if the opposing lawyer is strangely pleasant or easygoing. Assume that everything they say and do is intentional and designed to influence your response.

- Speak slowly and deliberately. Remember that everything spoken during a deposition—including stuttering or faltering—is recorded. Slow and deliberate speech will make your testimony appear more professional and credible when it is read later by a judge.

- Do not bring any documents with you unless you were specifically told to do so. You do not want to provide the opposition with any information that they do not already have.

- Always pause after each question before answering. This way, you have time to consider the question, and you will be sure that the question has ended. There is no real time limit for answering a question, so take as much time as you need. Answering questions quickly might also encourage the opposing lawyer to ask more questions than they otherwise would, which will work against you. Also, permitting a pause before answering will allow your attorney the chance to object to the question. It is too late to object after you have begun to answer.

- Do not volunteer information. Answer exactly what is asked and nothing more. Attorneys may also continue to look you in the eyes long after you've completed your answer in hopes that the uncomfortable silence will cause you to continue talking.

- Always ask for clarification if you do not fully understand the question. Never guess the meaning of a question.

- Do not speculate. If you do not know the answer to a question, say that you do not know the answer.

- Request breaks whenever you feel you need one.

- Do not be afraid of questions that require a "yes" or a "no" answer, even if you think you will sound bad. You do not need to defend yourself at a deposition with a lengthy explanation.

- Do not attempt to memorize answers to anticipated questions. You will not sound natural and there is no way to know in advance what you will be asked.

In summary, inspectors who are deposed should prepare themselves for the unfamiliar environment in which they will provide sworn testimony.

Inspectors as Expert Witnesses

What Is an Expert Witness?

Some home inspectors who want to expand their business do so by performing consulting work. "Consulting" means to advise paying clients according to one's particular area of expertise. One way for residential and commercial property inspectors to offer consulting services is to act as an expert witness.

An "expert witness" is someone with expertise in a particular area who is called to testify during litigation. A "fact witness" is a person whose testimony is limited to giving facts. An "expert witness," by contrast, is allowed to give his or her professional opinion.

An expert witness provides an Expert Witness Report after performing an inspection. The goal is to provide a report so convincing that the opposition will decide to settle out of court, saving the client the cost of continued litigation.

Although an expert witness may be hired by either a defendant or a plaintiff, or by the court, s/he is supposed to be a neutral third party. This means that the inspector has no interest in the outcome of the case, and his or her testimony is unbiased.

What Qualifications Do I Need?

There is no single qualification, and the exact qualifications you'll need will depend on the nature of the court case. The first step in entering a case as an expert witness is to establish your credentials.

Qualifying to perform as an expert witness means that you must be able to show knowledge, skill, experience, training, education, and/or other expertise that may be meaningful to a party attempting to prove its side in a lawsuit.

When developing this portion of your business, a prospective client will probably be looking for an expert witness who:

- is a practitioner in the subject at issue;
- is an instructor in the subject at issue;
- has published peer review articles, textbooks, and/or guidelines in his or her area of expertise; and/or
- presents well in front of a jury.

What Does an Expert Witness Do?

The process for the expert witness works something like this:

The Referral

When you receive the referral, usually in a phone call, the prospective client will want to know your qualifications. You should have an updated *curriculum vitae* (CV), which is a detailed résumé, and a copy of your Expert Witness Agreement (including a fee schedule), ready to email. Be prompt. You want them to know that you can take care of business. During this phone call, you should ask for any relevant photos and documents, including a description of the litigation.

At this time, you should also start a project log, writing down important contact information, such as dates and phone numbers, and recording who you spoke with and what was discussed. Make sure to enter any major decisions.

Laws regulating the recording of telephone calls vary by state. In states where it's legal to electronically record phone calls, such equipment is inexpensive and can help you keep track of what's said.

Case Evaluation

After reviewing the preliminary information, the first decision you'll make is whether to accept the work at all. It may be that the prospective client will ask you to support a position that you are unable or unwilling to. If you feel comfortable about taking the case, notify your client.

The Agreement

Typically, you'll be approached by the attorney of one of the litigants. It's a good idea to insist that your contract name the attorney as your client, instead of the litigant. This will increase your chances of getting paid. If the case goes to court and your client loses, you may not be at the top of your client's "must pay" list.

- The "Services" portion of the agreement should describe the expert witness services you are to provide, including your fee schedule. This section should contain a number of disclosures describing the limitations of your expert witness service.

- The "Confidentiality" section should describe both the confidentiality which will be offered by the expert witness, and the limitations of the expert witness's liability concerning confidentiality.

- The "No Conflicts" section should state that the expert witness has no conflict of interest in the legal matter and is able to form an opinion free from bias.

- The section on "Legal Matters" may delineate items such as a "Hold-Harmless" clause. It should define the jurisdiction under which the contract was written, and describe where and how disputes will be handled.

- The "Termination" section describes the conditions under which the contract may be terminated, and the results of termination under different circumstances.

Expert witness fees vary with the situation and with the person providing the service. The client is typically required to pay an initial retainer, which might be $1,200.00 or more, depending on the amount of time the expert witness estimates the work will take.

Other types of fees may include:

- file review and research;

- travel time;

- inspection and investigative services (which you should bill at a two-hour minimum);

- report preparation;

- pre-trial preparation;

- deposition (also billed at a two-hour minimum);

- requested courtroom appearance (billed at a half-day or a full day); and

- miscellaneous expenses (such as meals and/or accommodations, or a *per diem*).

Once the agreement has been signed, arrangements will have to be made to perform the inspection. If you want a specialist to be there for any reason, you should schedule accordingly.

The Inspection

Your demeanor during the inspection is important. Frivolity is out of place. You should remain professional and neutral, especially if the opposition has representatives at the inspection who are unfriendly.

A tactic you may encounter is that the opposition may try to intimidate you. They may provide representatives with an overbearing presence, or they may place themselves in positions that make it difficult for you to do your job. The penalties for actually interfering with you during your inspection are harsh enough that you should not allow yourself to be intimidated. If you have a small voice recorder, you should use it to record the inspection, along with any confrontations or efforts to interfere with your inspection.

If the opposition succeeds in rattling you, under no circumstances should you lose your temper. Keep in mind that there's a good chance that any incident that arises may be described in court. You want to be portrayed as rational and in control of your emotions.

You should ask questions of anyone you like, but think twice about answering questions too freely. Don't give out information to the opposition, and don't go into too much detail with your client. You may change your mind about what you're seeing as you continue to investigate.

You should walk into the inspection as informed as possible. During the inspection, you should be working from a checklist and notes that you created during your preparation. Unlike home inspections, the property you inspect as an expert witness may be far from where you live. You may not be able to return easily, so you need to be prepared. To that end, you should take a lot of high-definition digital photos. Taking and storing photos is cheap in the digital age. Taking high-resolution photos means that you may be able to zoom in to look at something in more detail.

Report Preparation

Once the inspection is completed, you'll be ready to begin compiling your Expert Witness Report.

Based on the matter at issue, you should develop a hypothesis and show in your report why yours is the true hypothesis. You can include anything you think is necessary in your report.

The report may contain the following:

- a title page;
- a table of contents;
- your credentials;
- the Request for Inspection;
- any relevant building codes and standards;
- definitions of terms used in the report;
- the main body or narrative of the report;
- any miscellaneous reference material;
- a copy of the plaintiff's Complaint;
- a copy of the defendant's Response to Allegations;
- all relevant photos and diagrams (with captions as to location/area of the subject property);
- your conclusion; and
- any explanatory footnotes and/or bibliography of your reference materials.

The goal is to make your report overwhelming to the opposition while still maintaining your status as a neutral third party. If you testify to something that's later proven to be untrue, you'll lose credibility, which is crucial in finding work as an expert witness.

When the complaint consists of multiple allegations, you should organize your responses clearly and separate the information as necessary.

Opposition's Response

Once you've submitted your Expert Witness Report, you and the opposing expert witness will have a chance to review and respond to the other's report. If that fails to elicit a settlement, the next step will be to go to trial.

Deposition

Early in the proceedings, you may be asked to provide sworn testimony via a deposition, which is conducted outside of court. During the deposition, the expert witness must answer a series of oral questions by the opposition's attorney. The client's attorney will have a chance to cross-examine you in order to make clarifications.

In Court

In court, you need to be well-prepared. You should have reviewed your report carefully, especially if much time has passed since you wrote it. Try to anticipate the areas of the report that the opposition will attack, and have answers ready for questions they might ask.

You'll be coached on appropriate behavior by your client or their attorney. If you have any questions about the process, don't hesitate to ask. It's better to resolve them before you find yourself all alone on the witness stand.

Once you're on the stand, you'll first be asked about your qualifications and credentials. After the court and the opposition accept them, you'll give your testimony. You may be asked to give factual information. You may have to answer specific questions. And you may be asked for your professional opinion.

Final Billing

Your billing schedule should be included in the section of your agreement that outlines your fees. Send your client invoices on a regular basis until payment is received.

Conclusion

Requirements for expert witnesses vary by state. If you're considering offering expert witness services, you should discuss with your attorney any details that may affect your inspection business.

Tip: Use InterNACHI's Hold-Harmless Clause as a marketing tool (www.nachi.org/harmless).

Visit this link www.nachi.org/expert-witness-agreement to download InterNACHI's sample Expert Witness Agreement.

InterNACHI Attorney: "Code-certified" claims can lead to unexpected problems for inspectors.

InterNACHI's attorney, Mark Cohen, has issued a statement reminding InterNACHI members to be cautious in advertising themselves as "code-certified" or "ICC-Certified."

Cohen's warning comes in the wake of a recent court ruling in which a home inspector who marketed himself as "code-certified" was held liable to a customer for misrepresentation after a local government determined that the home he had inspected was not "up to code."

Training offered by the International Code Council (ICC) can be beneficial to home inspectors, but Cohen says home inspectors should be careful not to suggest or imply that their home inspections will ensure that the residence is in compliance with all applicable codes. Codes vary from one jurisdiction to the next, and whether something is "up to code" is often a judgment call made by a government employee. Unless an inspector intends to warrant that the property is in compliance with all codes, the inspector should make clear in his advertising and in his contract that the inspection seeks to identify defects, but does not attempt to identify code violations.

Cohen warns inspectors to use care in advertising their services, saying, "Statements contained in an advertisement or on a website may form the basis for subsequent claims of misrepresentation by customers who did not understand the inspector's role."

Read the announcement online at www.nachi.org/codecertifiedwarning

Legal: Links and Online Information

Online Inspection Agreement System

Use InterNACHI's free Online Inspection Agreement System. It allows for electronic signatures and is legally binding. Find it here: www.nachi.org/onlineagreement

Documents, Agreements and Sample Legal Language

- InterNACHI's Residential Inspection Agreement: www.nachi.org/newagreement
- Online Inspection Agreement System: www.nachi.org/onlineagreement
- Expert Witness Agreement: www.nachi.org/expert-witness-agreement
- Employment Agreement with Non-Compete Clause: www.nachi.org/employmentagreement
- Independent Contractor Agreement: www.nachi.org/independentcontractoragreement
- Hold-Harmless Clause: www.nachi.org/harmless
- General Release: www.nachi.org/release
- Personal Guaranty: www.nachi.org/personalguaranty
- Payment at Closing Authorization: www.nachi.org/closing2007
- Third-Party Service Provider's Permission-to-Contact Clause: www.nachi.org/tpsp
- Client Satisfaction Survey: www.nachi.org/survey
- Leave-Behind Letter: www.nachi.org/leave-behind-letter
- Estimated Life Expectancy Chart: www.nachi.org/life-expectancy
- Mold Inspection Agreement: www.iac2.org/agreement
- Mold Waiver: www.nachi.org/moldwaiver
- Radon Inspection Agreement: www.nachi.org/radonagreement
- Radon Test-in-Progress Notice: www.nachi.org/radon-test-in-progress
- Radon Waiver: www.nachi.org/radonwaiver
- Well Water Sampling Agreement: www.nachi.org/waterqualitysamplingagreement
- Universal Four-Point Insurance Inspection form: www.nachi.org/4point
- Log Home Disclaimer language: www.nachi.org/loghomedisclaimer
- Commercial Inspection Agreement: www.nachi.org/comsop.htm#10
- Request for Documents and Person(s) with Knowledge sample language: www.nachi.org/comsop.htm#11
- Professional Services Contract: www.nachi.org/comsop.htm#12
- Energy Audit Contract: www.nachi.org/energy-audit-contract
- Thermal Imaging Addendum to Residential Inspection Agreement: www.nachi.org/iraddendum
- Thermal Imaging Addendum to Commercial Inspection Agreement: www.nachi.org/comsop.htm#13

- WDO (Wood-Destroying Organism) Inspection Report Form: www.nachi.org/wdo-report
- InterNACHI's Standard Accessibility Inspection Report for Existing Commercial Buildings: www.nachi.org/comsop.htm#14
- InterNACHI's Observed Green Features Report for Existing Commercial Buildings: www.nachi.org/comsop.htm#15
- MoveInCertified.com's Green Certified Checklist: www.moveincertified.com/green
- Release and Hold-Harmless Agreement (for turning on utilities): www.nachi.org/utilities
- Winterization/De-Winterization Services Agreement: www.nachi.org/winterization-agreement
- InterNACHI's Standard Licensing Agreement for InterNACHI Use of Vendor Course Materials: www.nachi.org/nachicanuse

Inspection Legal Case Library

Read about inspection-related lawsuits in the Inspection Legal Case Library. These case summaries are designed to help inspectors and their defense attorneys. Read them at www.nachi.org/inspection-legal-case-library

Inspector Support

Links and Online Information

Receipt for Dues

Download and print off your tax-deductible receipt for your membership dues at www.nachi.org/receiptfordues

Net Profit Optimizer

Improve your bottom line with InterNACHI's free, online Net Profit Optimizer.

Visit www.nachi.org/netprofit

Message Boards, Blog, News, and Consumer Assistance

- Visit **InterNACHI's Inspector Blog** at www.nachi.org/blog. The blog contains information and news for both inspectors and consumers.
- Visit **InterNACHI's interactive Message Board** at www.nachi.org/forum. The board allows inspectors to interact, post pictures, and discuss inspection topics. Forum categories include:
  - Ethics
  - Legal Advice
  - Marketing
  - Computers and Technology
  - Report Writing
  - General Inspection Discussion (www.nachi.org/forum/f11)
  - Miscellaneous Discussion (www.nachi.org/forum/f13)
  - Legislation, Licensing and Legal Issues (www.nachi.org/forum/f14)
  - Special Discounts for InterNACHI Members (www.nachi.org/forum/f32)
  - NACHI.TV (www.nachi.org/forum/f63)
  - InterNACHI Blog (www.nachi.org/forum/f69)
  - Seller Inspections & Move-In Certified™ (www.nachi.org/forum/f62)
  - Thermal Imaging, Infrared Cameras & Energy Audits (www.nachi.org/forum/f58)
  - Green Building Inspections (www.nachi.org/forum/f59)
  - Exterior (www.nachi.org/forum/f16)
  - Interior (www.nachi.org/forum/f18)
  - Electrical (www.nachi.org/forum/f19)
  - HVAC (www.nachi.org/forum/f20)
  - Plumbing (www.nachi.org/forum/f22)
  - Structural (www.nachi.org/forum/f23)

- Commercial (www.nachi.org/forum/f53)
- Ancillary Services & Additional Topics (www.nachi.org/forum/f21)
- Hardware, Software & Publications (www.nachi.org/forum/f31)
- Education (www.nachi.org/forum/f25)
- Canada Inspectors (www.nachi.org/forum/f48)
- Puerto Rico Inspectors (www.nachi.org/forum/f68)
- California Inspectors (www.nachi.org/forum/f57)
- Texas Inspectors (www.nachi.org/forum/f71)
- Florida Inspectors (www.nachi.org/forum/f73)
- Oklahoma Inspectors (www.nachi.org/forum/f78)
- Minnesota/MAHI Inspectors (www.nachi.org/forum/f85)
- Ohio Inspectors (www.nachi.org/forum/f84)
- CMI/MICB Discussion (www.nachi.org/forum/f55)
- IAC2 Forum (www.nachi.org/forum/f50)
- Inspector Classified Ads
- InterNACHI's Emergency Forum (www.nachi.org/forum/f79) for inspectors on the job who need help right now.

- Visit InterNACHI's **What's New** page at www.nachi.org/whats_new to find out what's new in the inspection industry.

- Participate in **AskNACHI.org** at www.asknachi.org to contribute and help consumers with their inspection questions.

Emergency Forum

Need emergency help from inspection experts while you're on the job site?

Try out our Emergency Forum!

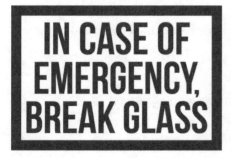

This forum is for time-sensitive emergencies only. If you need help using the InterNACHI website, or for any other questions, email FastReply@nachi.org instead.

It is not to be used to host discussions, make announcements, or for seeking help with off-site inspection report writing. This forum is dedicated solely to helping fellow members who are on an inspection site and need IMMEDIATE help with an issue. We also have various subject matter experts who have agreed to monitor this forum.

Visit the Emergency Forum at www.nachi.org/forum/f79

Report Review

InterNACHI's Report Review Committee reviews members' inspection reports, checks them for adherence to our Standards of Practice, makes suggestions for improvements, and returns them to the inspector. Working members who have yet to perform any fee-paid inspections must submit four mock inspection reports to the Report Review Committee before performing any fee-paid inspections. A mock inspection is an inspection performed for no fee. It can be performed on the member's own home, a friend's home, a family member's home, another inspector's home, or at an InterNACHI-sponsored mock inspection. This is a membership requirement for members who have never done a fee-paid inspection. ITA provides free mock inspection reporting forms for InterNACHI members. The forms and the Report Reviews are free. Visit www.nachi.org/reportreview

AutoCorrect Tutorial

Take this free AutoCorrect tutorial for report writing in MS Word: www.nachi.org/tutorials/tutorial

FetchReport™

Upload your inspection reports to the Internet for your clients to view and print at www.fetchreport.com Making your reports FetchReport™-friendly is totally free. As the inspection industry moves toward doing more work for home sellers, and as inspectors are seeking more ways to add value to their services without additional cost, a robust and unified upload and download system with multiple benefits has now been universally adopted.
FetchReport.com has already procured agreements from nearly every inspection software company, report form vendor, and testing laboratory to become FetchReport-friendly over the next several months. Uploading reports to FetchReport.com offers a number of advantages for everyone.

Advantages for the Real Estate Agent:

- they receive the inspection reports faster and can share them with repair contractors to get estimates faster;
- they can download, read and print the reports easily;
- they can provide potential buyers a link (from the pages on their website that promote a particular property) to access all the home's reports for seller inspection marketing purposes;
- they can become acquainted with an easy-to-use, unified system for all the home sales they are involved with, regardless of which inspector they use, regardless of how each inspector generates the reports, regardless of what supporting documentation or laboratory reports are desired, and regardless of what type of inspections are performed; and
- they can provide added value (in terms of third-party discount coupons and gift certificates) to their clients through reports uploaded to FetchReport.com.

Advantages for the Client:

- clients can receive the inspection reports faster and can provide others with access;
- they can download, read and print the reports easily;
- sellers can provide potential buyers a link to access all the home's reports for seller inspection marketing purposes;
- potential buyers can access past inspection reports when considering whether or not to tour a home; and
- clients enjoy added value (in terms of third-party discount coupons and gift certificates) found in reports uploaded to FetchReport.com.

Advantages for the Inspector:

- inspectors can upload their reports easily;
- they can control who gets access to uploaded reports:
- they can upload the reports under one unified system, regardless of what software or forms they used to generate the report;
- they can upload information from various types inspections, laboratory analysis reports, and supporting documentation using one unified system; and
- they can provide added value (in terms of third-party discount coupons and gift certificates) to their inspection reports.

FetchReport hopes to soon provide so much added value to uploaded reports that consumers (who have no need for an inspection otherwise) order one anyway, just to acquire the downloadable gift certificates, and they can enjoy added marketing exposure to potential clients who view reports of inspections performed on homes they considered buying but did not purchase.

Four other uses for FetchReport that are developing: use of the system by home insurance companies; use of the system for marketing foreclosed homes to online buyers; use of the system to move toward pay-per-view report downloading; and use of the system by real estate companies to mass-market listings. InterNACHI's free, online, signable electronic inspection agreement system is FetchReport-friendly, and MoveInCertified.com uses FetchReport technology exclusively. The entire system is totally free. Visit www.nachi.org/fetchreportfriendlyseal

Inspector Safety Equipment

Inspectors should always bring with them gear that can protect against the hazardous situations inherent in inspections.

Ironically, the process of inspecting for safety defects can itself compromise the safety of inspectors and their clients. InterNACHI Inspectors can use the following types of equipment to help ensure that inspections proceed problem-free.

- **Coveralls:** Coveralls are made from a variety of materials, often canvas or Tyvek®, a tear-resistant, flexible plastic widely used to make items such as postal mailers, banknotes and even DVDs. While canvas is puncture-resistant, Tyvek® is disposable and lightweight, as well as anti-static, breathable and chemical-resistant. However, it should not be used near heat or open flames. Both canvas and Tyvek® provide effective barriers against splashes, asbestos, chemicals, lead dust, and other harmful substances.

- **Flashlights:** Inspectors should bring at least two flashlights with them before entering dimly lit attics and crawlspaces. This precaution will eliminate the possibility that one flashlight will lose power, forcing the inspector to feel his way back out. The multitude of dangerous elements that potentially lie in attics and crawlspaces is startling—from exposed nails and broken glass, to dangerous reptiles, insects and mammals. No one should ever enter these areas without a flashlight.

- **Goggles:** Goggles can protect against many types of harmful airborne substances, such as mold spores and sawdust. Inspectors should be sure to wear goggles or some other type of eye protection while inspecting electrical panels, which can emit dangerous sparks or arcs.

- **Roof equipment:** Inspectors who must walk on rooftops (especially those who perform roof, wind and hail inspections) regularly risk fall-related injuries. Some equipment that can keep them from stumbling off a roof are:

  - **roof shoes:** Shoes form the only constant point of contact between the inspector and the roof, and the bond between them needs to be firm. Some companies make shoes that are specially designed for roof work, but these are not always necessary. Whatever type of shoes inspectors decide to wear, they should be flat and have high-traction rubber soles. Footwear with heels can become caught on roof surfaces, potentially causing the inspector to trip and fall;

  - **ladder tie-offs:** Inspectors should bring with them straps to use to attach their ladders to the roof or structure. This attachment will help prevent the ladder from being blown away by a strong wind, embarrassing the marooned inspector. Also, a ladder tie-off can potentially prevent the ladder from slipping away from the building beneath the weight of the climber.

  - **personal tie-off:** Inspectors may want to attach themselves to the roof as an added security measure.

  A few notes about this procedure:

    - Some roofs do not allow for the implementation of this safety measure. Roofs must have a protruding, sturdy, accessible place as a connection point, such as a chimney.

    - The strap must have as little slack as possible. Rolling down 15 feet of steep roof and then plunging another 10 feet before being halted in mid-air is still going to hurt. Plus, the dangling inspector will need to somehow climb back up.

    - It is best to attach the strap to a harness designed for that purpose, rather than a tool belt or limb.

    - It is dangerous to tie the strap to a car on the other side of the house. While the car might hold the inspector in place during a fall, it would not hold the inspector in place if someone were to drive the car away. A riding lawnmower is also a poor choice for an anchor.

- **Gloves:** Rubber or leather gloves are important for inspecting electrical panels to reduce the chance of accidental shock. Also, they should be worn in crawlspaces and basements. A certain amount of crawling on all fours through these areas will be necessary during inspections, and gloves will certainly make this activity safer. Gloves should not be loose.

  Visit www.InspectorOutlet.com to purchase Comfort Crawl Gloves, which are the world's first padded forearm-protection gloves designed for crawling on rough surfaces.

- **Respirators:** Respirators are necessary safety equipment for inspectors. Choices include a full-face respirator, which covers the eyes, nose and mouth, and a half-face respirator. Full-face respirators may provide greater protection against certain toxins because they protect the mucous membranes around the eyes, but they are generally less comfortable. Wearers may find that the mask's air filtration makes it hard to breathe, especially when the inspector must crawl and bend using physical movements that may restrict breathing. Respirators that have HEPA filters are excellent personal protective equipment since, by definition, they trap at least 99.97% of small particles.

- **Road cones:** Inspectors may want to consider placing road cones some distance behind their vehicles to prevent others from parking too close behind. Large, unwieldy items such as ladders are more safely removed when there is ample room in which to maneuver. Nothing causes tension like a Realtor who gets knocked in the head after parking snugly behind the inspector's truck. Also, as universal symbols of caution, road cones will alert passing motorists and pedestrians of the need to maintain a safe distance.

- **"Danger" signs:** A sign can be placed near dangerous areas in which the inspector is working to warn clients and others of potential hazards. In 2008, an inspector in Seattle was sued because his client fell through an opening in a floor leading to a crawlspace that he was inspecting, and the client broke his arm in three places. The lawsuit alleges that the inspector was guilty of "negligence and misconduct" because he failed to notify the client of the potential hazard.

To avoid such liability and to ensure the safety of all persons present at an inspection, InterNACHI has created compact, lightweight "STOP—Inspector at Work" signs for inspectors to use at job sites. These signs are specifically designed to be placed on ladders and near crawlspace entrances that are being inspected. Made of strong, durable plastic, they fold up flat and fit securely over the rung of the inspector's ladder. Using them may also provide legal leverage for inspectors who are held responsible for harm inflicted to their clients during an inspection.

In summary, inspections can be dangerous for inspectors, as well as their clients. Safety equipment should be brought to all inspections to help avoid injury and liability issues.

Take InterNACHI's free "Safe Practices for the Home Inspector" course at www.nachi.org/education

Take InterNACHI's free online Ladder Safety video course at www.nachi.org/ladder-safety-training-video-course

Using a Trophy Office and Shop to Promote Your Inspection Business

What does your bricks-and-mortar office say about you, your business values, and your clientele—especially the ones you're trying to attract?

Certain businesses cater to wealthy clients in posh areas that require impressive offices. Your office is a direct reflection of your values and aesthetics, but you don't have to operate beyond your profit margin to make a good impression. Consider having an upscale office space to help you maintain a professional image that will attract high-end clients, as well as give you a home base to trumpet your achievements.

Whether your business is expanding or you have an established office that's in need of a makeover, consider the following factors as you create your business storefront.

Rent or Buy?

Perhaps the first question to consider is whether it's time for you to stop paying rent on your commercial office and simply buy the property, or buy or rent a different office space. Here are some questions to help you determine whether owning commercial property is right for your business.

- **Will the building help or hinder your growth?** Take a look at how fast your company has grown since you started it and try to predict how much space you will require in the future. You don't want to be limited to the small storefront you're in now if you're growing fast. On the other hand, if your building has adjacent spaces occupied by other tenants, you might be able to gradually grow in place by taking over neighboring leases.

- **Can you pay the mortgage?** Calculate whether your monthly costs would rise if you took on a mortgage. Is it much higher than the rent you're paying? If your business can't afford an increased expense, it could create cash-flow problems.

- **Can you make the down payment?** A commercial building purchase may require a large down payment, usually around 20%. If this payment puts your business in a cash crunch, it might be safer to hold off on property ownership.

- **How much control do you need?** You may eventually need to drastically alter your space as your company grows and discovers its own identity. For instance, you may want to paint all the walls blue, knock down walls, or install heavy machinery that would be difficult or expensive to remove. Most landlords will not allow these sorts of alterations, especially if they are prohibited in your lease agreement. Purchasing a building will give you far more control over your own business and remove obstacles that would prevent its growth.

- **Will write-offs be possible?** If your business is profitable, property ownership can lessen your tax burden. You may be able to write off a portion of the building's cost each year in the form of depreciation. Another possibility is to buy the building personally and then rent it to your company, which is an ownership structure that has some tax advantages.

- **Is a good building available?** Research the market to see whether it's a better idea to buy your existing building or find a more desirable location nearby. Keep in mind that moving and altering a new location will add to your short-term business costs and require advertising to let customers know where you've gone. An experienced commercial real estate agent should be able to help you with this research.

- **Are you cut out to be a landlord?** Maybe you're fed up with dealing with a landlord, but are you ready to become one? If your building has other tenants, you'll need to deal with all sorts of problems that arise and make difficult decisions, ranging from building improvements to rent increases. Do you have the time to accommodate these additional responsibilities? If you don't have the patience or time and you still want the property, consider hiring an experienced property manager.

- **What is the building's potential as an investment?** Distance yourself from your business for a moment and remember that property ownership is itself an investment. You might need to sell the building in the future, which can make you money even if the business fails. For instance, you may want to purchase a building that you know won't attract much foot traffic if you think the building's value will increase enough to make up for the lack of revenue. Is the building in a thriving commercial district that's popular and full of tenants, or is it mostly empty? Investigate the price trends.

Will you be in the location long enough for it to increase in value?

The decision to switch from being a renter to a buyer of commercial real estate requires time for research in order to develop the most feasible plan for your finances and your long-term business goals. A commercial real estate professional can help with the financial questions, and a structural engineer and commercial inspection subcontractors can help with the physical and structural questions in your decision-making process.

When you're ready to upgrade your business to a new space, here are some factors you should consider before making an appointment to look at any properties.

Location

Find a commercial property that is **centrally located.** Travel expenses may be deductible, but time is still money, so don't spend too much on commuting. You also don't want to spend more time away from your family than you already do.

Convenience is important both for productivity and professionalism. Be sure you're close to other businesses that provide your own business with necessary supplies and materials. In addition to inspection tools, you'll need printer cartridges, copier paper, and other miscellaneous office supplies. Imagine running out of printer paper and not having convenient access to supplies while you have a client waiting for a copy of his/her contract. Even if such things happen to everyone from time to time, your client is sure to remember this lack of preparation, which translates to a lack of professionalism.

In addition to stores and other businesses that you must rely on for your daily operation, consider nearby **amenities**, such as restaurants in different price ranges, where you and your staff can grab a quick lunch or where you can entertain business contacts.

Do you want **a shop adjacent to or attached to your office?** Most inspectors find this addition vital to their productivity. Find out what kind of zoning is required to accommodate the activities you want to conduct, and look for a location that will provide both an inviting office for clients and a shop that's out of sight for projects. If you find a rental space that's large enough that's not already set up as a shop, you can negotiate with your landlord on outfitting it to your needs. (There are tips to follow on how to make this happen for your business.)

Expenses & Lease Terms

With the addition of increased rent, utilities and insurance, perhaps upgraded equipment and furniture, and the cost of revised letterhead and marketing materials, your **operating expenses** will spike. Can you afford them, based on the revenue you're generating? If you use an accountant (or even if you don't), find out what business expenses and capital assets are deductible from your income tax. You may be able to afford more for your upgraded office than you thought you could.

Is the commercial property owner amenable to **negotiating lease items**, such as build-outs, rent deductions, early release from the agreement, or a break on utilities? When small business owners shut their doors or move their enterprises into their homes, exploit this aspect of cyclical economic downturns and negotiate with your prospective (or even your current) landlord on any details you can.

Can you **share a rental space** with a complementary business? What factors of compatibility are important to you for maintaining productivity and professionalism? Also, find out what areas of the premises are defined under your lease agreement, in addition to your responsibility for shared spaces.

Once you've found an upgraded commercial space to move into, you'll need to make to-do and to-buy lists in order to make your new office functional, while minimizing lost time for productivity. It can take up to a month of packing and planning before you're ready to move into your new space and be running at optimal speed again.

Commercial Real Estate Terms Inspectors Should Know

If your inspection business has outgrown your home office, consider leasing or purchasing commercial property. In addition to determining your new office's size and location, and the budget you'll need for monthly costs, you should familiarize yourself with some basic terms of the transaction. Always consult with a trusted commercial property broker and attorney familiar with such deals before signing on the dotted line.

- A **broker** is the go-between for a purchaser and seller (or landlord and prospective tenant). The property owner generally pays the commission or fee for the broker, who must be licensed by the state.

- An **appraisal** is the financial equivalent of an inspection. An appraisal is conducted by a state-licensed professional that includes an analysis of the property's value based on market trends and sales in the immediate surrounding area. An appraiser's written report is required for all property sales.

   Appraisals are essential for determining fair market values of properties, as well as property tax assessments.

- The rental agreement for a commercial property is commonly referred to as a **lease**. The owner is considered the lessor, and the tenant is known as the lessee. The lease generally stipulates the length (or term) of the lease, the rent and due date each month, and other general terms of occupancy, as well as specific prohibitions or responsibilities of the tenant. It's important that the tenant understands what his duties and financial responsibilities are for the property, and which ones are his landlord's (such as property and component maintenance, etc.) before signing the document.

   Additionally, there are a few different types of lease agreements that use alternate formulas for arriving at the amount of monthly rent:

   ◦ A flat lease (or straight lease) stipulates the flat amount of rent for the entire length of the lease, along with any renewal date, in which case the terms of the lease (including the rent) may change.

   ◦ A percentage lease uses a percentage of the tenant business's net or gross sales to help determine the monthly rent. This is a popular type of lease used for commercial retail properties, and the percentage of sales is charged in addition to a minimum base rent.

   ◦ A net lease—also referred to as a "triple net" or "net-net-net" lease—requires the tenant to pay additional fees on top of the basic rent. These fees may be for property taxes, maintenance, insurance, etc.

   Prospective tenants should especially note if there is an escalation clause in the lease. This allows the landlord to raise the rent based on any number of factors, including cost-of-living increases (based on a percentage as determined by the state in which the property is located), or planned or unexpected expenses during the term of the lease.

- Some commercial property owners allow a tenant to **sublease** a portion of the property, especially if it is larger than the tenant needs. The tenant is still responsible for the terms of the lease agreement. It's the equivalent of the tenant taking on a roommate, or becoming a landlord himself. It's always advisable for the primary tenant to make sure that his sublessee's business or occupancy is complementary to his own, including hours of operation, number of employees, whether there is adequate parking, noise barriers, shared kitchen and/or restroom accommodations, etc.

- Owners will sometimes modify properties based on a prospective tenant's specs. These tailored improvements, called "**build-outs**," are used in advertising for the property as **built-to-suit**.

  The owner makes his/her money back based on a long-term lease agreement, possibly one with an escalation clause.

- **Turn-key** properties are move-in ready, with little or no modifications or build-outs required in order for the tenant to commence business almost immediately upon occupancy.

- **Concessions** are benefits offered by the seller or landlord to help close the sale or finalize the lease. Common concessions include paying a tenant's moving expenses, build-outs, and discounted rent for a period of the lease.

In summary, there are aspects to leasing and purchasing with which you should become familiar before moving your business out of your home.

Commercial Leases

Don't sign on the dotted line for your commercial rental space before reviewing your lease carefully, preferably with the assistance of an attorney and a commercial property broker.

In addition to the type of lease, the rent amount and the length of occupancy, some considerations and terms you encounter in your commercial lease may include the following:

- Since you have probably already incorporated your inspection business to avoid personal liability (following InterNACHI's advice in other articles), make sure your company name—and not your own name—is listed on the lease agreement as the **lessee**.

- Similarly, avoid any request for **personal guarantees** in the lease agreement, as they can place both your personal and business assets at risk.

- Never underestimate the potential for misunderstandings, especially in legal matters. A case in point is defining the **premises** of the rental property. Your friendly prospective landlord may have proudly taken you on a tour of a spacious building with many amenities, such as a large parking area, a lobby, a kitchen and restroom facilities—but which of them actually constitute the premises that are subject to your lease agreement? They must be spelled out, especially if there are neighboring tenants who will share some of these areas.

- A **use clause** stipulates the specific space of the property that is subject to the lease agreement, and any surrounding area that is off-limits to the renter. The use clause may also stipulate what kind of activities may and may not be conducted in the rental space, such as activities that produce a lot of fumes or noise. Depending on where the property is located—zoned commercial or mixed-use— the property itself may seem ideal, but your ability to conduct business properly may be inhibited based on location and/or use limitations. Make sure that you and your landlord are in agreement about what kinds of activities will be conducted—and where—on the property, both during and outside of business hours. Also, try to keep the use clause as broad as possible. Realize that your plans may change as your company grows and you may require flexibility to use your space for purposes that could not have been anticipated.

- If your prospective landlord leases to several tenants in one area (such as in an industrial park or strip mall), you may want to ask for an **exclusivity clause**. This will prevent the landlord from renting to competing businesses in proximity to your own. This clause is added primarily for retail renters, but many inspectors engage in side-businesses which may make such a stipulation worthwhile.

- Especially if the premises are part of a larger rental property, the renter should know when and under what circumstances the landlord may have **access** to their property.

- Consider the **lease length**. A long-term lease can limit rent increases and give your business long-term stability, while a short-term lease allows you the flexibility to move sooner if you dislike the location. There are usually ways to break a lease, but you should not go into a lease agreement with the intention of breaking the lease.

- The renter should find out whether there is a **security** system in place, and what his responsibilities and rights are. For example, is he responsible for setting an alarm, or alerting a security officer? If so, under what circumstances? Are there fees for calls to secure the premises, or for false alarms?

  Also, if no security system or plan is in place, the renter may want to install or hire one, and these additions should be subject to negotiation, as well as added, using specific language, to the lease agreement.

- A landlord may insist on **annual rent increases** based on the percentage increase of the Consumer Price Index (CPI). If such a request is made, you should try to arrange that the CPI does not kick in for at least two years. Also, try to arrange an upper limit on the amount of each year's increase.

- Some leases require the tenant to **obtain permission** from the landlord before making improvements or alterations to the premises. These provisions are typically too restrictive and you should attempt to negotiate the terms. For example, try to get the right to make non-structural alterations or improvements that cost less than $2,500 without the landlord's consent.

In summary, you should familiarize yourself with lease terms that affect typical commercial businesses (as well as your specific enterprise), and what the short-term and long-term ramifications are for your various options.

Utilities

Make sure the power is turned on before you move into your new business office. Commercial accounts may take more lead time for service providers to get you up and running.

Some considerations include:

- **Electrical Receptacles:** A commercial space has less wiggle room on local electrical codes than a residence. Arrange your work area to accommodate the necessary electrical equipment and appliances such that you're not stringing extension cords across high-traffic footpaths or stairs, or overloading individual outlets. Make sure your receptacles and power strips provide the proper grounding. Commercial spaces are subject to municipal and county fire marshal inspections, and infractions can lead to serious fines and disruption of your workday.

- **Heating & Cooling:** If your space isn't equipped with HVAC, make provisions to have these added. If renting, negotiate with your landlord about these upgrades. You want your workspace to be as comfortable as possible year-round.

Communications

We all have different abilities and tolerances for learning about and using high-tech devices. Learning to use various types of electronic hardware and software can improve job efficiency and communications. Increased efficiency reduces costs, and these savings can then be passed along to your clients, which is something you can mention (to your advantage) in your marketing materials. If you want your employees to learn to incorporate high-tech tools into their jobs, keep their stress levels low by supplying them with trouble-free devices and good instruction.

Among the basics are:

- **Phones:** Many small businesses are transitioning from landlines to exclusively cell phones for their obvious portability, but you may want to maintain a no-frills landline to make local calls in order to keep your main business line free, to ensure that you have reliable connectivity and clear audio quality, and to make emergency calls. Don't forget to add a professional-sounding outgoing message, and to check for messages regularly. To improve your conversion rate (the percentage of initial calls that are converted into work), a live person answering the phone is always better than a recorded greeting and voicemail. Consider retaining an answering service if you can't afford office staff. Call-forwarding to a dedicated cell phone or landline can allow you to have a family member answer phones with the name of your company. Be sure to list any appropriate new phone numbers on your company's website.

- **Internet Access:** If you're opting for a landline, adding Internet access can lower your monthly costs by taking advantage of bundled service discounts. If going all-cellular, you'll want to arrange for password-protected wireless service. Consider the fastest connection offered in your area so that you can make the most of your business day. Some service providers also offer VOIP (voice-over-Internet protocol), which allows you to make phone calls online and listen to voicemail messages via email.

- **Laptops & Tablets:** Carrying a laptop in the field, especially one that is Internet-enabled, will facilitate communication with your office staff, clients, vendors, and everyone else you deal with. The advantage of online communication is not only the great variety of information that can be transferred instantly, but that everyone with whom you communicate is only one click away from your website and other online marketing devices. Skype™ is a free communications application that allows you to see the person with whom you're speaking, along with anything they want to show you, using a remote camera or the camera installed on their computer.

Space & Use

- **Work Areas:** While a cramped home or starter office may have been sufficient for doing quick work online and then dashing off to an appointment, think long-term for making your upgraded office functional for yourself and hospitable to clients. That means investing in office furniture that is solid and aesthetically neutral. Beyond desks, chairs and furniture for larger meeting areas, bookcases can house reference manuals, industry publications and code books. For marketing purposes, your technical library should be visible to prospective clients who visit. Filing cabinets dedicated to your business can store hard-copy reports, photos and contracts. There's no need to spend big bucks at office furniture and supply stores; try shopping for second-hand items online (Craigslist is a good local resource) and at thrift stores. (More guidelines for buying used furniture follow.) If buying new, always negotiate with the salesperson for a corporate account that provides built-in discounts; today's economic climate favors the buyer for retail items, especially if you're in the market for more than a single desk or chair. Spread out in your new space as much as you can. Organization is the key to productivity.

- **Non-Work Areas:** For meeting clients and hosting the occasional business function at your office, you want your new or upgraded office space to be comfortable but professional-looking. Again, there's no need to go into debt to meet this goal. As other businesses close or downsize, it's possible to find second-hand items in classic styles with plenty of life left. Look for simple but sturdy desks, tables, chairs and lamps, and avoid styles, colors and patterns that look dated, especially if they're priced to move. They should be clean and devoid of blemishes that can't be easily repaired. Keep reception and meeting areas uncluttered.

- **Privacy & Confidentiality:** If you've been on a particularly dirty project and you need to change into clean clothes, make sure you have a private area. If you're having a conversation over the phone or in person, the details of which should not be broadcast to employees, clients or neighboring tenants, make sure you have a separate area in which to conduct such confidential business. Partitions and noise barriers can help with this. Likewise, you may wish to have a locking file cabinet or safe in which to store expensive equipment, and irreplaceable and confidential hard-copy records and downloaded computer files.

- **Shop Area:** If you have the space to have a shop adjacent to your office, it will also go a long way to enhancing your professional image with clients. Most inspectors find this setup ideal, as it will be a huge time-saver for making minor adjustments and repairs to office-related and job-related materials and equipment. Make sure that your location and your lease provide for storing and using equipment that can be noisy while in operation during business hours (and off-hours, if you're located near a residential area), as well as any hazardous materials, including paints, finishes, bonding materials and cleaners.

Potential clients may be impressed by a professional-looking, efficiently run office, but an attached shop can also be a sales tool, especially if you perform contracting or repair work on items that you don't inspect or that are beyond the constraints of the Standards of Practice that you follow in your inspection business. That gives the impression that your services are in demand!

Bear in mind that if you use your shop as a sales tool, it should be safe and clean, including visible personal protective equipment (PPE), as well as dust-removal equipment for any saws, sanders, etc.

Tip: Install a glass window where potential clients can view your shop area from your office or waiting area.

Provisions for the Office & Shop

- **Office Supplies:** Copier paper, toner, printer ink cartridges, paper clips and pens can deplete your budget in a hurry, so buy only what you estimate you'll need for the first three months. This will help you budget long-term more precisely. Remember, too, that if you have employees in your new space, you're responsible for providing them with the tools they'll need to perform their jobs properly, so don't make them scrounge for the basics in order to get their daily work done. Failing to account for simple provisions like these can be morale-killers, along with a lack of secondary supplies.

- **Secondary Supplies:** If you're sharing kitchen and/or restroom facilities with a neighboring business, find out who is responsible for supplies, and maintain an appropriate budget. If responsible only for your own, consider buying in bulk at shopping clubs, or work out a deal with a local vendor who supplies neighboring businesses. Remember to make scheduled stops for essentials, such as coffee, tea, soft drinks, snacks, condiments and restroom supplies, so that you can avoid last-minute impulse purchases, which tend to be more expensive.

- **Kitchen:** Even the most basic hotel room now provides a mini-fridge, coffee maker and microwave oven, so think of your own fundamental comforts and that of your clients (and your employees, if you have any), and outfit an area dedicated to these needs. Eating lunch in the office a few days a week will also save you petty cash and increase productivity.

- **Emergency Supplies:** Whether you have other employees or not, the responsibility of using a commercial business space dictates that you have a fully stocked first-aid kit on hand. Additionally, local fire codes will probably also require you to have several of these, depending on the size of your commercial space and/or number of employees, along with a fire extinguisher and flashlight, as well as signs for all exits. Depending on your comfort level, work schedule, and the climate of your geographical region, you may want to stock a personal emergency kit that contains extra batteries, canned goods, blankets and a sleeping cot, bottled water, spare toiletries, and extra footwear and clothing.

- **Office Equipment:** If your business has expanded to the point that you're considering investing in capital equipment, such as a computer system and/or copier, investigate whether leasing is a better deal than an outright purchase. Be wary of purchasing these items second-hand. Manufacturers tend to upgrade their models every couple of years, and finding knowledgeable service technicians and replacement parts can make what appeared to be a good deal at the outset an expensive and obsolete heap of plastic and metal that you'll have to pay a fee to dump. Always negotiate on long-term service contracts. Demand an upgrade if the machine you've contracted for develops chronic problems, which can lead to aggravation and downtime. Conversely, if the machine you're leasing is problem-free, negotiate for a less expensive service contract, since there are few or no service calls.

- **Shop Equipment & Supplies:** As mentioned earlier, organization is key to productivity, and the same rule applies to shops. Remember that more than one person may be using the shop, which is why it should always be clean, orderly, and have a home for every tool, bucket, bottle, can, nut and bolt. You may find occasion to conduct some of your business with a client in the shop area, so it should always be presentable, even if there's a project in progress.

- **Proper ventilation and drainage** should be provided for fumes, vapors and liquids. It should also be appropriately soundproofed from the rest of the office area and nearby tenants. If possible, a mop sink should be installed for extra-dirty wash-ups so that the restroom in the office area is not used and unnecessarily soiled between regular cleanups.

- **Locking tool chests** will ensure that expensive and specialized tools remain on the premises. If the shop has a back door, it should be locked and integrated with the office site's security system. Maintaining a separate supply inventory for the shop will also be useful to combine shopping trips, requiring less time to stock up on office essentials.

Office Maintenance

Your office requires regular maintenance just like your home and vehicle. If your staff is enlisted to take care of cleaning the reception area, meeting room, kitchen, bathroom and/or shop, make sure you devise a regular schedule and that they understand that they should clean any messes that happen during the interim.

If you or your staff won't be taking care of this, hire only a licensed and bonded janitorial service that will contract with you to clean your premises during regularly scheduled times. Make sure it is bonded to protect your business against theft or loss due to their acts or negligence. If you are required to provide brooms, mops, trash bags and cleaning supplies, make sure these are on your weekly shopping list.

Also, be sure to notify the cleaning crew and their supervisors of any areas on site that are off limits, and that this information is also specified in your contract with the service.

Comfort & Convenience

- **Décor:** Carefully consider your clientele when choosing personal items and artwork to decorate your office. Your personal touches help establish the corporate culture of your business, even if it's a corporation of just one. Any fine art and prints, and even hunting and fishing trophies, should be subtle and not the central focus of the office. Remember: Your office is not your man-cave away from home, so leave the joke-themed and off-color items at home where they belong. Items should be framed and mounted using tasteful and low-key frames and plaques. A hobby store's framing department can choose these for you, which is an affordable option for most.

  Be sure to display items that speak to your professional achievements. Frame and display certificates for Continuing Education course completions and professional association memberships. Download your InterNACHI Membership Certificate (nachi.org/getcertificate) and your course Certificates of Completion at nachi.org/certificatesofcompletion.

  Portfolio pictures from jobs are essential for your walls, especially those showing you shaking hands with happy clients (which is a good reason to always have a camera available out in the field), as well as positive reference letters thanking you for your good work. Keep a photo album in your meeting room. You can also display industry-related awards and your own marketing materials; these are, in themselves, works of art worth showing off, and they also speak to your professional accomplishments.

  Another way to give the impression of personal stability and your investment in the community is to display family photos. If you put them on your desk rather than on the wall, be sure they're facing so that your visitors can see them. Or you can place them on a bookshelf or credenza behind your desk and chair so that they'll naturally face outward.

  Additionally, if you've received any awards from local newspapers or certificates from organizations not directly related to your business activities, hang these proudly alongside your professional accolades. Your identity includes not just what you do in your professional life, but also what you do as a member of your community, including volunteer work. Even local sports trophies count!

  Along with personal artwork and trophies, you can display industry-related conversation-starters. These are great for breaking the ice when meeting new clients and for relieving tension if the conversation may involve some stressful topics. For example, you might have a mold of one of the largest hailstones to ever hit the area, or evidence of some other natural disaster or on-the-job oddity. Again, don't clutter your office, but appoint it tastefully with items that speak to your commitment to both your industry and your community. As always, keep these items (as well as the rest of your office) tidy and dust-free.

  And if your office has a waiting area, be sure to subscribe to some trade magazines and keep them on the table. This leaves clients with the perception that you stay abreast of the latest industry-related news and trends. Remember to always keep the reception and waiting areas tidy. Your clients expect a quiet, clean and orderly place to meet with you and conduct their business with you.

  Tip: Hang a framed copy of the International Association of Certified Home Inspectors' Code of Ethics on the wall. Find InterNACHI's COE at www.nachi.org/code_of_ethics

- **Lighting:** Natural daylight isn't always available in office spaces, but don't underestimate the effect of lighting for reasons other than just to see what you're doing. It can affect mood and productivity in direct and indirect ways. Some offices and warehouses provide basic overhead fluorescent-tube lighting, which can be adequate but garish (and even noisy), so consider augmenting those sources with low spot lighting using desk lamps and wall sconces. Energy-efficient bulbs come in colors of the visible spectrum that are easier on the eyes and reflect a glow that "warms up" the area to appear more inviting. Of course, they're better for the environment, as well as your budget, in the long run.

- **Plants:** Live plants can add an important touch that exudes relaxation, comfort, and a green consciousness. If you don't have the time to take care of office plants yourself, a plant or floral service is a good investment. For a business-friendly monthly rate, it will first deliver and then monitor the weekly health and watering of your foliage. This is a simple way to advertise that you understand the aesthetic importance of live greenery. It emits the message that you have taste and value quality. Quality means comfort. If you don't think this is true, think back and rate your own comfort level in offices and waiting rooms that you visited that had no foliage, some foliage, dying foliage, lush foliage, and fake silk plants. Healthy greenery has an instantly calming effect, and the more stressful and/or high-end the business, the nicer the plants you'll find in the lobby. These plants don't have to overtake the office environment, and they should never show signs of neglect, which is much worse than not having any live plants at all. Avoid silk plants; no silk plant actually looks real, and the message it transmits is that you either: a) don't pay attention to the finer details of the indoor environment; or b) think that cheapness is an acceptable substitute for quality.

Security

- Provisions for **securing your business premises** should be clearly spelled out in your lease. Follow a ritual at the end of the day to make sure that all doors and windows are properly closed and locked, and if you have shades or drapes, make sure they're closed at night, too. A security system is a sound investment. Adequate lighting for the immediate exterior, as well as the parking area, is a safety as well as liability concern. Additionally, get acquainted with local law enforcement, and find out whether their regular patrols include the location of your workplace, especially if it's in a more industrial area, rather than in an office building in the middle of town.

- Other physical safety concerns include **locking filing cabinets and safes**. If many people have access to the same work documents, they may get easily misplaced if they aren't treated as documents that need to be secured. This can delay work and frustrate clients. Additionally, if you have firearms on the premises, they should be kept unloaded in a lockable case and safely stowed. The local police department will have information to help you stay within the law, especially if you have employees on the premises and clients who visit. Again, it's not just a question of safety—it's also one of liability.

- Security includes backing up your **computer data**. You can easily do this using a thumb drive, writable CDs, or an external hard drive. There are web-based storage options, too. If you're a larger company, you may have a central server that backs up all networked data. You can also pay a monthly fee to have your data backed up and stored off-site, which is a lifesaver in case of a catastrophic power outage.

Personal Safety at a Commercial Property

For any kind of a commercial investment, such as a condo filled with renters and owner-occupants, or a light-industrial complex filled with small businesses, tenants as well as owners have a mutual responsibility to ensure a safe environment that promotes both peace of mind and business-as-usual. Here are some tips that you can act on now to make your commercial property safe.

Lock it up!

You may be 20 feet away from your vehicle while you're working at your desk, but property crimes are crimes of opportunity, and criminals don't like to work, so don't make it any easier for them to loot your vehicle by leaving it unlocked—or by leaving valuables in plain sight, even in a locked car. Additionally, lock home and office doors, and use security locks on windows that allow them to open, but not too much. Pull drapes and shades on windows when the sun goes down and when unoccupied – don't announce your absence by leaving your premises on display.

Light it up!

Owners should ensure that there is adequate lighting in the parking facility, whether a parking structure, individual garages, carports or assigned parking spaces.

Injuries due to inadequate lighting can lead to liability issues and expensive legal hassles. Motion-detector security lights should be installed at every unit's entrance. They save energy, and alert residents and tenants when someone is in the immediate vicinity. These lights are generally hard-wired into the building's electrical system, but portable sensor lights can be added to the perimeter of the building to make dark areas and those obstructed by vegetation better lit to discourage nighttime trespassers.

Stairs and Walkways

These should be kept clear of debris and obstructions, such as lawn-care equipment. Sidewalk cement in poor repair can present a tripping hazard, leading to injury and costly legal ramifications. If sidewalks have graded steps, install photo-sensor stake lights at the edges to capture the sun's energy during the day so they can provide illumination at night.

Security Systems

There are many approaches to this issue, depending on the structure of the complex, the cost involved, and the level of desired protection. Some condos and industrial parks prohibit additional locks on doors that may prevent owners from entering a tenant's home or office in case of an emergency. Some gated communities go the extra mile and hire personnel to regularly patrol the area. Most small businesses have electronic security systems that must be activated and disabled, and which will automatically alert local first-responders in case of a breach. Whether you're a tenant or an owner, make sure the terms, as well as the limitations, of the security system are spelled out in your lease. Also, make sure that you post window decals and lawn signs alerting potential trespassers of the risk they'd be taking. Again, most property crimes are crimes of opportunity, so don't make a criminal's job any easier by failing to use simple deterrents.

Be alert!

Know your neighbors. Know their hours of operation. Pay attention to the vehicles that are regularly parked in the lot. If someone seems out of place, acts as if he's lost, or is spending an inordinate amount of time on the property without entering a unit or conducting any business, consider contacting the authorities. Always exercise caution when approaching such people to question them, but do be mindful of their presence to determine whether they actually belong on the premises.

In short, safety is everyone's concern. Regardless of your monetary investment, you can't put a price on a safe workplace and a secure residence.

Miscellaneous Considerations

- **Children & Pets:** One of the benefits of owning your own business is that you can take your children and pets to work with you. Children require constant attention, so make sure your attention isn't divided, leading to a potential accident, or creating an unprofessional atmosphere. Also, don't expect your employees to double as your babysitter. In terms of pets, some of them don't adjust well to strangers or unfamiliar surroundings, and some clients and employees may have allergies and even phobias. What's okay around the house won't necessarily work in the workplace, even if you're the boss, so think like a businessperson and make decisions based on what's best for your business.

- **Music:** Your choice of music in the office, if you have any, can make as big an impression as your office décor, so make it low-key, quiet enough to conduct conversations both in person and on the phone, and neutral in terms of content.

- **Recreational & After-Hours Activities:** If you have alcohol on the work premises, it's important that such beverages be kept in an appropriate and lockable location that cannot be accessed by uninvited (or underage) personnel or visitors. Its presence should not be advertised. Your lease or a local ordinance may prohibit alcohol consumption on site during regular business hours. Other non-work activities, such as smoking, watching TV or playing video games, may be allowed during certain times, but make sure they're confined to specific areas so that the professional atmosphere of your workplace is maintained. Not every client will appreciate a loose or laid-back inspector. If you engage in any recreational activities on site after hours, be sure your offices are locked to outside visitors, requiring them to knock or ring a bell for permission to enter.

Running a Green Office

Most small business owners have their hands full just trying to stay on top of their current workload, as well as marketing themselves, and inspectors are no exception. But whether you lease an office or are a new commercial property owner, everyone can make some simple and painless improvements to their workplace and work habits that will minimize their carbon footprint and save money. As an added bonus, demonstrating to visiting clients that you run a green business is a great marketing tool for anyone in the inspection industry, since saving on home energy is such a solid trend now. If you practice what you preach, you'll have that much more credibility in the industry.

Here are some tactics that you can start using today:

- Use recycled paper for your contracts, reports and marketing materials, and make sure you use a logo that tells your customers so. "Printed on 90% post-consumer waste" (or whatever applies) can provide your prospective clients with a positive heads-up that you're environmentally conscious. Recycled paper and cardstock are also generally cheaper, which can lower your costs for office supplies. Also, if you must print out something and it's for internal use only, use the reverse side of paper that you would otherwise throw away.

- Also, while it may be difficult or impossible for inspectors to develop an entirely paperless office, you can drastically reduce the amount of paper you use and store by creating and storing documents electronically. Hard-copy documents can be scanned and stored using one of several types of devices, including multi-function copiers.

- Recycle your printer cartridges. Most printer services and retail outlets will accept used ones and reward you with a discount on your next purchase.

- Get organized. Maximize your time by minimizing your driving trips around town. Shop online, when possible. You'll save wear and tear on your vehicle, and you'll spare the air of your emissions.

- Pay your bills online. This decreases what you spend on postage, and cuts down on the mail you receive, much of which winds up in the trash anyway, such as promotional inserts and window envelopes.

- Buy e-books, such as the ones published by the International Association of Certified Home Inspectors and sold by www.InspectorOutlet.com. Save on storage space.

- If it's cold in your office, add a layer of clothing, rather than turn up the heat. Likewise, if it's warm, open a window instead of turning on the A/C. If ventilation to the outdoors is not practical, consider running the A/C intermittently rather than continuously throughout the day. Be sure to use fans to assist with air movement, as well as shades to block the sunlight through windows.

- If you don't already have a low-flow toilet at your office, place a brick in the tank of your toilet to save on water used for flushes. If you need to install a new toilet, consider buying a dual-flush type.

- Find ways to let natural light into your workspace to cut down on the use of electric lights. Where practical, change your incandescent bulbs to energy-saving compact fluorescent bulbs (CFLs) and T8 fluorescent bulbs, which can reduce your lighting energy costs by up to 75%.

- Use cups, plates and silverware in your office kitchen, rather than paper products. If you buy disposable products, consider purchasing the newer biodegradable plastics made of corn. Also, purchase paper supplies in bulk, which will reduce your shopping trips, as well as your expenses.

- When upgrading tools and equipment, donate what you no longer use, if selling is impractical. Many thrift stores, including outlets run by Habitat for Humanity, will gladly accept a worn tape measure, flashlight, and even work boots. Just make sure that items such as ladders are safe before passing them along.

- Many office supply stores that sell office technology, such as Staples, OfficeMax® and Kinko's, will accept your outmoded cell phones, computers and printers to dispose of at bulk savings to them, or they will refurbish them for resale or donation. Tech hardware disposed of in landfills is among the most toxic sources of soil and groundwater contamination today because of the chemicals contained in their components and the results of the biochemical breakdown of their materials. If you don't want to pay a fee to dispose of these items responsibly, take them to a recycling center or retail outlet that will gladly take them off your hands.

- Before hauling something out to the Dumpster, consider re-purposing it. An oak door can be converted into a work table in the shop area, and foamboard can be used as a bulletin board. Old t-shirts make handy rags for the office and work truck.

- Make sure your computers, printers and copiers are set to energy-saving or sleep mode when not in use for extended periods. Also, consider routinely unplugging electrical items at the end of the day, since coffee makers, lamps and power strips that are turned off but remain plugged in continue to draw current.

- Before making a purchase, look online at websites such as Craigslist and Freecycle to see if you can find what you need for less than new, or even free. Several different categories on these sites offer tools and office equipment and products at second-hand prices for sometimes brand new items, which can save you money that you can put toward more meaningful purchases.

- If you want to buy new office furniture, consider buying chairs, desks, tables and bookcases made from wood that has been reclaimed or that originates from sustainably harvested forests. Look for certifications on wood products from the Forestry Stewardship Council and the Rainforest Alliance. In addition to sparing living trees, reclaimed and sustainably harvested wood has the advantage of being free of formaldehyde and volatile organic compounds (VOCs), which is better for your health, as well as the planet's.

- Make your business website robust. Take advantage of the marketing tips and tools included in this book so that your prospective clients can find the information they need about you and your services online. This will save them time (and aggravation), and will impress them with your technological savvy. For many people, using technology to its fullest potential is equivalent to being green, and this method of marketing yourself can set you apart from your competition. Give your prospective customers a genuine sense of yourself and your (green) business ethic by creating a specific and indelible web presence. Hiring a pro to do this may be the best investment you'll ever make in your business and your future.

Moving into a new commercial space is an exciting step forward for your business. Make your move stress-free with careful planning before you pack up the first box.

And remember: Your goal is to create an impression for your client that says that you value quality first, both on the job and in your own work environment.

Tip: Visit InterNACHI's Green Resources page for both inspectors and consumers at www.nachi.org/green

Affordable Ways to Outfit Your Business

While inspectors and other small business owners generally want to avoid incurring additional debt whenever possible, financing expensive purchases of essential items for your business—including for your office and on the job—will help you maintain a positive cash flow. This is essential for any company's survival, especially in a stagnant economic climate that's seeing so many small businesses close their doors.

Perhaps you need to outfit a new office with a copier, computer system or furniture. You might need field gear and specific tools. Inspectors who are in the market for heavy equipment or other high-ticket capital purchases for their expanding businesses would do well to finance such acquisitions using a commercial equipment loan. In some cases, the inspector may opt for a lease instead. Before paging through any online catalogs and loading up the virtual shopping cart, the inspector should do some homework first to find the best financing deal to maintain financial flexibility and a healthy bank account.

Buy or Lease?

Depending on the equipment, financing a lease instead of a purchase may make more sense. For example, items based on technology, such as computers and copiers, tend to undergo manufacturers' updates and revamps more frequently than, say, furniture and other items that are built to last. When a piece of equipment will stand the test of time, it's a reasonable move to finance its purchase. If the item is subject to planned obsolescence, it's savvier to lease. For commercial equipment, there are several considerations that the inspector should explore.

Financing a Commercial Equipment Loan

With the changes in lending practices of banks and the Small Business Administration, which provides both small and large banks greater incentive for lending to small businesses, more opportunities are opening up for inspectors wanting to expand their businesses and finance major purchases. Once you've decided to finance a purchase, and depending on the item and the amount you want to borrow, as well as the lender, you may be required to provide financial records to prove your creditworthiness and to secure the lowest rate.

You may want to seek the assistance of a broker who can research your loan options and match you with the best lender. Brokers' fees can add 3% to 5% to the cost of your purchase.

Financing a Commercial Equipment Lease

There are a few different options available when it comes to leasing, and most lenders offer them.

- A **deferred lease** allows you to skip the first two or three months of payments, as well as any down payment. This is useful for people with strong credit and the need to acquire expensive commercial equipment right away, but without the cash flow for immediate loan servicing. Once the repayment kicks in, the amount tends to be higher than with other types of leases.

- A **step-up lease** is similar to a deferred lease, but no initial payments are skipped; they are simply lower, and the amount increases as the term progresses. Start-ups, and small business owners whose cash-flow situation is sluggish but not dire, opt for this type of lease, with the advantage that subsequent payments are increased, compared to the first several payments, but they're still manageable.

- A **skip lease** allows the borrower to skip different months of repayment during the loan term while interest still accrues. This is a typical choice for inspectors who experience seasonal slow periods, and prevents them from defaulting on their lease agreements or having the financed equipment repossessed.

There is no right or best option across the board for the inspector or any small business when it comes to commercial loans. Your smartest choice will depend on your company's unique circumstances, as well as the equipment you have your eye on. But some generalities regarding commercial equipment financing can be summed up in the following lists.

The Upside of Purchasing:

- You own the equipment.
- You may be able to write off the purchase during the first year.
- Commercial loan rates are generally manageable, especially if your credit history is solid and you use an SBA-backed lender. Generally speaking, the more high-ticket the item is, the lower the interest rate will be, and the loan term will tend to be longer, as well.
- The item is considered a capital asset, which speaks to your company's overall financial fitness.

The Downside of Purchasing:

- Because the item starts depreciating in value after the first year (check IRS rules and regulations), the buyer may not be able to secure 100% financing using a commercial loan, and s/he may be required to finance part of the purchase out of pocket as a down payment.
- A commercial loan generally means that the item purchased is named as collateral, so it can be repossessed if the borrower defaults on the loan.

The Upside of Leasing:

- Up-front cash for the application and other fees is minimal, usually between 10% and 20%.
- Business owners with weak credit histories can obtain leases more easily than commercial loans for financing purchases.
- You can contract on a short-term basis for more high-end equipment whose cost would ultimately be prohibitive as a financed purchase.
- The lease payments can be expensed (under a true lease).
- Maintenance on the item is taken care of by the vendor.

- Depending on the item leased, it can generally be upgraded at the end of the term with a lease renewal. This is especially important for computer systems and service vehicles.

- At the end of the contract under a true lease, the item may be purchased outright at the fair market value or at a discounted rate.

The Downside of Leasing:

- In the long run, leases are more expensive than other types of financing because of their higher interest rates charged over a comparatively shorter loan term.

- Additional charges for delivery, setup, training, and service calls may be built into the financing agreement, which means that you'll be paying interest on these add-ons.

- If you purchase the item at the end of the lease term using a conditional sale or rent-to-own lease, also known as a finance lease, you can't take advantage of tax breaks, since you will own the item by the end of the lease term.

- Breaking a lease before the end of the contracted term can cost the borrower significant penalties.

- Without manageable terms for your lease agreement, default means repossession, which can interrupt your business's daily operation. It also means a ding on your credit score.

The first purchase an inspector may wish to make is a computer that can be used to calculate a cost-benefit analysis to see how financing a lease or purchase of major equipment will affect the company's cash flow. Whether going with a trusted and experienced broker or going it alone and using one of the many online resources available, inspectors and other small business owners owe it to their bottom line and long-term stability to perform their own due diligence when making the important decision to secure financing for commercial equipment for their companies.

Purchasing or Leasing the Right Truck

Reliable, respectable transportation is essential for the inspector. Purchasing the right work vehicle to carry equipment, as well as doubling as a mobile office, is becoming somewhat easier, ironically, as the American car industry is suffering through tough economic times. Securing the most favorable commercial truck loan will get the inspector on the road more quickly.

Many commercial lenders will smooth the way for borrowers whose business credit has yet to be firmly established, or whose credit may be damaged, by offering flexible loan options, as well as holding the title to the vehicle as collateral. Many heavy-duty truck manufacturers, such as Kenworth, GMC and Peterbilt, work with commercial lenders to offer pre-owned vehicles and special financing.

While it's tempting for the inspector to find the biggest and most flashy vehicle s/he can possibly afford, it's important to be realistic and think long-term about one of the largest and most expensive equipment investments tied to the business. The right truck can cost anywhere from a modestly priced $20,000 vehicle to something costing over six figures.

So, consider the following:

- Will this vehicle be used mainly for business, or will it double as the primary vehicle for the owner and possibly the family, too? Either scenario will affect both business taxes and insurance rates, so it's important to decide, before purchasing, how the vehicle will be used on a daily basis.

- As fuel costs continue to remain high, with only occasional temporary dips, consider both the type of fuel you want to use and the average miles per day you will probably add to the odometer. Diesel, ethanol and hybrid options will influence your operating costs down the line, as well as your purchasing decision up front. Research these options carefully, and don't dismiss newer technologies just because they're unfamiliar.

- New or used? Your credit rating, financing options and personal preference will all factor into which part of the car lot you'll be shopping in, either on site or on the Internet. Consider the safety features and special extras in newer vehicles (such as GPS navigation, storage, plug-ins for laptops and cell phones, etc.) that will keep you roadworthy for years to come. Some of these newer vehicles may have been recently repossessed and will qualify as pre-owned for a lower sticker price and easier financing.

- Shopping for the right loan is as important as shopping for the right truck. Affordability is affected not just by how much the bank is willing to lend you, but by whether you can maintain the monthly payments. The percentage rate and loan structure are critical in determining whether you can afford the vehicle of your choice. Remember that if you default on your truck loan, not only will its repossession damage your credit rating, but it will also damage your ability to conduct your day-to-day business. Make sure you consider the monthly amortization schedule of your loan, and bargain for the best option that dovetails with your expected business revenue. If you have a balloon payment due during a slow period, renegotiate with your lender before signing any documents. Many online lenders have streamlined the loan process, and many dealers offer the same sort of convenience. Make them compete for your business by taking time to research your best long-term options.

- Another loan option includes leasing rather than purchasing your service vehicle. The primary feature of a lease is that the dealer is responsible for maintenance, and you can upgrade at the end of the term. But for commercial vehicles, the more attractive plus is that if the vehicle is used strictly for business, the monthly payments are tax-deductible. Other advantages of leasing include a usually favorable purchase price or buyout at the lease's termination, or leasing another, newer vehicle, possibly with updated features and improved fuel efficiency, which is another smart move for any small business owner.

Purchasing a new or new-to-you work vehicle is a stressful as well as exciting decision, so mitigate that built-in anxiety by doing your homework and considering all your options before committing to a new rig for the road.

Truck Signage

Good vehicle signage promotes your brand. Truck signage is the easiest marketing you can do all day without having to lift a finger. It works while you're working. The larger your service area, the more people will see it. The smaller your service area, the more people will recognize it and become familiar with it, along with the services it advertises. Truck signage demonstrates that you're a professional. When you have truck signage, you carry your branding with you to every job, every day.

A study by American Trucking Associations, Inc., showed that a truck sign creates almost 5 million visual impressions a year. For inspectors located in major cities, their driver's-side signage may be seen up to 44,000 times per day. Truck ads are the oldest form of mobile advertising still used today, dating back to 1912, when delivery trucks needed to distinguish themselves in the narrow streets of New York City.

Every inspector should invest in truck signage to advertise his/her inspection business. Given the massive exposure gained just by driving around, it really is a marketing no-brainer.

Truck signs are especially important in jurisdictions that restrict the use of yard signs. Mobile signage goes where you go, and the design options are virtually unlimited.

Some inspectors (especially multi-vehicle firms) have their vehicles professionally painted. A newer innovation is custom vinyl applications that are semi-permanent. These are the ultimate marketing tools for dedicated work vehicles, and even for vehicles that do double-duty as a family vehicle. Some may find painting cost-prohibitive, or just enjoy the flexibility of having top-quality magnetic signage to use on different vehicles or upgrades without having to have a new vehicle re-painted. With the improved variety and quality of magnetic signage available now, it's an economical alternative to having your information professionally painted on your truck. Because they're sturdy, weatherproof, and can be exactly replicated again and again as necessary, magnetic signs are a sound investment in your business marketing that will recoup the expense in drive-by advertising, which is a unique method that all inspectors should take advantage of.

Note: When you use InterNACHI's Member Marketing Department (nachi.org/marketing) to design your logo, they provide a vector file of your logo that can be scaled to any size for vehicle graphics.

Three Words: Quality, Quality and Quality

Make sure that your sign is high-quality. Whether you opt for permanent paint or the magnetic type, a cheap sign—or, worse, a homemade one—can do more damage to your professional reputation than not having any type of mobile marketing at all. Your signage should be professionally executed, and not by your neighbor's kid who loves to draw. Effective marketing materials are not only impeccably rendered, but they also follow certain principles of design. You do not want to go the DIY route for truck signage. What may appeal to the individual inspector may make a poor sign that most viewers will struggle to make sense of quickly in traffic. So, make sure you pay attention to proper spelling, grammar, punctuation and capitalizations, too.

Use Your Truck as a Billboard, Not as a Brochure

Your sign should include your company name, your logo, your phone number, your web address, and, optionally, your general service area, along with a brief and simple list of the services you offer. Some inspectors may insist on including "Licensed & Insured," which is another indication of legitimacy and professionalism, especially in jurisdictions that regulate inspectors.

However, resist the temptation to include everything but the kitchen sink. Don't cram a lot of details into your sign, such as your qualifications, or an exhaustive list of your ancillary inspecting services.

Also, unless you have a short and snappy tagline, you may want to omit that, too. You have to make your impression quickly, so, unlike a business brochure, less is more for vehicle signage. For all these considerations that need to strike the right balance between visual appeal and information, it's best to have your sign professionally designed.

Tip: Some inspectors design their signage to include blank areas in anticipation of mounting exterior brochure holders that say "Free! Take one!"

Make the Most of Your Mobile Billboard

Since magnetic signs are affordable and easily transferable, consider purchasing two signs: one for the driver's side and one for the passenger side. That effectively doubles your exposure. And don't neglect the tailgate of your truck. That smaller area may require a specialized sign that's different from your main sign, but inspectors should take advantage of drivers stopped behind them in traffic who will have ample time to read the signage. This can increase your business's visibility by more than 60%.

Tip: If you are in a city with high-rises, consider putting your logo or an ad on the roof of your van or truck cab so that people in tall buildings can see it.

Some Do's & Don'ts for Work Vehicles

Do:

- Make sure your vehicle is clean inside and out before your first appointment of the day. Many inspectors wash their vehicles first thing every morning.

- Check every day that your magnetic signage is secure and properly positioned, or you'll give the impression that you're a fly-by-night operation.

- Be a courteous and conservative driver. Don't speed or tailgate such that other drivers may find your driving aggressive. Since you'll have your contact information splashed all over your vehicle, you may create negative consequences with your driving that will hurt you personally and professionally—and possibly legally, as well.

Don't:

- Don't use your vehicle for personal expressions that evoke politics, religion or humor, or identify you with non-professional associations that may have controversial reputations. Avoid (most) bumper stickers, novelty items hanging from the trailer hitch or sitting on your dashboard or attached to your antenna, as well as questionable images on mud flaps, and flags that are not of your state, province or country. It's simply not appropriate to display such items at your workplace—or your workplace on wheels—and doing so may create unwanted notions about you and your work ethic and unnecessarily alienate potential clients. Can you afford to say no to new business? Just as inspectors should use discretion and good judgment in choosing their work wardrobe by avoiding t-shirts and hats emblazoned with logos, images, jokes and text that some may find offensive or which may be misunderstood, the same advice holds true for your work vehicle. Err on the conservative side by sticking to business; your clients will appreciate your no-nonsense approach.

- Don't neglect to keep the interior (as well as the exterior) of your vehicle clean. You may have to eat three meals a day inside your truck while you juggle a hectic schedule, but police your mess as you go and keep your vehicle tidy. Your clients may notice your messy vehicle and, fairly or not, they will likely form opinions about you and your work habits based on both your appearance and that of your vehicle. It's unavoidable because it's human nature, so do what you can to make a good impression throughout the day.

Remember that in everything you do in your workday, you are representing your business, so make the most of it by marketing wherever you go and invest in truck signage. You'll be surprised at how effective it can be.

If You Have a Fleet

If you have a fleet of work vehicles with signage, exploit it. If you have a company meeting at a restaurant, have your employees drive your fleet in a parade to the restaurant and park out front. This attention-grabbing exposure is free.

Tip: Direct people to take your free brochure ("Take my free brochure!") and use them in conjunction with exterior vehicle brochure holders.

More Ancillary Inspections

Besides the typical add-ons of inspection services (such as radon testing, mold sampling, WDO/termite inspections, pool and spa inspections, commercial property inspections, etc.), consider the following inspection and consulting options to enhance your income.

Become a HUD 203K Consultant

A 203K consultant is a professional who is responsible for advising clients on the complicated 203K process. They make sure the required paperwork is filled out and filed correctly so that homeowners can obtain a 203K loan. Many 203K consultants are inspectors who wish to widen the scope of their business. Inspectors already have much of the knowledge and training required to become a 203K consultant.

The 203K program was created in 1961 as a way to obtain money to complete necessary repairs and to refinance or purchase a home. The program's complexity prevented it from being used effectively until 1994 when consultants were first introduced to the field. In order to become an approved 203K consultant, applicants must be approved by the U.S. Department of Housing and Urban Development (HUD). Approved candidates are placed on the Federal Housing Administration's 203K Consultant Roster, which guarantees that the consultant has met the qualifications as prescribed by the FHA.

Read "Become a HUD 203(K) Consultant" online at www.nachi.org/203k-consultant

Move-In Certified™ Seller Inspections: Streamlining Real Estate Transactions

Seller inspections (sometimes referred to as pre-listing inspections) are becoming more popular because they virtually eliminate all the pitfalls and hassles associated with waiting to do the home inspection until a buyer is found. In many ways, waiting to schedule the inspection until after a home goes under agreement is too late.

Seller inspections are arranged and paid for by the seller just before the home goes on the market. The seller is the inspector's client. The inspector works for the seller and generates a report for the seller. The seller then typically makes multiple copies of the report and shares them with potential buyers who tour the home for sale. Seller inspections are a benefit to all parties in a real estate transaction. They are a win-win-win-win situation. Home inspectors should consider offering seller inspections and marketing this service to local listing agents.

InterNACHI encourages its members to take advantage of its pre-branded and recognized Move-In Certified™ Seller Inspections. Visit www.moveincertified.com for more details, including how to obtain low-cost yard signs and other marketing items that will help the pre-inspected home for sale stand out in the neighborhood.

Advantages for the Home Inspector:

- Seller inspections allow the inspector to catch inspection jobs upstream, ahead of real estate transactions and the competition.

- Seller inspections are easier to schedule and are not under the time constraints of a sales agreement's inspection contingencies.

- Working for sellers is typically less stressful than working for buyers who are about to make the purchase of a lifetime.

- Sellers can alert the inspector to problems that should be included in the report, answer questions about their homes, and provide Seller's Disclosure Statements.

- Repairs of problems found during seller inspections often necessitate the need for re-inspections by the inspector.

- Seller inspections put a sample copy of the inspector's product—the report—in the hands of many potential buyers who will need a local inspector soon.

- Seller inspections put a sample copy of the inspector's product—the report—in the hands of many local buyers' agents who tour the home.

- The inspector is credited, in part, with the smoothness of the real estate transaction by the buyer, seller and agents on both sides.

- The liability of the inspector is reduced by putting more time between the date of the inspection and the move-in date of the buyers.

- The liability of the inspector is reduced because the inspector's clients are not buying the properties inspected, but, rather, moving out of them.

- The buyer might insist on hiring the seller's inspector to produce a fresh report, since the seller's inspector is already familiar with the home.

- Seller inspections provide inspectors the opportunity to show off their services to listing agents.

- Seller inspections provide examples of the inspector's work to the listing agent of each home, which might encourage those agents to have other listings pre-inspected by the inspector.

- Most sellers are local buyers, so many sellers hire the inspector again to inspect the homes they are moving into.

Advantages for the Home Seller:

- The seller can choose a certified InterNACHI inspector, rather than be at the mercy of the buyer's choice of inspector.

- The seller can schedule the inspections at the seller's convenience.

- It can alert the seller of any items of immediate concern, such as elevated radon gas levels or an active termite infestation.

- The seller can assist the inspector during the inspection, something not normally done during a buyer's inspection.

- The seller can have the inspector correct any misstatements in the inspection report before it is generated.

- The report can help the seller price the home more realistically if problems exist.

- The report can help the seller substantiate a higher asking price if problems don't exist or have been corrected.

- A seller inspection reveals problems ahead of time, which:
  ○ can make the home show better;
  ○ gives the seller time to shop for competitive bids and make repairs;
  ○ permits the seller to attach repair estimates or paid invoices to the inspection report; and
  ○ removes over-inflated buyer-procured estimates from the negotiating table.

- The report might alert the seller to any immediate safety issues found, before agents and visitors tour the home.

- The report provides a third-party, unbiased opinion to offer to potential buyers.

- A seller inspection permits a clean home inspection report to be used as a marketing tool.

- A seller inspection is the ultimate gesture in forthrightness on the part of the seller.

- The report might relieve a prospective buyer's unfounded suspicions, before they walk away.

- A seller inspection lightens negotiations and 11th-hour re-negotiations.

- The report might encourage the buyer to waive the inspection contingency.

- The deal is less likely to fall apart, the way they often do, when a buyer's inspection unexpectedly reveals a last-minute problem.

- The report provides full-disclosure protection from future legal claims.

Advantages for the Real Estate Agent:

- Agents can recommend certified InterNACHI inspectors, as opposed to being at the mercy of buyers' choices in inspectors.

- Sellers can schedule the inspections at their convenience, with little effort on the part of agents.

- Sellers can assist inspectors during the inspections, something not normally done during buyers' inspections.

- Sellers can have inspectors correct any misstatements in the reports before they are generated.

- The reports help sellers see their homes through the eyes of a critical third party, thus making sellers more realistic about asking price.

- Agents are alerted to any immediate safety issues found, before other agents and potential buyers tour the home.

- Repairs made ahead of time might make homes show better.

- Reports hosted online entice potential buyers to tour the homes.

- The reports provide third-party, unbiased opinions to offer to potential buyers.

- Clean reports can be used as marketing tools to help sell the homes.

- The reports might relieve prospective buyers' unfounded suspicions, before they walk away.

- Seller inspections eliminate "buyer's remorse" that sometimes occurs just after an inspection.

- Seller inspections reduce the need for negotiations and 11th-hour re-negotiations.

- Seller inspections relieve the agent of having to hurriedly procure repair estimates or schedule repairs.

- The reports might encourage buyers to waive their inspection contingencies.

- Deals are less likely to fall apart, the way they often do, when buyers' inspections unexpectedly reveal last-minute problems.

- Reports provide full-disclosure protection from future legal claims.

Advantages for the Home Buyer:

- The inspection is already done.

- The inspection is paid for by the seller.

- The report provides a more accurate, third-party view of the condition of the home prior to making an offer.

- A seller inspection eliminates surprise defects.

- Problems are corrected, or at least acknowledged, prior to making an offer on the home.

- A seller inspection reduces the need for negotiations and 11th-hour re-negotiations.

- The report might assist in acquiring financing.

- A seller inspection allows the buyer to sweeten the offer without increasing the offering price by waiving inspections.

Suggested language follows for:

- inspectors to add to their seller inspection reports;

- sellers to use to encourage buyers to perform their own fresh inspections; and

- agents to use to encourage buyers to perform their own fresh inspections.

Please note: Just as no two home inspectors and no two reporting systems are alike, no two inspection reports are alike, even if performed on the same property at the same time.

This seller or pre-listing inspection report was performed for my client, the home seller, with his/her full cooperation and assistance. It assumes his/her full disclosure. My client may choose to share my report with others, but it was performed solely for him/her. Although ABC Inspections performs all inspections and writes all reports objectively without regard to the client's personal interests, the performance of additional, fresh inspections (which, of course, could reveal and report conditions differently) should be considered.

Common Myths About Seller Inspections:

Q. *Don't seller inspections kill deals by forcing sellers to disclose defects they otherwise wouldn't have known about?*

A. Any defect that is material enough to kill a real estate transaction is likely going to be uncovered eventually anyway. It is best to discover the problem ahead of time, before it can kill the deal.

Q. *Isn't a home inspector's liability increased by having his/her report seen by potential buyers?*

A. No. There is no liability in having your seller permit someone who doesn't buy the property see your report. And there is less liability in having a buyer rely on your old report when the buyer is not your client (and has been warned not to rely on your report) than it is to work directly for the buyer and have him be entitled to rely on your report.

Q. *Don't seller inspections take too much energy to sell to make them profitable for the inspector?*

A. Perhaps, but not when the inspector takes into account the marketing benefit of having a sample of his/her product (the report) passed out to agents and potential buyers who are looking to buy now in the inspector's own local market, not to mention the seller who is likely moving locally and is in need of an inspector, plus the additional chance of re-inspection work that is generated for the inspector.

Q. *A newer home in good condition doesn't need an inspection anyway. Why should the seller have one done?*

A. Unlike real estate agents, whose job is to market properties for their sellers, inspectors produce objective reports. If the property is truly in great shape, the inspection report becomes a pseudo-marketing piece, with the added benefit of having been generated by an impartial party.

Q. *Don't seller inspections and re-inspections reduce the number of buyer inspections needed in the marketplace?*

A. No. Although every inspection job an InterNACHI member catches upstream is one his/her competitors might not get, especially if the buyer waives his/her inspection and/or the seller hires the same inspector to inspect the home s/he is buying, the number of inspections performed by the industry as a whole is increased by seller inspections.

Sample Letter for Inspectors to Send to Listing Agents:

Dear Jane Smartagent:

I am Joe Goodspector of ABC Inspections. I am writing to encourage you to contact me about pre-inspecting your listings. The advantages to your real estate business and your home-selling clients are many:

- *You can recommend me, a certified InterNACHI inspector, to do the inspection, as opposed to being at the mercy of buyers' choices in inspectors.*
- *Your sellers can schedule the inspections at their convenience, directly with me, with little effort on your part.*
- *Your sellers can assist me during the inspections, something not normally done during buyers' inspections.*
- *Your sellers can have me correct any misstatements in my reports before I generate them.*
- *My reports help sellers see their homes through the eyes of a critical third party, thus making sellers more realistic about asking price.*
- *I will alert you to any immediate safety issues I find before other agents and potential buyers tour the homes I inspect.*
- *Repairs made ahead of time might make your listings show better.*
- *My reports provide third-party, unbiased opinions to offer to potential buyers.*
- *My reports can be used as marketing tools to help sell the homes.*
- *My reports might relieve a prospective buyer's unfounded suspicions, before they walk away.*
- *Seller inspections eliminate "buyer's remorse" that sometimes occurs just after an inspection.*
- *Seller inspections reduce the need for negotiations and 11th-hour re-negotiations.*
- *Seller inspections relieve you of having to hurriedly procure repair estimates or schedule repairs.*
- *My reports might encourage buyers to waive their inspection contingencies.*
- *Your deals are less likely to fall apart, the way they often do, when buyers' inspections unexpectedly reveal last-minute problems.*
- *My reports provide full-disclosure protection from future legal claims.*

Of course, I always stand ready to perform inspections for your buyers. However, I would like to meet with you in person to explain how I can help streamline your real estate transactions. This seller inspection service I offer might also be used to procure future listings and/or sell homes that are already on the market. Please contact me.

Joe Goodinspector

ABC Inspections
(123) 456-7890

A good question to ask when presenting to a group of real estate agents:

Have any of you had a deal fall apart at the 11th hour over an inspection report?

Every hand will go up.

Sample Letter for Inspectors to Send to Home Sellers:

Dear Mr. Homeseller:

I am Joe Goodinspector of ABC inspections and I noticed you are selling your home. I am writing to encourage you to contact me about inspecting your home before any more potential buyers tour it. The advantages of having it inspected now are many:

- *You can have me, a certified InterNACHI inspector, do the inspection, rather than be at the mercy of the buyer's choice of inspector.*

- *You can schedule the inspection with me at your convenience.*

- *I might be able to alert you to any items of immediate concern, such as radon gas or active termite infestation.*

- *You can assist me during the inspection, something not normally done during a buyer's inspection.*

- *You can help me correct any misstatements in my inspection report before I generate it.*

- *The report can help you realistically price your home if problems exist.*

- *The report can help you substantiate a higher asking price if problems don't exist or have been corrected.*

- *My report will reveal problems ahead of time, which:*

  - *might make your home show better;*

  - *gives you time to make repairs and shop for competitive contractors;*

  - *permits you to attach repair estimates or paid invoices to the inspection report; and*

  - *removes over-inflated buyer-procured estimates from any future negotiations.*

- *My report might alert you to any immediate safety issues found, before agents and visitors tour the home.*

- *My report provides a third-party, unbiased opinion to offer to your potential buyers.*

- *A seller inspection permits a clean home inspection report to be used as a marketing tool.*

- *A seller inspection is the ultimate gesture in forthrightness on your part.*

- *My report might relieve a prospective buyer's unfounded suspicions, before they walk away from your home.*

- *A seller inspection lightens negotiations and 11th-hour re-negotiations.*

- *My report might encourage your buyer to waive the inspection contingency.*

- *Your deal is less likely to fall apart, the way they often do, when a buyer's inspection unexpectedly reveals a last-minute problem.*

- *My report provides you with full-disclosure protection from future legal claims.*

I would like to talk with you in person to explain how I can help streamline your real estate sale. And, of course, I always stand ready to inspect the home you are buying, as well. Please contact me.

Joe Goodinspector

ABC Inspections
(123) 456-7890

The talking points within such sample letters can be used by inspectors to create separate brochures that promote his/her seller inspection services.

In summary, seller inspections streamline the real estate sales process for all parties involved. InterNACHI recommends that every home be inspected before being put on the market (listed), and recommends annual inspections for homes that aren't for sale.

InterNACHI has entered into an exclusive agreement with **OverSeeIt.com** to market solely InterNACHI inspector-performed seller inspections directly to home sellers across North America, which began in the fall of 2006.

InterNACHI members are reminded to add this service to the services they offer by clicking on it at www.nachi.org/ancillary

InterNACHI members are reminded to upload their reports to FetchReport.com

Read this article online at www.nachi.org/sellerinspections

11th-Month Builder's Warranty Inspections

It's easier than you think to parlay a one-time home buyer's inspection into a second inspection. For clients who have had their new home built, offer them an 11th-Month Builder's Warranty Inspection to check items before the builder's one-year warranty expires. Help them create a list of items that can be addressed by the contractor so that they don't have to go out of pocket for repairs.

You can also use it to solicit new clients even if you didn't inspect their new-construction home right after they built it.

Annual Home Maintenance Inspections

It's never too late to offer your clients a copy of *Now That You've Had a Home Inspection*, InterNACHI's best-selling home maintenance book, also available in Spanish. It's loaded with tips and how-to instructions for seasonal home maintenance, just for homeowners. This is the perfect tool to use to market your Annual Home Maintenance Inspections to help your clients keep their new home in top condition. Learn more at www.nachi.org/now

Owens Corning Roof Inspection Program

The Roof Data Technician Program, developed by InterNACHI, Owens Corning and Lowe's®, provides an additional revenue stream for InterNACHI members in the U.S. who are hired by Owens Corning as part of a roof warranty claim-resolution process.

Each job takes about 30 to 45 minutes to complete. Payments range from $100 to $140 per job, depending on distance and difficulty. There's no cost for InterNACHI members to participate in this program, and you don't have to be a certified home inspector—just a member of InterNACHI. The online training, scheduling, and report software are provided by InterNACHI for free. The roofing materials are provided by Lowe's® for free.

Visit www.nachi.org/owens-corning-roof-warranty-program-press-release to watch a video and learn more about this easy way to increase your income as an InterNACHI member.

How to Quadruple Your Inspection Business in Two Years

If you want to seriously grow your business within the limited time frame of two years from now—an endpoint that's virtually around the corner—but think that it's absurd that you could actually quadruple it that quickly, you need look no further for mathematical proof of the possibility than the story of the wheat and the chessboard.

The Wheat and the Chessboard (*aka* "The Mathematician and the King")

When an Indian mathematician named Sissa created the game of chess at the end of the 5th century AD, he presented it as a gift to his king. The king was so thrilled that he told Sissa to name his reward for the amazing gift—anything he had was his for the asking. Sissa, perhaps in feigned modesty, asked the king merely for some wheat. The king thought he was getting the better end of the deal by far and asked Sissa how much wheat, thinking this a meager and even insulting prize. Sissa said that he would like to use the chessboard to count out his reward: one grain of wheat on the first square, then doubled to two grains of wheat on the second square, and then doubled again to four grains of wheat on the next square, and so on, until all 64 squares of the chessboard were accounted for. Amused, the king ordered his servant to retrieve a bushel of wheat to count out Sissa's reward.

What the king didn't realize until halfway through this exercise was that Sissa's reward was becoming so enormous that the kingdom was in threat of losing its entire wheat stores, and more. The king's accountant pleaded for him to reverse his promise, explaining that, with 64 squares on the chessboard, and doubling the number of grains of wheat on each successive square (1 + 2 + 4 + 8, etc.), the total number of grains would equal 18,446,744,073,709,551,615—far more wheat than that held by the entire continent.

This story beautifully and simply illustrates the theory of exponential growth.

Exponentially Grow Your Business

Of course, there are limits to growth at this pace, as the king quickly discovered. And any inspector would balk at the notion of growing his or her business year after year after year, *ad infinitum*. But you can do this, too. You can grow your business exponentially. It is possible to grow your business at a rate that you never thought possible and yet keep it manageable so that it doesn't eclipse everything else in your life. You can double your business next year, and you can quadruple it in two years.

Here's How

Any inspector can do this, regardless of his or her current average number of inspections. All you have to do is to get every past client to refer one inspection to you. If you can get 100 referrals from 100 former clients, you will have effectively doubled your business. During the second year, repeat what you did during your first year (having a larger base of past clientele), and so on. This is exponential growth.

Putting the Plan into Play

The question now becomes: How do I get my past clients to refer to me?

You can get your past clients to refer you using the following marketing strategies:

1. Send each past client three copies of the *Now That You've Had a Home Inspection* home-maintenance book with your business card attached to each one, and a brief letter asking your former client to pass along each book to someone they know (family member, friend, neighbor, co-worker) who is buying, building, or selling their home, or even just planning to in the near future. Even if just one of these three books results in an inspection appointment, you'll have met your goal for growth. And while you may be tempted to opt for a less expensive alternative, such as mailing

out a half dozen of your brochures and business cards instead, the likelihood of those ending up in the trash is high, whereas no one will throw away a book. (And this assumes that you've already given your past clients their own copy of *Now That You've Had a Home Inspection*—you wouldn't want them to keep for themselves what you want them to give away to someone else.) You can't get much cheaper than $2.70 a copy anyway. If you're a savvy inspector, you're already giving the *Now* book to each of your current clients as a value-added bonus with their inspection report.

2. Offer each of your past clients an Annual Home Maintenance Inspection. Especially if any of them is a recent first-time home buyer and in need of extra help figuring out the ins and outs of homeownership, this will effectively double your rate of inspections. It's a strategy that can be repeated year after year, on top of your new business.

   In addition to recurring business from repeat customers, inspectors can capitalize on offering Annual Home Inspections by alerting the client's neighbors. The neighborhood is really a built-in local market, so inspectors should take advantage of this kind of close-proximity marketing opportunity. Find out how to accomplish this by reading "Marketing Tip for Inspectors: Hit Up the Neighbors with Your Annual Inspections" found earlier in this book.

3. Get a Custom Inspection Video made (like the one you can order at www.InspectorOutlet.com) and email the link to all of your past clients, and ask them to forward it to people who may be interested in your services. Your video can highlight any services you want to advertise, including your Annual Home Maintenance Inspection. But don't stop there. You can advertise your 11th-Month Builder's Warranty Inspection for people building new homes, your Pre-Listing Seller Inspection for those putting their homes on the market, your Aging-in-Place Inspection for seniors and those with limited mobility, your Pool & Spa Inspections, your Wood-Destroying Insect Inspection, Radon Testing, your package of Wind Mitigation, 4-Point and Roof Certification Inspections, your Home Energy Inspection... the possibilities are limited only by your initiative.

Why Did Sissa the Mathematician Ask the King for Grains of Wheat?

The beleaguered ruler came to the conclusion that it would be less expensive to surrender his kingdom than to make good on his promise to Sissa. And that's what happened... Sissa was crowned king.

The theory of exponential growth is profitable, indeed.

Before you lament your slow week (or month), or the sluggish rate of new construction in your service area—before you tell yourself that you've run out of new clients and, consequently, new business—always remember that your past clients are your best source of new business. And if you leave them satisfied, they're also your best advertising. Always be marketing. In addition to inspecting, it's the work you need to be doing to grow your business.

Why Inspectors Should Take Continuing Education Courses (even when it's not required)

Some jurisdictions require inspectors to meet minimum Continuing Education requirements each year. However, even if your state or province does not, there are still good reasons for taking such courses regularly.

- First and foremost, obviously, is the fact that **taking courses can help you become a better inspector**. Smart inspectors who are serious about their business will stay on top of their game by continually learning. Furthermore, building design innovations and the growing number of new building products mean that there's always something new for the inspector to know.

- **An inspector who keeps current with the industry will almost always have greater credibility with consumers**. Taking Continuing Education courses and training strengthens an inspector's credentials, and the inspector's credentials are important in marketing his/her services. Many inspectors display their Certificates of Completion from all their courses on their websites and on their office walls.

- **An inspector who has completed many Continuing Education courses provides a measure of protection for the real estate agent who referred the inspector**. Often, when an inspector gets sued, the agent also gets sued for a negligent referral. It's difficult for a plaintiff to succeed in such a claim if the inspector is able to produce a long list of robust courses that s/he has completed.

- **Attending live classes or taking online Continuing Education courses can strengthen an inspector's credibility in court**. In states where Continuing Education coursework is mandatory, an inspector's failure to meet the state's requirements could result not only in administrative action, but could also be considered as evidence of negligence in a civil suit filed against him/her. Even in states and provinces that have no mandatory education requirements, an inspector's failure to keep current in the field will diminish his/her credibility if s/he ever testifies in court or at a deposition.

  A judge or jury is far more likely to find an inspector's testimony persuasive if s/he regularly takes Continuing Education courses.

- **Finally, like it or not, inspectors must sometimes testify as experts**. Failure to keep current in the field could result in a ruling that disqualifies the inspector as an expert altogether. An inspector who appears as an unprepared witness who gives shoddy testimony will have his/her words reverberate throughout the legal and inspection communities, since that testimony may become a matter of public record.

An interesting case that illustrates this point is *Pettit v. Hampton and Beech, Inc., 922 A.2d 300* (Conn. App. 2007). In this case, the plaintiffs asked the court to disallow an inspector's testimony because they alleged he was not qualified to give an expert opinion on the cost of repairs. The court overruled the plaintiff's objection and qualified the inspector as an expert, in part, because of his Continuing Education activities. In another case, *GSB Contractors, Inc. v. Hess, 179 S.W.3d 535* (Tenn. App. 2005), the court qualified the inspector as an expert, in part, because of his Continuing Education and teaching background.

To sum up, there are many good reasons for inspectors to take Continuing Education courses. InterNACHI's online inspection courses are approved, accredited and free. So, inspectors really have no excuse for failing to avail themselves of InterNACHI's educational offerings. For a full list of available courses, visit www.nachi.org/education

The bottom line is that knowledge is power. The more you know, the more you can do, and the more you can do, the more you can earn.

Inspection Excellence Through Education and Camaraderie

"Just as iron sharpens iron, one man sharpens another."

—Proverbs 27:17

Members of the International Association of Certified Home Inspectors (InterNACHI) are the most educated and best-trained inspectors in the world, and InterNACHI is committed to keeping it that way. Toward that end, InterNACHI has taken steps to encourage its members' pursuit of inspection excellence, and we have accomplished this without additional charge to members. We believe that fees deter professional development, and that the best way to encourage the continuing education of our membership is by supporting variety, accessibility and affordability in educational options.

InterNACHI members start off by fulfilling certain requirements before they can even apply for membership. They have access to the InterNACHI University, which is free. InterNACHI's Code of Ethics Course is free and open to all. InterNACHI's Online Exam Preparation Tool, with a pool of more than 2,000 multiple-choice questions and answers, is the largest in the world, and free. InterNACHI's online, searchable Inspection Glossary is the largest in the world and is free and open to all.

InterNACHI's Standards of Practice Course, which reveals where an inspector may be veering off course, is self-evaluating and is free and open to all. InterNACHI's online Continuing Education is free.

InterNACHI's 25 Standards course is free. InterNACHI's online Roof Inspection course is free. InterNACHI's online Electrical Inspection course is free. InterNACHI's Inspecting Foundation Walls and Piers course is free. InterNACHI's online Structural Inspection course is free. InterNACHI's online Commercial Inspection course is free. InterNACHI's Advanced Radon Measurement Service Provider course is free. InterNACHI's Deck Inspections course is free. InterNACHI's Vermiculite Insulation mini-course is free. InterNACHI's TPR Valve Discharge mini-course is free. InterNACHI's Emergency Egress course is free. InterNACHI's Safe Practices for the Home Inspector course is free. InterNACHI's Plumbing Inspection course is free. InterNACHI's Polybutylene Plumbing course is free. InterNACHI's Commercial Standards of Practice course is free. InterNACHI's Green Building course is free. InterNACHI's Log Home Inspection course is free. Our online, comprehensive Moisture Intrusion Inspection course is free. InterNACHI's WDO Inspection course is free.

InterNACHI's Online Inspector Examination, with over a trillion different versions, taken over 385,000 times, and which generates a custom inspector-weakness pie chart upon completion, is graded instantly, is open to all, and is free.

InterNACHI's one-day HVAC Inspection, Mold Inspection and Electrical Inspection seminars are open to all and free to members. InterNACHI, far more than any other source, provides educational events around the world, which are free and open to all.

InterNACHI refuses paid advertisements in order to enhance trust in our information. InterNACHI's interactive photo message board, with over 450,000 topics, is the industry's largest and most popular, very educational, and is free and open to all. InterNACHI's Message Board protects free speech so that visitors can determine the truth. InterNACHI publishes "What's New," an inspection industry update, online, open to all, and free. InterNACHI's local chapter meetings typically present technical speakers, are open to all, and free. InterNACHI provides report review services for free. InterNACHI's annual convention is very educational, with three days of six continuously running classes, and are all free. InterNACHI permits all outside/for-profit Continuing Education providers to advertise their courses to our members on InterNACHI's websites for free. InterNACHI maintains a Question of the Day thread, open-to-all, and free. InterNACHI negotiates member discounts on nearly every Continuing Education provider's courses. InterNACHI's meetings distribute a wide variety of educational literature to all for free. InterNACHI's staff, committee members, chapter leaders, veteran members, special-expertise members, and advisory boards are constantly helping members one-on-one for free. InterNACHI members typically provide fellow members with free ride-alongs on actual inspections. InterNACHI employs some of the world's leading trainers and makes them available to members for free. InterNACHI does not charge for or unduly withhold approval of any organization's Continuing Education courses, even those offered by other inspection associations.

InterNACHI's 275,000+ page website is, itself, very educational. InterNACHI opened the first of six actual House of Horrors in December of 2005, which provides real, hands-on training and is due to release a virtual House of Horrors, an online Wood-Destroying Organism Inspection course, and an occupant hazard-recognition primer, and "What's Wrong Here?" panels—all very educational and all free. InterNACHI's Online Inspector Examination's main purpose, besides testing competence, is to alert members to their weaknesses. The same is true for InterNACHI's Code of Ethics Course, designed to alert members to possible infractions. And the same is true for InterNACHI's Standards of Practice Course, designed to alert members to areas they are over- and/or under-inspecting. All three are pre-application requirements and all are free.

InterNACHI's Inspection Article Library is free. InterNACHI's Inspection Graphics Gallery is free. InterNACHI even has online, educational, inspection-related crossword puzzles, open to all and free, of course.

A variety of accessible and affordable educational options encourage and enhance the professional development of all our members, but our most precious educational tool is our spirit of camaraderie. InterNACHI members continue to pursue, achieve and maintain inspection excellence in an atmosphere of members helping fellow members.

Please join us in this spirit.

Online Education: Better Than Classroom Education

Do classroom home inspection courses harm consumers?

Online written and video courses are perfect for educating and improving the competence of home inspectors and providing options for their primary and Continuing Education.

Advantages of online courses over live classroom courses include:

- **Cost of Course:** Online courses are inexpensive or free. Dollar for dollar, an inspector can complete many online courses for the same cost as a single classroom course. The more education an inspector has, the better s/he can serve his/her clients. Compared to online courses, classroom courses harm consumers by exhausting the Continuing Education budgets of inspectors faster than online courses.

- **Cost of Travel:** There are no travel or hotel costs associated with online courses. In contrast, relevant classroom courses, which are few and far between, cause the inspector to incur out-of-pocket travel and accommodation costs. Again, the more education an inspector has, the better s/he can serve served his/her clients. Compared to online courses, classroom courses harm consumers by exhausting the Continuing Education travel budgets of inspectors faster than online courses.

- **Cost of Lost Work:** An inspector need not take off work to complete online courses. Online courses can be taken at night, on the weekends, or whenever an inspector doesn't have any inspections scheduled. In contrast, classroom courses are often offered only during the day and require the inspector to suffer lost business income. Again, the more education an inspector has, the better s/he can serve his/her clients. Compared to online courses, classroom courses harm consumers by exhausting the Continuing Education budgets of inspectors faster than online courses.

- **Cost Advantage to Consumers:** Online inspection courses are simply more affordable to inspectors. With reduced course costs come an increase in the number of courses an inspector can afford to complete each year, with a corresponding rise in the level of inspector competence. Increasing the level of inspector competence is a direct benefit to consumers. Lower-cost education also gives inspectors the opportunity to pass on savings to consumers. Compared to online courses, classroom courses harm consumers by delaying the inspector's professional progress.

- **Accessibility:** Online courses are available all the time, anytime, from anywhere. In contrast, classroom courses for the inspection industry are few and far between. Compared to online courses, classroom courses harm consumers by limiting access to education for inspectors.

- **Collaboration in Development:** Online course development often includes collaboration among many experts and inspectors from around the world. For example, it is not unusual for InterNACHI's online courses to be the product of dozens of contributors. Compared to online courses, classroom courses harm consumers by often lacking in international collaborative development.

- **Expert Instruction:** Online course developers can hire many experts to contribute to each course. Often in online video courses, the instruction is presented by one or more renowned experts. In contrast, classroom instructors, though perhaps competent to teach about a particular subject, are rarely international experts. Compared to online courses, classroom courses harm consumers by denying renowned expert instruction to inspectors.

- **Number of Instructors:** Online courses often utilize more than one instructor, with more than one area of expertise. In contrast, most classroom courses are taught by only one instructor. Compared to online courses, classroom courses harm consumers by limiting the number of expert instructors per course.

- **Accuracy:** Online courses are reviewed for accuracy before being released. Online courses are also subjected to industry-wide peer review forever. In contrast, classroom instruction is rarely reviewed by anyone. (The author of this article personally knows of a physics professor who had been teaching the use of an incorrect formula for over 30 years before the error was caught.) Compared to online courses, classroom courses harm consumers by failing to correct misinformation given to inspectors in a timely fashion.

- **Current Course Material:** Downloadable, printable online course material is reviewed, edited and improved over time. In contrast, classroom texts are less frequently updated. Compared to online courses, classroom courses harm consumers by being less able to provide inspectors with current course material.

- **Pictures & Video:** Online courses contain pictures and on-location video that permit the inspector to virtually accompany the instructors on inspections of many actual structures and components. In contrast, classroom courses can't take inspectors into crawlspaces or on roofs. Compared to online courses, classroom courses harm consumers by failing to provide inspectors with virtual, real-situation training.

- **Pace:** Online courses move at each inspector's desired pace. Online courses can be stopped and re-started. Online video can be paused. In contrast, classroom courses move at only the instructor's speed. Compared to online courses, classroom courses harm consumers by being unable to teach at each inspector's own pace.

- **Wasted Time:** Online courses are edited to cut out set-up time, off-topic discussions, bathroom breaks, lunchtime, etc. In contrast, classroom courses include much wasted time. Compared to online courses, classroom courses harm consumers by diluting the training time with things that don't increase inspector competence.

- **Schedule:** Online courses are available when each inspector wants to take them. In contrast, classroom courses have inflexible schedules that require inspectors to attend when it is inconvenient, when the inspector is ill, when the inspector is tired, etc. Compared to online courses, classroom courses harm consumers by forcing inspectors to study and learn at a preset schedule.

- **Quizzes & Exams:** Online courses contain numerous short quizzes that assure the inspector has learned each section before moving on to the next. These quizzes are graded instantly, and often alert the inspector to incorrect answers immediately. Some even have built-in intelligence, which recognizes each inspector's unique areas of weakness, and reviews those areas until the inspector grasps them. Classroom courses typically have fewer quizzes, without instant grading. Compared to online courses, classroom courses harm consumers by being less diligent about assuring that each inspector has learned and understands every concept being taught.

- **Review:** Online courses permit inspectors to go back and review areas of weakness. For example, InterNACHI's online video courses permit the inspector to rewind and replay them over and over. In contrast, classroom material is typically covered only once. Compared to online courses, classroom courses harm consumers by being unable to allow inspectors go back and repeat material to strengthen his/her particular areas of weakness.

- **Repeat:** Online courses permit inspectors to take the course over again. In contrast, classroom courses are typically taken only once. Compared to online courses, classroom courses harm consumers by being all but impossible for inspectors to re-take over and over.

- **Instant Grading:** Online courses contain quizzes and final exams that are graded instantly. Instant grading permits the inspector to be alerted to areas of weakness while still engaged in the course. In contrast, classroom courses typically don't grade instantly. Compared to online courses, classroom courses harm consumers by being unable to instantly grade each quiz and exam.

- **Consistent Grading:** Online courses and quizzes are graded consistently over time and around the world. In contrast, classroom courses grade easier or harder, depending on where and when the inspector takes each course. Compared to online courses, classroom courses harm consumers by being unable to grade inspectors consistently.

- **Advanced Courses:** It is financially feasible to offer advanced courses online. An online course need only be developed once, yet can run for years. In contrast, classroom courses usually must be of an introductory nature to attract enough students to pay for an instructor each time it is offered. Compared to online courses, classroom courses harm consumers by being unable to financially sustain advanced course offerings.

- **Specialty Courses:** It is financially feasible to offer specialty courses online. An online course need only be developed once, yet can run for years. In contrast, classroom courses usually must have a common-enough appeal of subject matter in order to attract enough students to pay for an instructor each time it is offered. Compared to online courses, classroom courses harm consumers by being unable to financially sustain specialty course offerings.

- **Choice:** Online courses offer inspectors a wide variety of choices in both level and subject matter. In contrast, classroom courses are fewer and farther between. Compared to online courses, classroom courses harm consumers by being less likely to offer the training inspectors need, when and where they need it.

- **Communication:** Online courses often provide an Internet forum for all current students, graduates, instructors, experts, developers and interested parties from around the world to interact with each other and discuss the course. These course-specific forums provide continuing education to inspectors long after completing the course. Classroom courses harm consumers by rarely providing such widespread, post-course interaction.

In summary, online courses allow inspectors to study and learn at little or no cost, without having to travel or lose business, when and where they want, with well-developed, accurate courses, taught by experts, using updated course material, pictures and video, at their own pace and schedule, with the ability to review and repeat, and with the assurance they'll end up with a thorough understanding of the chosen topic.

Home inspection licensing board members or government bureaucrats who steer inspectors away from online course offerings by rejecting their Continuing Education approval based solely on their method of Internet delivery create a disincentive to inspector skill-set improvement, which ultimately harms consumers. And because much of an inspection report includes safety issues, the harm may also be physical, instead of merely financial.

In some cases, the harm may result in the actual death of either the inspector or the consumer.

A New York Times article supports InterNACHI's education model:

U.S. Department of Education Study Shows Online Education Better Than Classroom Education

by Steve Lohr
The New York Times

A recent 93-page report on online education, conducted by SRI International for the Department of Education, has a starchy academic title, but a most intriguing conclusion:

"On average, students in online learning conditions performed better than those receiving face-to-face instruction."

The report examined the comparative research on online-versus-traditional classroom teaching from 1996 to 2008. Some of it was in K-12 settings, but most of the comparative studies were done in colleges and adult continuing-education programs of various kinds, from medical training to the military.

Over the 12-year span, the report found 99 studies in which there were quantitative comparisons of online and classroom performance for the same courses. The analysis for the Department of Education found that, on average, students doing some or all of the course online would rank in the 59th percentile in tested performance, compared with the average classroom student scoring in the 50th percentile.

That is a modest but statistically meaningful difference.

"The study's major significance lies in demonstrating that online learning today is not just better than nothing — it actually tends to be better than conventional instruction," said Barbara Means, the study's lead author and an educational psychologist at SRI International.

Read the rest of the NYT article online at www.nachi.org/online-beats-classroom

Download the U.S. Department of Education's findings at
www.nachi.org/documents/US-Department-of-Education-Online-Education-Report.pdf

InterNACHI commends the following fine organizations for their consumer-protection policies toward online education of home inspectors: www.nachi.org/education

Below are the names, addresses and phone numbers of home inspection licensing board members and government bureaucrats who summarily withhold Continuing Education approval of online courses and, thus, are responsible for the financial and physical harm, and perhaps even death, of their fellow citizens:

As of today, no InterNACHI online course approvals have ever been rejected by anyone.

Find all of InterNACHI's current curriculum available through InterNACHI University, as well as a list of accreditations to date, listed in this book and online at www.nachi.org/education

Exams That Harm

Inspector exams with too many difficult-to-answer questions are harmful to consumers.

InterNACHI has administered more inspection exams than all other sources combined. It is also the leader in gathering home inspector-competence evaluation data, right down to the pass/fail rates of every question ever asked. View the results at exams.nachi.org/oe/stats.php

Often, we will hear someone in the industry complain that "the questions should have been more difficult to answer" on this or that exam. On the surface, it may appear that an exam is improved to the benefit of the consumer if the questions are made to be more difficult. Let us dispel this myth now.

For the purpose and ease of discussion, let's assume that we have a 100-point true/false exam. Because a multiple-choice question often has at least one clearly wrong answer choice, a multiple-choice question is not much different (and only a bit more difficult) mathematically than a true/false question. Let's also assume that we have two exam-takers. One—we'll call him Mr. Veteran—knows 10 times what the other—we'll call him Mr. Newbie—knows about home inspections.

Now, we all know that if we make the exam too easy, Mr. Veteran and Mr. Newbie will score similarly, just as if we asked a Pulitzer Prize winner and a 6-year-old how to spell the word "cat." This is known as "proof by extremes." In the inspection industry, an exam that is too easy is harmful to consumers because it makes a weak distinction between Mr. Veteran and Mr. Newbie... and they both pass.

But what happens if the questions in the exam are too difficult to answer? Let's find out using another proof by extremes. Let's say we create a 100-point true/false home inspection exam that has so many *difficult-to-answer* questions that Mr. Veteran only knows the answer to 20 of the 100 questions. That's a pretty hard exam! Mr. Veteran will have to guess the answer to 80 of the questions. On average, he will score 60: 20 for the ones he knows the answer to, plus half of the 80 that he guesses at. Mr. Newbie knows a tenth of Mr. Veteran. So, he knows the answer to only two questions. On average, he will score 51: two for the ones he knows the answer to, plus half of the 98 he guesses at.

Now, if you flip a coin 10 times, you should get heads five times, on average. But, often, if you flip a coin 10 times, you will get more than five heads or fewer than five heads. The same is true for the questions our exam-takers are guessing at. Sometimes, Mr. Veteran will score worse than 60, and sometimes Mr. Newbie will score better than 51. Using an online binomial calculator, one finds that one in 10 Mr. Newbies will score as well as the average Mr. Veteran, and that one in 10 Mr. Veterans will score as low as the average Mr. Newbie, all based solely on chance! Often, Mr. Newbie will score better than Mr. Veteran simply because the score on an exam that contains a large percentage of *difficult-to-answer* questions, that neither exam-taker knows the answers to, is determined solely by luck. That's not too good for consumers.

But, wait—it gets worse for consumers! As we make the questions more difficult to answer, the percentage of questions that our exam-takers have to guess at goes up, which increases the reliance of the score on chance, which, in turn, increases the odds that Mr. Newbie will score as well or even better than Mr. Veteran, which weakens the exam's ability to determine who is competent and who isn't, which is worse for consumers.

In fact, on an exam full of so many *difficult-to-answer* questions that Mr. Veteran only knows the answer to 10 of the 100, Mr. Veteran will (on average) score only 4.5 points better than Mr. Newbie.

But, wait—it gets worse for consumers! By making the questions more *difficult-to-answer* and increasing the chances that Mr. Newbie will be able to pass by being lucky, we also increase the chance that Mr. Veteran will fail due to bad luck. If the exam is used for certification (which gives the exam-passer a market advantage, and denies the exam-failer the market advantage), or, worse... if the exam is used for licensing (which puts the exam-passer into the market, and prohibits the exam-failer from entering the market), an exam with more *difficult-to-answer* questions increases the ratio of Mr. Newbies-to-Mr. Veterans in the marketplace by increasing the number of Mr. Newbies and decreasing the number of Mr. Veterans, which is horrible for consumers.

But, wait—it gets worse for consumers! If the exam is used for licensing, Mr. Newbie need not score anywhere near as high as Mr. Veteran to earn the right to wave the exact same government-issued credential (license) as Mr. Veteran has. This is especially true when the licensing exam uses a low passing cut-off score (like the NHIE does). The government displays both Mr. Veteran and Mr. Newbie as *equally licensed* in the eyes of the consumer, even though, in reality, their levels of competency differ greatly.

But, wait—here's where it gets better for consumers. InterNACHI's exams don't rely much on chance. InterNACHI's exams contain what some would describe as easy-to-answer questions that every Mr. Veteran should know the answer to. InterNACHI's exams are sometimes criticized for containing such questions. What these critics don't understand is our superior scoring system. If the exam-taker answers these questions correctly, he gets no credit for them, because we can't tell if he answered the questions correctly because he is a Mr. Veteran, or if he is a just a lucky Mr. Newbie. However, if the exam-taker answers them incorrectly, we assume that he is very likely a Mr. Newbie, and the exam-taker is severley penalized (in terms of score) for failing to answer them correctly. For, you see, it is much easier to determine incompetence than competence. This system, combined with InterNACHI's high passing cut-off scores, result in InterNACHI's exams being superior to other exams at distinguishing between competent and incompetent inspectors, who can't rely on chance and luck.

Online Inspector Exam

Take InterNACHI's free, **Online Inspector Examination:** www.nachi.org/aboutexam

InterNACHI inspectors must take this exam every three years in order to maintain their membership in good standing.

InterNACHI's Free, Online Continuing Education Courses for Inspectors

InterNACHI's online courses have been taken hundreds of thousands of times and are great learning tools. Each final exam is different (more than 4 trillion different versions), and each contains built-in intelligence to help alert test-takers to their weaknesses.

Here are some important features that make InterNACHI's online courses superior to existing Continuing Education options:

• All online courses are free to members.

• The courses are written in pure XHTML code for quick loading. The courses load fast on old computers, even those using dial-up modems.

- The courses are designed using a hierarchal menu, coupled with sequential page navigation. This provides the student with the option to easily repeat areas of weakness.

- The courses permit the student to start, stop and restart any part of the course as often as desired.

- There are a variety of images referenced within the courses, including diagrams, illustrations and photos of actual defects.

- Some illustrations can be enlarged for clearer viewing by clicking on them.

- Some text is integrated into InterNACHI's Inspection Glossary at www.nachi.org/glossary. Rolling over blue-colored terms provides their definition.

- Some final exams use multiple-choice questions that reference images.

- The courses' quizzes and final exams have numerous advantages over traditional exam systems, such as:

  1. The courses, quizzes and final exams incorporate built-in intelligence, which identifies and strengthens each student's unique subject weaknesses.

  2. Not only is each question weighted with regard to score, but each answer is weighted, as well as the correctness of each answer being weighted.

     a. Answers to easy questions are weighted such that the student is penalized, in terms of score, for answering incorrectly, but rewarded modestly for answering correctly.

     b. Answers to difficult questions are weighted such that the student is rewarded, in terms of score, for answering correctly, but not penalized for answering incorrectly.

     c. Answers to questions regarding basic safety and questions that every inspector should know the answers to are weighted such that the student is severely penalized, in terms of score, for answering incorrectly.

- Upon passing a final exam, the student can print out a Certificate of Completion that is auto-generated in his/her own name. (www.nachi.org/certificatesofcompletion)

InterNACHI members who desire that InterNACHI automatically submit proof of completion of an online or video course to their state for Continuing Education credit need only give us their state license number by clicking here: www.nachi.org/state-licenses

The student's (InterNACHI member's) information is recorded on InterNACHI's servers for membership-compliance verification, and automatically logs course completion into InterNACHI's online Continuing Education Log.

Here's a list of InterNACHI's current online courses:

- Safe Practices for the Home Inspector
- Home Inspection Business Course
- How to Perform Roof Inspections
- How to Perform Residential Electrical Inspections
- Structural Issues for Home Inspectors
- Residential Structural Design for Home Inspectors
- Residential Plumbing Overview for Inspectors
- How to Perform Exterior Inspections
- How to Inspect the Attic, Insulation, Ventilation and Interior

- How to Inspect HVAC Systems
- How to Inspect Fireplaces, Stoves and Chimneys
- How to Perform Deck Inspections
- How to Inspect Pools and Spas
- Log Home Inspection
- How to Inspect Septic Systems
- Green Building Inspection
- How to Perform Energy Audits
- The House As a System
- Energy Movement for Inspectors
- Comfort and Climate for Inspectors
- Indoor Air Quality for Inspectors
- How to Perform Mold Inspections
- Advanced Radon Measurement Service Provider Course
- Wood-Destroying Organism Inspection
- How to Inspect for Moisture Intrusion
- Lead Safety for Renovation, Repair and Painting (RRP)
- 25 Standards Every Inspector Should Know
- Customer Service and Communication for Inspectors
- Commercial Property Inspection Prerequisite
- Inspecting Commercial Electrical Systems
- Inspecting Portable Fire Extinguishers
- Introduction to InterNACHI's Residential Standards of Practice
- InterNACHI Membership Code of Ethics Course
- Inspecting Foundation Walls and Piers
- Advanced Electrical Inspection Training
- Advanced HVAC Training for Inspectors
- How to Perform Deck Inspections
- How to Inspect Manufactured and Mobile Homes
- Advanced Inspection of Crawlspaces
- Infrared Thermography Inspection Training
- Building Science and Infrared Thermal Imaging
- Performing a Home Energy Audit
- Inspecting Means of Egress
- Inspecting Water Heater Tanks
- Advanced Mold Inspection Training
- Advanced Stucco & EIFS Inspection Training for Home Inspectors

- Calculating Envelope Energy Loss
- How to Perform Wind Mitigation Inspections
- Illinois Standards of Practice and Legal Issues for Home Inspectors
- Indiana Licensure Law & Regulations for Home Inspectors Course
- Indiana Online Pre-Licensing Course for Home Inspectors
- Texas TREC Standard Inspection Form and Report Writing
- 8-Hour Texas TREC Standards of Practice/Legal/Ethics Update
- Texas TREC Wood-Destroying Insect Inspection, Treatment & Reporting
- Wind and Hail Damage Inspections
- Wind & Hail Roof Inspection and Replacement
- Ladder Safety Training
- Exterior Safety for Inspectors and Contractors
- Professionalism Training
- General Roof Inspection
- 10 Steps to Performing a Roof Inspection
- Lead-Safe Work Practices
- Inspecting Asphalt Shingle Roofs
- Inspecting Wood Shingle and Shake Roofs
- Inspecting Tile Roofs
- Inspecting Metal Roofs
- Inspecting Slate Roofs
- Appliance Inspection for Home Inspectors
- TREC Standards of Practice for Inspecting Appliances
- Inspecting HVAC Energy Efficiency
- Home Energy Blower Door Training
- Fundamentals of Inspecting the Exterior
- Nevada Home Inspectors Standards of Practice and Legal Rules
- Defect Recognition and Report Writing
- Webinars for Home Inspectors
- Home Energy Score for Real Estate Professionals
- Saving Home Energy for Real Estate Professionals
- Home Energy Efficiency for Real Estate Professionals
- Florida Adjusters
- Florida Mold Assessor & Remediator CE Course
- Australia: Introduction to Home Inspections
- Australia: Introduction to the Australian Standards of Practice
- Mexico: Introducción a la Inspección Residencial de Pre-Compra

- South Africa: Introduction to Home Inspections
- South Africa: Roof Inspections
- South Africa: Soils, Substructures, and Superstructures
- South Africa: Standards of Practice
- Vermiculite Insulation
- Emergency Egress
- Water Heater Discharge Piping

Continuing Education for Real Estate Professionals

Inspectors should be sure to let the real estate professionals they deal with know that they can obtain some of their required Continuing Education for free through InterNACHI. Give your local real estate agents the opportunity to fulfill their CE requirements conveniently online at no charge. Check our Education Resources page often for the added courses and latest state approvals at www.nachi.org/education

- **Home Energy Score for Real Estate Professionals**

  www.nachi.org/home-energy-score-real-estate-education-course

  This online course teaches real estate professionals about how the U.S. Department of Energy's Home Energy Score helps homeowners understand the energy performance of their homes, and how they compare to other homes nationwide.

- **Saving Home Energy for Real Estate Professionals**

  www.nachi.org/saving-home-energy-real-estate-education-course

  This online course teaches real estate professionals how to understand the value of home energy inspections for current and prospective homeowners, and how to provide informative options to help homeowners cut their energy use, reduce their carbon footprint, and increase their homes' comfort, health and safety.

- **Home Energy Efficiency for Real Estate Professionals**

  www.nachi.org/home-energy-efficiency-real-estate-education-course

  This online course teaches real estate professionals how to understand the value of home energy inspections for current and prospective homeowners, provide informative options to help homeowners cut their energy use, reduce their carbon footprint, and increase their homes' comfort, health, and safety, and help homeowners make informed decisions about purchasing new HVAC equipment or improving existing equipment for more efficient operation.

Free Real Estate Agent Marketing Cards

Get your free Real Estate Agent Marketing Cards from www.InspectorOutlet.com. These cards are state-specific and include the web addresses for the free and approved online Continuing Education courses for real estate professionals. The cards also include room for your name and InterNACHI ID number so the agent can log in to take the free courses. Visit www.InspectorOutlet.com to order your free cards so that you can start handing them out and mailing them to every agent you know.

NACHI.TV

Take NACHI.TV's online video courses and watch NACHI.TV's episodes at www.nachi.tv

InterNACHI and NACHI.TV have teamed up to create next-generation online education with NACHI.TV streaming video technology and InterNACHI's state-of-the-art online education and testing systems. You need not be a member of InterNACHI—these courses are open to all. Non-members are charged a nominal fee to view most of the for-credit videos.

Each course includes:

- free downloadable course materials (yours to keep);
- a free online final exam;
- a free printable Certificate of Completion; and
- InterNACHI, MICB, IAC2, and state Continuing Education approval.

InterNACHI requires that each inspector-member taking an online video course log in with his/her unique identification code at the start of the course, when s/he begins watching the video portion of the course, and when s/he begins the final exam. This identification is linked both to individual email and mailing addresses. Our video partner (Reports, Inc.) stores information regarding the time each inspector viewed that video. This information is stored with that inspector's unique Internet Protocol (IP) address and is verified by InterNACHI before allowing the inspector to take the final exam. Finally, InterNACHI stores the time of the final exam, how long the inspector took to complete the timed exam, his/her final score, as well as each question asked and which answer the inspector provided for that question. All this information is stored securely over distributed databases and can be verified by InterNACHI at any time.

These courses don't just tell inspectors how to do it; these video courses show inspectors how to do it. NACHI.TV online video courses include topics such as:

- Performing a Home Inspection
- Inspecting Portable Fire Extinguishers
- Commercial Inspection Training
- Commercial Inspection of a Dentist's Office
- Commercial Inspection of a Warehouse
- Commercial Inspection of a Warehouse's Electrical System
- Home Inspection Fundamentals: The Exterior
- Inspection of a House with Structural Defects
- Performing a Roof Inspection
- Marketing and Sales
- Introduction to Energy Audits
- Building Science and Thermography
- Performing Your Best Inspection
- HVAC Training for Inspectors

- Home Inspectors' Electrical Wall of Defects
- Electrical Inspection Training promotional video
- Mold Inspection Training
- How to Perform Mold Inspection promotional video
- Inspecting Tankless Water Heaters
- IAC2 Mold Inspection Training and Certification
- Inspection with an IR Camera
- Inspection Tips and Techniques
- Advanced Inspection of Crawlspaces
- How to Inspect Notches, Holes and Cuts in Solid Lumber
- Drain and Duct Inspections
- Introduction to Infrared Thermography Inspection
- A Consumer's Guide to Wells and Water Quality
- Green LEED-Rated Home Inspection
- Inspecting Water Heater Tanks
- Inspecting Means of Egress
- Consumer's Guide to Infrared Thermography
- Fireplace and Chimney Inspections
- Law and Disorder with Joe Farsetta
- Interview with Joe Farsetta and Nick Gromicko
- Search Engine Optimization Tutorial
- Inspecting a Stairway
- Inspecting a Straw Bale Home
- EPA Green Building Inspection
- Structural Inspection of a Home
- Wind and Hail Inspections for Home Inspectors
- Wind and Hail Roof Inspection and Replacement
- How to Perform a Deck Inspection
- Ladder Safety Training/Demonstration
- Professionalism Training
- Safety for the Exterior
- General Roof Inspection
- Lead-Safe Work Practices for Home Inspectors
- Inspecting Asphalt Shingle Roofs
- Inspecting Wood Shingle and Shake Roofs
- Inspecting Tile Roofs
- Inspecting Slate Roofs
- Inspecting Metal Roofs

- Inspecting Roof Slope and Pitch
- What Really Matters in a Home Inspection
- Write a Home Energy Report™ in 3 Minutes
- Carpenter Ant Infestation
- Inspection Video Tips with Nick Gromicko
- 10 Steps to Performing a Roof Inspection with Ben Gromicko
- Home Energy Inspections with Nick Gromicko
- Advanced HVAC Inspection Training for Home Inspectors
- InterNACHI's Monthly Webinars for Home Inspectors
- Home Inspection Training Video #1 with Ben Gromicko
- Home Inspection Training Video #2 with Ben Gromicko
- Performing a Home Energy Audit promotional video
- Performing a Garage Inspection
- Find a Crack in the Heat Exchanger with Ben Gromicko
- Performing a Home Energy Rating
- Inspection Tips and Techniques
- Structural Inspection of a House
- Inspecting Skylight Flashing
- Photovoltaic Solar Panel Systems Inspection
- Well Water Meter Demonstration
- Home Energy Blower Door Training
- How to Inspect Decks Video Course promotional video
- Infrared Camera Inspection for Home Inspectors
- Stucco & EIFS Inspection Tips for Home Inspectors
- Advanced Stucco & EIFS Inspection Training for Home Inspectors
- A Consumer's Guide to Stucco & EIFS Inspections
- Commercial Office Inspection
- Commercial Inspection of a Bakery
- Inspecting Modular Homes
- Septic System Fundamentals for Home Inspectors
- Inspecting a U.S. EPA Green Building in Denver
- Inspecting a Log Home in Colorado
- Drainpipes and Duct Inspection with a Video Camera
- Inspector Success with Michael Pagoulatos
- Moisture-Free Warranty promotional video
- A Consumer's Guide to Infrared-Certified® Inspectors
- Home Inspector Marketing Tips with Mike Crow
- Electrical Inspection Training Video with Joe Tedesco, Part 1

- Electrical Inspection Training Video with Joe Tedesco, Part 2
- Electrical Inspection Training Video with Joe Tedesco, Part 3
- Home Inspection with Kenton Schaff
- Home Inspection with Greg Bell
- Fundamentals of Inspecting the Exterior with Mike Nelson
- Walk on Concrete Tile Roofs with Kenton Shepard
- Fall Protection Demonstration for Home Inspectors with Kenton Shepard
- InterNACHI Standards of Practice for Home Inspectors
- InterNACHI Online Agreement System for Members
- Home Maintenance Checkups
- Florida Pre-Licensing Courses
- Video Tip of the Week
- Subscribe to InterNACHI's YouTube Channel at youtube.com/internachi

InterNACHI's Free, Live Online Classes & Webinars for Home Inspectors

Join InterNACHI's Director of Education Ben Gromicko for free Continuing Education classes broadcast live online. Register for these free, accredited classes and webinars at www.nachi.org/class. Can't watch live? You can also visit this link to watch archived classes and webinars.

Exam Preparation

- **InterNACHI's State Exam Prep Tool**

  www.nachi.org/qa

  This practice exam contains more than 2,000 questions found on state and local home inspector exams. The correct answer is revealed after each question is answered.

- **InterNACHI's Advanced Residential Code Inspection Exam Prep Tool**

  www.nachi.org/residential-code-inspection-exam-prep

  This simulated ICC Exam helps inspectors prepare to be municipal code officials or licensed general contractors. It contains 200 sample questions. The correct answers are revealed after each quiz is taken.

- **InterNACHI's Advanced Commercial Property Code Inspection Exam Prep Tool**

  www.nachi.org/commercial-code-inspection-exam-prep

  This simulated ICC Exam helps inspectors prepare to be municipal code officials or licensed general contractors. It contains 300 sample questions. The correct answers are revealed after each quiz is taken.

More courses and course accreditations and approvals are added each month, so visit www.nachi.org/education often.

Join as a Student Member

Not an inspector yet? You can join as a Student-Member and take all of InterNACHI's free and accredited online Continuing Education courses for a low monthly fee. When you're ready, you can join InterNACHI as a certified member after fulfilling the membership requirements, and then transfer your credits to your Continuing Education Log. Join as a Student Member now at www.nachi.org/join

Certificates of Completion and Education Transcript

- Download and print your **Certificates of Completion** when you complete any of InterNACHI's free, online courses at www.nachi.org/certificatesofcompletion These are great for marketing purposes.

- Add your **Education Transcript** to your inspection website at www.nachi.org/my-transcript

- Download and print your **InterNACHI Membership Certificate** at www.nachi.org/mycertificate

- **Transfer the credits you earned** as a non-member to your InterNACHI University transcript at www.nachi.org/transfer-account

- Download and print your **IAC2 Membership Certificate** at www.iac2.org/certificate

- Download and print your **Infrared-Certified™ Certificate** at www.nachi.org/ir-certificate

Course Approvals & Accreditations

InterNACHI has been awarded more than 1,200 approvals and accreditations for its inspector educators, courses and exams. Here is a list of just some of the organizations and government agencies that have specifically recognized or accredited them and have issued approvals to InterNACHI:

- Alabama Building Commission
- Alabama Real Estate Commisssion
- Alaska Department of Commerce, Community and Economic Development, Division of Corporations, Business, and Professional Licensing, Home Inspector Program
- Alaska Real Estate Commission
- Alberta Government, Service Alberta
- American Association of Radon Scientists and Technologists (AARST)
- American Council for Accredited Certification (ACAC)
- Arkansas Home Inspector Registration Board
- Association of Real Estate License Law Officials (ARELLO)
- Australia InterNACHI
- Building Performance Institute (BPI)
- California Bureau of Real Estate
- California Department of Pesticide Regulation
- CanNACHI
- Chimney Safety Institute
- City of Boulder
- City of Toledo
- Clemson University

- Colorado Department of Agriculture
- Colorado Department of Regulatory Agencies, Division of Real Estate
- ComInspect Network
- Connecticut Department of Consumer Protection, Home Inspector Licensing Board
- Delaware Board of Home Inspectors
- Delaware Department of Agriculture
- Delaware Real Estate Commission
- Delaware State Housing Authority
- District of Columbia Real Estate Commission
- ENERGY STAR
- Environmental Solutions Association (ESA)
- EPA Indoor airPlus
- Exterior Design Institute
- Florida Construction Industries Licensing Board
- Florida DBPR Mold-Related Services
- Florida Department of Business and Professional Regulation, Bureau of Education and Testing
- Florida Department of Financial Services
- Georgia Department of Agriculture
- Hawaii Real Estate Branch, Professional and Vocational Licensing Division
- Hawaii Real Estate Commission, Department of Commerce and Consumer Affairs
- Home Inspectors of Tennessee Association
- Idaho Department of Agriculture
- Illinois Department of Financial and Professional Regulation, Division of Professional Regulation
- Indiana Professional Licensing Agency
- International Association of Certified Home Inspectors (InterNACHI)
- International Association of Certified Indoor Air Consultants (IAC2)
- International Association of Professional Contractors
- International Code Council (ICC)
- International Distance Education Certification Center (IDECC)
- Iowa Real Estate Commission
- Kansas Department of Health and Environment, Radiation Control Program
- Kentucky Public Protection Cabinet Office of Occupations and Professions Board of Home Inspectors
- Louisiana State Board of Home Inspectors
- Maine Department of Agriculture, Food & Rural Resources
- Maryland Department of Agriculture, Office of Plant Industries and Pest Management
- Maryland Department of Labor, Licensing and Regulation: Commission of Real Estate Appraisers, Appraisal Management Companies, and Home Inspectors
- Massachusetts Division of Professional Licensure
- Massachusetts Department of Agricultural Resources
- Master Inspector Certification Board

- Mexico InterNACHI
- Michigan Department of Labor & Economic Growth
- Michigan Department of Licensing & Regulatory Affairs
- Michigan Governor's Office, Michigan Saves Program
- Middle East InterNACHI
- Mississippi Home Inspector Board
- Mississippi Real Estate Commission
- Missouri Real Estate Commission
- Montana Board of Realty Regulation
- Montana Department of Labor and Industry, Business Standards Division
- Mountain Metro Association of REALTORs
- National Environmental Health Association (NEHA)
- National Radon Proficiency Program (NRPP)
- Nebraska Department of Public Health, Office of Environmental Health Hazards & Indoor Air
- Nebraska Real Estate Commission
- Nevada Department of Agriculture
- New Hampshire Home Inspector Licensing Board
- New Hampshire Real Estate Commission
- New Jersey Office of the Attorney General, Division of Consumer Affairs, State Board of Professional Engineers and Land Surveyors, Home Inspection Advisory Committee
- New Jersey Real Estate Commission
- New Mexico Department of Agriculture
- New York Department of State Division of Licensing Services
- New Zealand Real Estate Agents Authority
- North Carolina Office of State Fire Marshal
- North Carolina Real Estate Commission
- North Carolina Home Inspector Licensing Board
- North Dakota Real Estate Commission
- North Dakota Secretary of State
- Northwest Florida Home Inspectors Association
- Ohio Department of Agriculture
- Ohio Department of Commerce, Division of Real Estate and Professional Licensing
- Ohio Department of Health
- Oklahoma Department of Agriculture
- Oklahoma Real Estate Commission
- Oklahoma Residential & Commercial Inspection Association
- Oklahoma State Department of Health, Occupational Licensing Division, Construction Industries Board, Home Inspector Examiners
- Ontario Association of Certified Home Inspectors
- Oregon Construction Contractors Board

- Oregon Department of Agriculture
- Oregon Real Estate Commission
- Owens Corning
- Pasco County (Florida) Community Development Division's Home Buyer Assistance Program
- Pennsylvania Department of Agriculture
- PRO-LAB®
- Quebec Real Estate Brokerage Regulatory Organization
- Rhode Island Department of Business Regulation
- Rhode Island Division of Agriculture
- South Africa InterNACHI
- South Carolina Department of Labor, Licensing and Regulation, Residential Builders Commission
- South Carolina Department of Pesticide Regulation
- South Carolina Real Estate Commission
- South Dakota Real Estate Commission
- Tennessee Department of Agriculture
- Tennessee Department of Commerce and Insurance Division of Regulator Boards, Home Inspector Licensing Program
- Tennessee Radon Program
- Tennessee Real Estate Commission
- Texas Professional Real Estate Inspectors Association (TPREIA)
- Texas Real Estate Commission (TREC)
- U.S. Environmental Protection Agency (EPA)
- U.S. Department of Energy (DOE)
- U.S. DOE Energy Score Partner
- Utah Department of Agriculture
- Utah Department of Commerce, Division of Real Estate
- Vermont Agency of Agriculture, Food & Markets
- Virginia Department of Professional and Occupational Regulation, Board for Asbestos, Lead, Mold, and Home Inspectors
- Washington Department of Licensing
- Washington State Department of Agriculture
- Washington State Department of Licensing, Home Inspectors Board
- West Virginia Department of Military Affairs and Public Safety, State Fire Marshal's Office
- West Virginia Real Estate Commission
- Wisconsin Department of Regulation and Licensing
- Wyoming Department of Agriculture
- Wyoming Real Estate Commission

View InterNACHI's ever-growing list of accredited courses at www.nachi.org/education and their approvals at www.nachi.org/approved

Inspection Textbooks & Reference Tools

Inspection Textbooks

Purchase any of InterNACHI's books written specifically for inspectors. These books are sold online at www.InspectorOutlet.com

Titles include:

- 25 Standards Every Inspector Should Know
- How to Perform Residential Electrical Inspections
- How to Perform Roof Inspections
- Inspecting HVAC Systems
- Residential Plumbing Overview
- Safe Practices for the Home Inspector
- Structural Issues for Home Inspectors
- How to Inspect for Moisture Intrusion
- How to Inspect Pools & Spas
- How to Inspect the Exterior
- How to Perform Mold Inspections
- Advanced Radon Measurement Service Provider
- WDO Inspection Field Guide
- Inspecting the Attic, Insulation, Ventilation and Interior
- How to Perform Deck Inspections
- How to Run a Successful Home Inspection Business
- "Now That You've Had a Home Inspection" (for consumers)
- International Standards of Practice for Inspecting Commercial Properties (order for free at www.nachi.org/commercial-sop)

Whether you're new to the business, an inspector wanting more information, or a veteran of the industry looking to expand your knowledge, the InterNACHI Inspector Library is a must.

These titles and more are available as soft-cover books and/or PDF downloads at www.InspectorOutlet.com

Flash Cards

InterNACHI has also developed a series of affordable **flash cards**, which are excellent learning tools for exam prep, and available through www.InspectorOutlet.com:

- Residential Code Inspection Exam Prep Flash Cards
- Commercial Code Inspection Exam Prep Flash Cards

Video on USB Drive

InterNACHI sells its Home Inspection Training Video on a **USB drive**, which allows the inspector to view the video on a personal computer, laptop, or compatible tablet without having to be online and using an Internet connection. It's also available through www.InspectorOutlet.com

Standards of Practice and Codes of Ethics

These Standards and Codes will help guide your inspection protocol and business practices. Put them on your website to minimize your liability, and print off and include them with your inspection contract and/or report to keep your clients aware of your standard inspection's scope and limitations.

- InterNACHI's Standards of Practice for Performing a General Home Inspection (www.nachi.org/sop)

- InterNACHI's Code of Ethics for Home Inspectors (www.nachi.org/code_of_ethics)

- International Standards of Practice for Inspecting Commercial Properties (www.nachi.org/comsop)

- Commercial Code of Ethics (www.nachi.org/comsop.htm#9)

- Certified Master Inspector® Code of Ethics (certifiedmasterinspector.org/cmi/coe)

- Mold Inspection Standards of Practice (iac2.org/sop)

- InterNACHI's Standard Accessibility Inspection Report for Existing Commercial Buildings (www.nachi.org/comsop.htm#14)

- InterNACHI's Observed Green Features Report for Existing Commercial Buildings (www.nachi.org/comsop.htm#15)

- International Standards of Practice for Inspecting Commercial Fire Doors (www.nachi.org/comsop.htm#16)

- International Standards of Practice for Inspecting Fireplaces and Chimneys (www.nachi.org/comsop.htm#18)

- International Standards of Practice for Inspecting Radon Mitigation Systems (www.nachi.org/comsop.htm#18)

- International Phase I Standards of Practice for Inspecting Exterior Wall Cladding (www.nachi.org/ewcsop)

- Vendor Code of Ethics (www.nachi.org/vendor-ethics)

Tip: Order your free copy of the International Standards of Practice for Inspecting Commercial Properties at www.nachi.org/commercial-sop

Inspection Glossary

Visit InterNACHI's Inspection Glossary at www.nachi.org/glossary

It's online, alphabetized and searchable.

InterNACHI's Inspection Articles Library

Read original articles written just for inspectors and pass along informational articles for consumers from InterNACHI's vast and ever-expanding Inspection Articles Library at www.nachi.org/articles

These articles help educate inspectors (and consumers) about the many different issues associated with the inspection industry, information about the various systems and components found in homes, and news and trends in residential and commercial construction. Many of these articles are also available in Spanish and French.

Read all 145 articles in the "Mastering Roof Inspections" article series at www.nachi.org/mastering-roof-inspections These articles educate inspectors on the different types of roofs they'll encounter on inspections.

General Inspection & Consumer Articles:

- 10 Easy Ways to Save Energy in Your Home (consumer-targeted)
- 10 Easy Ways to Save Energy in Your Home (French)
- 10 Easy Ways to Save Energy in Your Home (Spanish)
- 15 Tools Every Homeowner Should Own (consumer-targeted)
- 15 Tools Every Homeowner Should Own (French)
- 15 Tools Every Homeowner Should Own (Spanish)
- A Caution Against Using XRF Alone for the Identification of Problem Drywall
- A Caution Against Using XRF Alone for the Identification of Problem Drywall (French)
- A Garage Inspection
- A Garage Inspection (French)
- A Garage Inspection (Spanish)
- Abrasive Blasting for Mold Remediation
- Acid Rain and Inspectors: Buildings at Risk
- Acid Rain and Inspectors: Buildings at Risk (French)
- Adjustable Steel Columns
- Adjustable Steel Columns (French)
- Adjustable Steel Columns (Spanish)
- Adobe Inspection
- Adobe Inspection (Spanish)
- Advantages of Solar Energy
- Advantages of Solar Energy (Spanish)
- Aerogel
- AFCI Testers
- AFCI Testers (French)
- AFCI Testers (Spanish)
- Aging in Place
- Aging in Place (French)

- Aging in Place (Spanish)
- Air Sampling for Mold Inspections
- Aluminum Siding Inspection
- Aluminum Siding Inspection (French)
- Aluminum Siding Inspection (Spanish)
- Aluminum Wiring
- Aluminum Wiring (French)
- Aluminum Wiring (Spanish)
- An Introduction to Foreclosures
- Ant Inspection
- Ant Inspection (French)
- Ant Inspection (Spanish)
- Anti-Scald Valves
- Anti-Scald Valves (Spanish)
- Anti-Tip Brackets for Freestanding Ranges
- Anti-Tip Brackets for Freestanding Ranges (French)
- Anti-Tip Brackets for Freestanding Ranges (Spanish)
- Arc-Fault Circuit Interrupters (AFCIs)
- Arc-Fault Circuit Interrupters (Spanish)
- Asbestos (consumer-targeted)
- Asbestos (French)
- Asbestos (Spanish)
- Asbestos Cement Siding Inspection
- Asbestos Cement Siding Inspection (Spanish)
- Attached Garage Fire Containment
- Attached Garage Fire Containment (French)
- Attached Garage Fire Containment (Spanish)
- Attached Garage Fire Hazards (consumer-targeted)
- Attic Pull-Down Ladders
- Attic Pull-Down Ladders (French)
- Attic Pull-Down Ladders (Spanish)
- Backdrafting
- Backflow Prevention
- Bamboo Construction and Inspection
- Barbeque Safety
- Barbecue Safety (French)
- Barn Inspection

- Barn Inspection (French)
- Barn Inspection (Spanish)
- Basic Waterproofing for Basements
- Basic Waterproofing for Basements (French)
- Basic Waterproofing for Basements (Spanish)
- Bat Infestation
- Bat Infestation (French)
- Bat House Inspection
- Bat House Inspection (French)
- Bathroom Ventilation Ducts and Fans
- Bathroom Ventilation Ducts and Fans (French)
- Bed Bugs: Inspecting for the New "House Herpes"
- Bed Bugs: Inspecting for the New "House Herpes" (French)
- Bidets
- Bidets (French)
- Biological Pollutants in the Home (consumer-targeted)
- Biological Pollutants in the Home (Spanish)
- Biowall Inspection (consumer-targeted)
- Bloom Boxes®
- Blower Door Testing
- Brominated Fire-Retardant Dangers
- Brownfields and Redevelopment
- Bug Zappers
- Building a Home (consumer-targeted)
- Building Cavities Used as Supply or Return Ducts
- Building Orientation for Optimum Energy (consumer-targeted)
- Bump Keys and What Inspectors Should Know About Them
- Bump Keys and What Inspectors Should Know About Them (French)
- Bump Keys and What Inspectors Should Know About Them (Spanish)
- Burglar-Resistant Homes
- Burglar-Resistant Homes (French)
- Burglar-Resistant Homes (Spanish)
- Buying a Foreclosure
- Carbon Monoxide Poisoning and Detectors
- Carbon Monoxide Poisoning and Detectors (French)
- Carbon Monoxide Poisoning and Detectors (Spanish)
- Carpet Beetles

- Carpet Beetles (Spanish)
- Carpet Mold: Identification, Prevention and Removal
- Carpeted Bathrooms
- Carpeted Bathrooms (French)
- Carpeted Bathrooms (Spanish)
- Ceiling Fan Inspection
- Ceiling Fan Inspection (French)
- Ceiling Fan Inspection (Spanish)
- Cement Substitutes
- Central Air-Conditioning System Inspection (consumer-targeted)
- Central Humidifiers
- Central Humidifiers (French)
- Central Humidifiers (Spanish)
- Central Vacuum Systems
- Central Vacuum Systems (French)
- Central Vacuum Systems (Spanish)
- Ceramic Tile and Stone Inspection
- Child-Proofing Windows and Stairs
- Child-Proofing Windows and Stairs (French)
- Child-Proofing Windows and Stairs (Spanish)
- Child Safety / Child-Proofing Your Home: 12 Safety Devices to Protect Your Children (consumer-targeted)
- Child Safety / Child-Proofing Your Home: 12 Safety Devices to Protect Your Children (Spanish; consumer-targeted)
- Child Safety / Child-Proofing Your Home: 12 Safety Devices to Protect Your Children (French; consumer-targeted)
- Chimney Inspection: Preventing Collapse
- Chinese Drywall
- Choosing a Manufactured Home (consumer-targeted)
- Choosing a Manufactured Home (Spanish; consumer-targeted)
- Choosing the Right Home Inspector (consumer-targeted)
- Choosing the Right Home Inspector (Spanish; consumer-targeted)
- Cisterns
- Cisterns (French)
- Closing Costs
- Clothes Closet Lighting
- Clothing Moths
- C.L.U.E. Reports
- Cockroach Inspection

- Collar Ties vs. Rafter Ties
- Collar Ties vs. Rafter Ties (French)
- Commercial and Home Inspector Safety: Carcinogens on the Job
- Commercial and Home Inspector Safety: Carcinogens on the Job (French)
- Common Electrical Conductor Types
- Compost Pile Hazards
- Composting Toilet Inspection
- Concrete Admixtures
- Concrete for Exterior and Structural Walls
- Condensation in Double-Paned Windows
- Condensation in Double-Paned Windows (French)
- Condensation in Double-Paned Windows (Spanish)
- Condensation Inspection
- Constituent Materials of Concrete
- Constructed Wetlands (consumer-targeted)
- Construction Methods and Materials for Noise Control
- Cool Roofs
- Cool Roofs (French)
- Cork Floor Inspection
- Cork Floor Inspection (French)
- Cost Segregation Studies for Commercial Properties
- Crawlspace Hazards and Inspection
- Crawlspace Hazards and Inspection (French)
- Crawlspace Hazards and Inspection (Spanish)
- Credit Reports
- Credit Reports (Spanish)
- Crib Safety and Inspection
- Daylight Saving Time
- Deck Inspections, Illustrated
- Deck Inspections, Illustrated (French)
- Deck Receptacles
- Deck Receptacles (French)
- Deck Receptacles (Spanish)
- Defensible Space
- Defensible Space (French)
- Defrost Cycle of a Heat Pump
- Depreciation of Investment Property

- Detecting Corrosion in Concrete-Encased Steel
- Disadvantages of Solar Energy
- Doing Damage During an Inspection: It's Your Job
- Drones and Inspections
- Dryer Vent Safety
- Dryer Vent Safety (French)
- Dust Mite Inspection
- Dust Mite Inspection (French)
- Earthquake Preparedness Inspection
- Earthquake Preparedness Inspection (French)
- Eco-Friendly Relocation (consumer-targeted)
- Edison's Early Accident
- Efflorescence for Inspectors
- Efflorescence for Inspectors (French)
- Elderly Safety
- Electric Fence Inspection
- Electric Fence Inspection (French)
- Electrical Safety (consumer-targeted)
- Electrical Safety (French; consumer-targeted)
- Electrical Service Panels
- Electrical Service Panels (French)
- Electrical Terms
- Electrical Terms (French)
- Electricity: Origins, Consumption and Costs
- Electromagnetic Fields (consumer-targeted)
- Emergency Preparedness: How Home Inspectors Can Help Their Clients
- Eminent Domain
- Energy Conservation
- Energy Efficiency
- Energy-Efficient Mortgages
- Energy-Efficient Space Heaters
- ENERGY STAR Program Criticized
- Engineered Wood Flooring
- Enhancing Energy Efficiency in Historic Buildings
- Estimating the Lifespan of a Water Heater
- Evaluating Homes Built Using Alternative Building Methods
- Evaluating Structural Framing

- Evaporative Coolers
- Exercise Equipment Dangers
- Exterior Design Features
- Exterior Design Features (Spanish)
- Eyebrow Dormers
- Factory-Built Fireplaces
- Fall-Arrest Systems
- FHA Loan Basics
- Fiberglass Insulation: History, Hazards, Alternatives
- Fire Extinguisher Maintenance and Inspection
- Fire Safety for the Home
- Fireplace Fuel
- Firestops
- Flood-Damaged Buildings
- For Home Inspectors: Evaluating Problems with Fasteners
- For Sale by Owner: Pros and Pitfalls
- Foreclosure Inspections: Trust Your Gut
- Formaldehyde
- Foundation Insulation (consumer-targeted)
- Free Negligent Referral Protection for Real Estate Professionals
- Free Negligent Referral Protection for Real Estate Professionals (Spanish)
- French Drain Inspection
- French-Language Inspection Articles
- Furniture and TV Tip-Over Hazards
- Galvanic Corrosion
- Garage Doors and Openers
- Garbage Disposals for Inspectors
- Generator Hazards and Inspection
- Geothermal Heating and Cooling Systems
- Ghosting
- Gravity Furnace Inspection
- Green Roof Inspection
- Green Lumber
- Greenhouse Inspection
- Grinder Pumps
- Ground-Fault Circuit Interrupters (GFCIs)
- Greywater Inspection

- Grounding Electrodes
- H-Clips for Inspectors
- Hand-Dug Well Inspection
- Hantavirus Danger in Homes
- Hard Water
- Hearths and Hearth Extensions
- High-Performance Buildings (consumer-targeted)
- Holiday Safety (consumer-targeted)
- Home Buyer Mistakes (consumer-targeted)
- Home Equity Loans and Lines of Credit
- Home Heating Oil Tanks
- Home Inspection Equipment
- Home Inspection Equipment (Spanish)
- Home Inspection Reports: What to Expect (consumer-targeted)
- Home Inspection Reports: What to Expect (Spanish)
- Home Inspector Safety & the Dangers of Arc Flashes
- Home Insurance (consumer-targeted)
- Home Repair Rip-Offs
- Home Safety for the Elderly (consumer-targeted)
- Home Safety for the Elderly (French)
- Home Winterization
- Homeowner Maintenance: Changing the HVAC Filter
- Homeowners Associations vs. the Green Homeowner
- Hot Water Recirculation Systems
- House-Moving
- House Numbers
- House Numbers (consumer-targeted)
- House Numbers (Spanish)
- House-Raising
- Household Hazards (consumer-targeted)
- Housewrap Inspection
- How Agents Can Reduce Their Liability
- How Agents Can Reduce Their Liability (Spanish)
- How Home Buyers Can Choose the Right Real Estate Pro
- How to Be a Successful Landlord
- How to Clean Algae and Moss Off Asphalt Shingles (consumer article sponsored by The Home Depot)
- How to Determine the Age of a Building

- How to Inspect the Refrigerator
- Hydroponics Inspection
- Ice Dams
- ICF Inspection and Termites
- Identifying and Describing Heating Systems
- Increasing Home Energy Efficiency
- Indoor Air (consumer-targeted)
- Inspecting EPDM
- Inspecting Floating Homes
- Inspecting for Defects in Older Buildings
- Inspecting Furnaces
- Inspecting Log Homes
- Inspecting Manufactured Stone for Water Damage
- Inspecting Off-Grid Photovoltaic Systems
- Inspecting the Bathroom Exhaust
- Inspecting the Dryer Exhaust
- Inspecting the Kitchen Exhaust
- Inspecting Underlayment on Roofs
- Inspecting Visible Masonry
- Inspector Safety: Three-Point Control for Climbing Ladders
- Installing Attic Insulation
- Insulation R-Value
- InterNACHI and the EPA Team Up to Monitor Lead Safety
- IR Cameras: An Overview for Inspectors
- IR Cameras: Electrical Inspections
- IR Cameras: Inspecting for Air Leaks
- IR Cameras: Inspecting for Moisture Intrusion
- IR Cameras: Inspecting Roofs
- Kerosene Heater Inspection
- Kickout Flashing
- Kitec® Fittings
- Knob-and-Tube Wiring
- Ladder Safety
- Ladder Safety (Spanish)
- Laminate Floor Inspection
- Landscape Shading (consumer-targeted)
- Lead Facts (consumer-targeted)

- Lead Facts for Inspectors
- Life Expectancy Chart
- Life Expectancy Chart for Homes in Florida
- Lighting Quality
- Lightning (consumer-targeted)
- Linoleum Inspection
- Lock Boxes
- Log Homes (consumer-targeted)
- Low-E Windows
- Lumber Grade Stamps
- Manufactured Homes (consumer-targeted)
- Marijuana Grow Operations
- Mastering Roof Inspections article series
- Material Defects Defined for Home Inspectors
- "McMansions" and Energy Inefficiency
- Measuring Roof Slope and Pitch
- Memo to Realtors: Inspecting Crawlspaces with Water
- Meth Labs
- Modular vs. Manufactured Homes
- Moisture Intrusion
- Moisture Meters
- Mold (consumer-targeted)
- Mortar Joints
- Mudjacking
- Net Metering
- Nightlights
- Noise Mitigation
- Non-Conforming Bedrooms
- Organic Solar Concentrators
- OSB vs. Plywood
- Outhouse Inspection
- Over-Occupancy Rental Laws for Inspectors
- Ozone Generator Hazards
- Paperless Drywall
- Pay for the Inspection at Closing (downloadable PDF for clients to sign)
- Paying a little extra for an InterNACHI inspector pays off!
- Paying a little extra for an InterNACHI inspector pays off! (French)

- Passive Solar Building Design
- Pellet Stoves for Inspectors
- Perlite
- Permanent Wood Foundations
- Pesticides (consumer-targeted)
- Pet Allergens
- Pilot Lights
- Pine Beetles
- Plants and Indoor Air Quality
- Playground Equipment Hazards and Inspection
- Plumbing Terms (consumer-targeted)
- Poison Ivy, Oak and Sumac
- Polybutylene for Inspectors
- Polyurethane Spray Foam Insulation
- Pool Alarms
- Pool Drain Hazards Inspection
- Pool Safety (consumer-targeted)
- Pool Water Pathogens
- Power Strips
- Pressure-Assist Toilets
- Private Water Wells (consumer-targeted)
- Property Appraisals
- PVC Health Hazards
- Radiant Heating Systems
- Radon Gas (consumer-targeted)
- Rainwater Catchment Systems
- Rebar
- Rehab a Home (consumer-targeted)
- Remodeling Is a Poor Investment Strategy (consumer-targeted)
- Rent-to-Own Home Leases
- Renters Insurance
- Residential Fire Sprinklers
- Reverse Mortgages
- Rockwool
- Rodent Inspection
- Roofing (consumer-targeted)
- Roofing Underlayment Types

- Rubber Flooring Inspection
- Rust Inspection and Prevention
- Safe Rooms
- Safety Glass for Inspectors
- Salvaged Building Materials Inspection
- Sauna Inspection
- Seller's Pre-Listing Inspection (consumer-targeted)
- Septic System Inspections
- Septic Systems (consumer-targeted)
- Settlement Information (consumer-targeted)
- Sewer Gases in the Home
- Sheet Vinyl Flooring
- Short Sales
- Shrinkage Cracks in Concrete
- Sinkholes
- Slash Piles
- Smoke Alarm Inspection
- Snow Guard Inspection
- Soil Contamination Inspection
- Soils and Settlement
- Solar Gardens
- Solar Heat-Gain Coefficient Ratings for Windows
- Solar Panel Fires and Electrical Hazards
- Solar Panel Rentals
- Solar Theft
- Solar Water Heaters
- Solid Brick vs. Brick Veneer
- Soy-Based Insulation
- Spill Switch Inspection
- Stairway Inspection
- Standpipes
- Static Electricity
- Steel Homes
- Steel Siding Inspection
- Steel Siding Inspection (Spanish)
- Straw Bale Home Basics
- Straw Bale House Inspection

- Structural Connection Design for the Home Inspector
- Structural Design Basics of Residential Construction for the Home Inspector
- Structural Design Concepts for the Home Inspector
- Structural Design Loads for the Home Inspector
- Structural Design of Foundations for the Home Inspector
- Structural Design of Lateral Resistance to Wind and Earthquake for the Home Inspector
- Structural Design of Wood Framing for the Home Inspector
- Stucco (consumer-targeted)
- Styrofoam Homes
- Sump Pump Operation and Inspection
- Surge Protectors
- Swimming Pool Barrier Regulations
- Tamper-Resistant Receptacles
- Tape Sampling for Mold Inspections
- Ten Tips to Speed Up Your Home Inspection (consumer-targeted)
- Termite Baits
- Termites (consumer-targeted)
- The Dark Side of Homeowners Associations
- The Duty to Warn: A Home Inspector's and Home Seller's Guide to Immediate Hazards
- The History of Concrete
- The Limitations of a Home Inspection
- The Potential for a Water Crisis
- The Small House Movement
- The Ten Best Places to Hide Valuables in Your Home (consumer-targeted)
- Thermal Imaging Reports
- Thermostats
- Three Deadly Mistakes Every Home Buyer Should Avoid (consumer-targeted)
- Tie-Downs for Manufactured Homes
- To Buy or to Rent?
- Tobacco Odor Removal
- Toilet Inspections
- Tornado Safety and Inspection
- TPR Valves and Discharge Piping
- Trampoline Safety and Inspection
- Tree Dangers
- Tree Swing Inspection
- Treehouse Inspection

- Trombe Walls
- Type B and Type L Vent Inspection
- Tyvek®
- U-Factors for Windows
- UFFI Insulation Inspection
- Ultrasonic Pest Repellers: Solution or Scam?
- Underground Fuel Storage Tank Hazards and Inspection
- Ungrounded Electrical Receptacles
- Unvented Roof Assemblies
- USDA Loans (consumer-targeted)
- VA Loan Basics (consumer-targeted)
- Vapor Barriers
- Venomous Pests: Inspector Beware
- Ventless Fireplace Inspection
- Vermiculite
- Vinyl Siding Inspection
- Visual Inspection of Concrete
- Wallpaper Inspection
- Water Damage (consumer-targeted)
- Water Damage and EIFS
- Water Heater Dating Chart
- Water Heater Expansion Tanks
- Water Quality (consumer-targeted)
- Water Stoves
- What Is a Green Home Inspection?
- What Really Matters in a Home Inspection (consumer-targeted)
- Wildfire Mitigation Strategies and Inspection
- Wildlife (consumer-targeted)
- Wind Mitigation
- Wind Turbines
- Wind Turbines and Lightning
- Windbreaks (consumer-targeted)
- Window Bars
- Window Falls
- Window Films
- Window Gas Fills
- Window Well Inspection

- Wood-Burning Stoves
- Wood Decay
- Wood Siding Inspection
- Woodpecker Damage Prevention and Inspection
- Zoning Ordinances for Inspectors

Articles for Commercial Property Inspectors, in Particular:

- Anatomy of a Commercial Property Inspection Report
- Baghouse Inspection
- Baghouse Inspection (Spanish)
- Barn Inspection
- Barn Inspection (French)
- Barn Inspection (Spanish)
- Boost Your Inspection Business with Truck Signage
- Building Permits
- Commercial and Home Inspector Safety: Carcinogens on the Job
- Commercial and Home Inspector Safety: Carcinogens on the Job (French)
- Commercial Water Towers
- Cost Segregation Studies for Commercial Properties
- Creating a Team of Experts for Your Commercial Property Inspection Business
- Deep Fryer Inspection
- Drones and Inspections
- Dry Cleaners for Commercial Inspectors
- Dust Inspection
- Fire Alarm Systems
- Fire Extinguisher Maintenance and Inspection
- Firestops
- Grease Trap Inspection
- Green Strategies for Commercial Buildings
- How to Buy Commercial Property Without Using Your Own Money
- Inspecting Slip-Resistant Flooring in Commercial Buildings
- InterNACHI and the EPA Team Up to Monitor Lead Safety
- Mastering Roof Inspections article series
- Occupancy Load Signs
- Performing Commercial Inspections
- Personal Safety at a Commercial Property
- Pest Birds
- Pricing and Billing for Inspectors

- Reserve Studies
- Rubber Flooring Inspection
- Rust Inspection and Prevention
- Sample Language to Stop Defamation of an Inspector
- Scaffold Inspection
- Shopping for a Commercial Loan? Avoid These Mistakes
- Steel Siding Inspection
- Visual Inspection of Concrete
- Window Films

Business, Marketing & Legal Articles for Inspectors:

- Asset Protection for Inspectors
- Avoiding Lawsuits
- Become a HUD 203K Consultant
- Boost Your Inspection Business with Truck Signage
- Can a Real Estate Agent Sign the Inspection Agreement on Behalf of the Client?
- Choosing a Domain Name
- Choosing the Right Home Inspection Business Insurance Provider
- Commercial Lending Proposals Will Benefit Home Inspectors
- Commercial Office Checklist
- Commercial Property: Buy or Rent?
- Commercial Real Estate Terms Inspectors Should Know
- Commercial Vehicles: Considerations for Inspectors
- Comparative Negligence Defense for Home Inspectors
- Creating Customer Profiles for Your Marketing
- Deposition Preparation
- Digits and Hyphens in Inspection Reports
- Do Classroom Inspection Courses Harm Consumers?
- Doing Damage During an Inspection: It's Your Job
- Drones and Inspections
- Exams That Harm
- "Farther" vs. "Further"
- Financing Commercial Equipment for Inspectors
- Forms of Inspection Business Ownership
- Free Negligent Referral Protection for Real Estate Professionals
- Free Negligent Referral Protection for Real Estate Professionals (Spanish)
- Greening Your Inspection Business
- Gromicko on Home Inspection Brochures

- Gromicko on Home Inspector Websites
- Here are some freebies that inspectors should never give out.
- Home Inspection Equipment
- Home Inspector Pro: Website Optimization and Online Marketing article series:
    - Google, Yahoo & Bing Local Listings
    - Choose Your Words Wisely
    - Adding Interactive Content
- Home Inspector Safety & the Dangers of Arc Flashes
- Home Inspectors as Independent Business Operators
- How Agents Can Reduce Their Liability
- How Agents Can Reduce Their Liability (Spanish)
- How InterNACHI Calculates its Continuing Education Credit Hours
- How to Get Real Estate Pros to Hand Out Your Card
- How to Make Your Own Liquid Level
- How to Quadruple Your Inspection Business in Two Years
- How to Sell to a Real Estate Professional
- How to Write a Mission Statement for Your Inspection Company
- I Formed a Corporation or Limited Liability Company. Now What?
- If a Home Inspector Misses Something
- Inspection Riddles
- Inspection Reports: Engage Your Senses
- Inspection Reports: Present or Past Tense?
- Inspector Attire
- Inspector Safety Equipment
- Inspector Selection, A Real Estate Agent's Duty
- Inspector Selection, A Real Estate Agent's Duty (French)
- Inspectors and Commercial Leases
- Inspectors as Expert Witnesses
- Inspectors: Do You Take Pride in Your Ride?
- Inspectors Working in the Dark
- InterNACHI and the EPA Team Up to Monitor Lead Safety
- Introduction to Blueprint Reading for Inspectors
- Magic Marker Marketing
- Market Your Inspection Business Using InterNACHI's Message Board
- Marketing for Inspectors: There's More to Design Than You Think
- Marketing Tip for Inspectors: eNewsletters for Inspectors
- Marketing Tip for Inspectors: Have more than one weapon and use the right one for the job.
- Marketing Tip for Inspectors: Hit Up the Neighbors with Your Annual Inspections

- Marketing Tip for Inspectors: Meeting Your Client for the First Time
- Marketing Tip for Inspectors: Online Promotional Videos
- Marketing Tip for Inspectors: Record Yourself on the Phone
- Material Defects Defined for Home Inspectors
- Memo to Realtors: Inspecting Crawlspaces with Water
- My Trick for Building Websites That Turn Visitors into Clients
- "No Visible Evidence" Language May Be Evidence Against You
- Online Education Better Than Classroom Education
- Pay for the Inspection at Closing (downloadable PDF for clients to sign)
- Paying a Little Extra for an InterNACHI Inspector Pays Off
- Personal Safety at a Commercial Property
- Press Releases for Inspectors
- Pricing and Billing for Home Inspectors
- Pros and Cons of Using Arbitration Clauses in Home Inspection Contracts
- Proving Negligence
- Put Your Inspection Business All Over the Internet
- Sample Language to Stop Defamation of an Inspector
- Sample Narratives
- Scheduling an Inspection
- Search Engine Optimization Tips for Inspectors
- SEO and the Inspection Industry (blog post)
- SEO and the Inspection Industry (article)
- Seven Ways to Use a Home Inspection Report
- Shopping for a Commercial Loan? Avoid These Mistakes
- "Sound Smart" Call Converter
- "That's a Lot of Money for a Few Hours' Work!"
- The Comparative Negligence Defense for Home Inspectors
- The Duty to Warn: A Home Inspector's and Home Seller's Guide to Immediate Hazards
- The "Red Phone" for Inspectors
- Thermal Imaging Reports
- Three Photos Every Inspector Should Include at the End of the Report
- To Exceed or Not to Exceed: That Is the Question
- To Exceed or Not to Exceed: That Is the Question (Spanish)
- Top 10 Inspection Industry Innovations of the Decade
- Warning About Advertising Oneself as "Code-Certified"
- "Watch My One-Minute Video"
- Water Heater Dating Chart
- Web Usability for Inspectors

- Website Legal Issues
- What Happens When Your Inspection Report Gets Recycled?
- What Makes You So Special?
- What the Department of Energy's Home Energy Scoring Program Means for InterNACHI Inspectors
- Why Inspectors Should Take Continuing Education Even When It's Not Required
- With One Click of a Button
- Work on Branding Your Inspection Business
- Writing Report Narratives
- Zoning Ordinances for Inspectors

InterNACHI's Inspection Graphics Library

Study the graphics in the **Inspection Graphics Library** at www.nachi.org/gallery These graphics are a visual way for inspectors to learn about proper installation and component identification, as well as useful visual aids to include in inspection reports and on your website. This educational library contains more than 1,600 high-resolution, inspection-related graphics to use in reports and on your website. Purchase InterNACHI's **Inspection Graphics Library** at www.InspectorOutlet.com

Inspector Images

Use InterNACHI's inspector images in your brochures, flyers and websites. They provide a professional, consistent look when you don't want to use photos. Download the images at www.nachi.org/images

Image Library of Major Pests in America

Browse the images in the **Major Pests in America Library** at www.nachi.org/padil

Defect Recognition

Try InterNACHI's free, online Photo Defect Recognition and Report-Writing Tutorial. The purpose of this photo tutorial is to help inspectors recognize the most common defects found on an inspection, and then see how to write a comment describing each defect as you would write it in an inspection report. Many inspectors spot obvious defects quickly, but then find it difficult to put what they see into words. The order of the categories within correlates with InterNACHI's Standards of Practice. Simply click each category, view the pictures of defects, anticipate the comment you would use to describe each defect, and click on the "Defect Description" link to see an example of how to word your finding. Categories include: roof; exterior; basement; foundation; crawlspace; structure; heating and cooling; plumbing; fireplace; attic; insulation; doors; windows; and interior. The tutorial is free. Find it online at www.nachi.org/defectrecognition

InterNACHI's Inspection Narratives Library

Learn to say it correctly. The library reduces the amount of time inspectors spend filling out reports. The quality of reports will improve and inspectors will enjoy reduced liability when using these 8,000+ narratives. Purchase the **Inspection Narratives Library** at www.nachi.org/narratives

More Benefits for Inspectors & Their Businesses

InterNACHI ID Card

Order your free InterNACHI photo ID card. Visit www.nachi.org/sampleid

InterNACHI Profile Editor

Update your profile on more than 4,500 websites at once with InterNACHI's Profile Editor. Visit www.nachi.org/profileintro

InterNACHI Member Marketing Department

Visit InterNACHI's Member Marketing Department at www.nachi.org/marketing. Keep your inspection calendar booked solid.

IAC2

Join IAC2, the International Association of Certified Indoor Air Consultants, by visiting www.IAC2.org IAC2 is the non-profit certifying body for home and building inspectors who have fulfilled certain educational and testing requirements, including those in the area of indoor air quality. Membership in IAC2 is free and there are no annual dues.

- Use your IAC2 logos at www.IAC2.org/logo
- Download and print your IAC2 certificate at www.IAC2.org/certificate
- Order your free IAC2 decals at www.nachi.org/IAC2-decals
- Find water, lead, mold and radon test kits promoting IAC2 members in 50,000 retail outlets at www.nachi.org/50000retailoutlets

Certified Professional Inspector (CPI)®

Use the Certified Professional Inspector (CPI)® professional designation at www.nachi.org/cpi. It's free.

Certified Master Inspector®

Become a Certified Master Inspector®, the inspection industry's highest professional designation. Visit www.certifiedmasterinspector.org

Infrared-Certified™

Become Infrared-Certified™ at www.nachi.org/ir

Consumer Verification Seal

Add the Consumer Verification Seal to your website. You can download it at www.nachi.org/webseal Earn your clients' confidence by letting them know you're certified by the world's largest inspection organization.

InterNACHI $10,000 Honor Guarantee™ Seal

Add the $10,000 Honor Guarantee™ Seal from www.nachi.org/honor to your website. Give your clients confidence by letting them know your honor is backed by the world's largest inspection organization.

First-Time Home Buyer-Friendly

Use InterNACHI's free First-Time Home Buyer-Friendly web seal. Download it from www.nachi.org/first-time

License Plate Covers

Order your free inspector license plate covers at www.nachi.org/plates

Inspection Vehicle Decals

- Order your free InterNACHI decals at www.nachi.org/decal
- Order your free IAC2 decals at www.nachi.org/iac2-decals
- Order your free Infrared-Certified™ decals at www.nachi.org/infrared-certified-decals
- Order your free Certified Master Inspector® decals at certifiedmasterinspector.org/cmi/decals

Sew-On Emblems

- Order your free InterNACHI emblems at www.nachi.org/emblem
- Order your free Certified Master Inspector® emblems at certifiedmasterinspector.org/cmi/emblem
- Order your free IAC2 emblems at iac2.org/sew-on-iac2-emblems

Ancillary Inspection Services

Add the ancillary inspections you offer to InterNACHI's many search engines. Learn more at www.nachi.org/ancillary Real estate agents use InspectorLocator.com to find a one-stop inspector who offers all the inspections needed, such as:

- Chimneys
- Commercial Buildings
- Green Certification
- Energy Loss
- Home Energy Inspection
- IAC2-Certified
- Lead Paint

- Log Homes
- Meth Testing
- Mold
- New Construction
- Pools and Spas
- Pre-Listing
- Radon Gas
- Septic Systems
- Sewer Lines
- Stucco/EIFS
- Thermal Imaging
- Water Quality
- WDO/Insects
- W.E.T.T. Certification

Report Forms & Checklists and Guidelines & SOPs for Ancillary Inspections

WDO Inspections

Offer Wood-Destroying Organism Inspections. Download the free reporting form at www.nachi.org/wdo-report

Accessibility Inspections

Offer accessibility inspection services on existing commercial buildings. Download the free reporting form at www.nachi.org/accessibility

Observed Green Features Inspections

Offer observed green features inspection services for existing commercial buildings. Download the free reporting form at www.nachi.org/comsop.htm#15

> **Tip:** Link to the free, online 20-question quiz for consumers at www.moveincertified.com/gogreen to find out how green their home is. It encourages consumers to hire InterNACHI members to perform full environmental inspections.

Home Energy Report™

Use InterNACHI's free software to generate a Home Energy Report™ in less than five minutes. Learn more at www.nachi.org/home-energy-inspection

Commercial Fire Door Inspections

Offer commercial fire door inspection services. Read the International Standards of Practice for Inspecting Commercial Fire Doors and download the free reporting form at www.nachi.org/comsop.htm#16

Fireplace and Chimney Inspections

Offer fireplace and chimney inspections. Read the International Phase I Standards of Practice for Inspecting Fireplaces and Chimneys and download the free reporting form at www.nachi.org/comsop.htm#17

Radon Mitigation System Inspections

Offer radon mitigation system inspections. Read the International Standards of Practice for Inspecting Radon Mitigation Systems and download the free reporting form at www.nachi.org/comsop.htm#18

Aging-in-Place Inspections

Offer aging-in-place inspections. Download the free inspection checklist at www.moveincertified.com/download/greencertifiedchecklist.pdf

Green-Certified Inspections

Offer Green-Certified inspections. Download the free inspection checklist at www.moveincertified.com/download/greencertifiedchecklist.pdf

Move-In Certified™ Seller Inspections

- Market Move-In Certified™ inspections to home sellers and real estate professionals. Learn more at www.moveincertified.com
- Add the Move-In Certified™ report-download box to your website. Get it at www.moveincertified.com/sitewidget
- Purchase our low-cost, full-color Move-In Certified™ flyers from www.InspectorOutlet.com

Tip: Use this free meth-testing kit by EMSL to test homes during a Seller Inspection www.emsl.com/index.cfm?nav=Pages&ID=519

Consumer Guide Videos

Add this code to your inspection business website so that consumers can watch these inspection-related episodes. They're free. www.nachi.org/consumer-guides

Inspector's Website of the Week

Check out the Inspector's Websites of the Week at www.nachi.org/websites. Submit your own business website.

HomeInspector.com

Give your inspection website a boost with HomeInspector.com: www.nachi.org/homeinspectordotcom

InspectorSEEK.com

Check to make sure you're listed at InspectorSEEK.com There is no charge for this listing.

InspectorNow.com

Check to make sure you're listed at InspectorNow.com and try the automated phone notification. This free, automated notification system alerts you by phone when a potential client needs an inspection.

CorrectInspect.com

Check to make sure you're listed at CorrectInspect.com There is no charge for this listing.

FindAnInspector.US

Check to make sure you're listed at FindanInspector.com There is no charge for this listing. FindanInspector.us explained.

InspectorLocator.com

Check to make sure you're listed at InspectorLocator.com InspectorLocator.com allows you to list various inspection services you offer. There is no charge for these listings.

OverSeeIt.com

Join OverSeeIt.com for free and offer renovation project and annual inspections.

North American Directory of Inspectors

Make sure you're listed in the North American Directory of Inspectors at www.nachi.org/directories There is no charge for this listing.

SEO Trackers

Enter your inspection website in InterNACHI's search engine optimizer at www.nachi.org/seotrackerintro The optimizer enters your website into more than 900 search engines and permits you to track its ranking.

InterNACHI's SEO Local Listing Tool for Home Inspectors found at www.nachi.org/local-seo-intro will help you get more search-engine returns and hits based on references to your company's name, address and phone number (NAP).

SEO Local Listing Tool

InterNACHI's SEO Local Listing Tool for Home Inspectors (www.nachi.org/local-seo-intro) will help you get more search engine returns and hits based on references to your company's name, address and phone number (NAP).

Website Click-Throughs

See how many inspection leads InterNACHI is generating for you at www.nachi.org/inspection-leads

ComInspect Network

Join the ComInspect Network at www.cominspect.com/for-inspectors for commercial building inspectors. Membership is free.

Discounted Business Insurance

InterNACHI members save thousands of dollars on general liability, E&O and other types of insurance. Check out all your options at www.nachi.org/insurance

Apply for an InterNACHI Visa® Card

InterNACHI.... it's everywhere you want to be. Apply for your InterNACHI credit card at www.nachi.org/credit-card

Free Merchant Account and Credit Card Swiper

Get the best rates, no-fee statements, unlimited processing, and free credit card swiper or terminal. www.nachi.org/free-merchant-account

Inspection Events

Attend one of InterNACHI's many events. It's great to meet fellow inspectors and inspection industry vendors. Check the updated schedule at www.nachi.org/events

Inspector Trade Show Displays and Tablecloths

Borrow a trade show display for your next home show or REALTOR® Expo. There is no charge to borrow a display. www.nachi.org/displays2008

Borrow a trade show tablecloth for your next home show or REALTOR® Expo. There is no charge to borrow a tablecloth. www.nachi.org/tablecloths

International Association of Professional Contractors

Are you a building contractor or subcontractor who does home inspections as a way to augment your current income, or are you transitioning from contracting to inspecting? Either way, you'll find lots of useful information by joining the International Association of Professional Contractors. Membership is free and there are no annual dues. Join now at www.contractorsassociation.org

Form your own InterNACHI member chapter.

It costs you nothing. Forming your own Chapter is easy and fun. We will help you. Besides, being an officer in your own local Chapter of the International Association of Certified Home Inspectors is great for your business. A chapter can be an INFORMAL Chapter and meeting (nothing more than a named InterNACHI meeting where attendees are charged for the cost of the room and food), or it can be a FORMAL CHARTERED Chapter (separate entity)... You decide. Many Chartered Chapters start off as informal chapter meetings and evolve into fully chartered InterNACHI Chapters later. InterNACHI will reimburse all cost overruns. Visit www.nachi.org/form

Set up your own InterNACHI Chapter website to promote you and your local members. It's free. In keeping with InterNACHI's efforts to give individual members more control in their local markets, InterNACHI is pleased to announce FREE chapter websites for every member. Any InterNACHI member can form his/her own local chapter, and now every member has one FREE chapter website which includes free hosting forever. Pick from any of dozens of site styles, and change styles anytime you want without disrupting the content you've added. Upload up to 10MB of images to display. Take online registration and payments for events and classes with our event-tracking system. Add as many custom pages as you'd like. Create pages with our easy-to-use interface—no need to know any code. The chapter sites are easy to create (all you need is your InterNACHI member username and password), and each site comes with a simple content manager so you can update it as you like, anytime you like. Chapter sites are free and hosting is free forever. Visit www.nachi.org/chaptersites

5-Year and 10-Year Pins

Order your free gold five-year or ten-year membership pin at www.nachi.org/5yearpin or www.nachi.org/10yearpin

PRO-LAB®

Stop by your local store and make sure the manager is carrying PRO-LAB® kits, which promote InterNACHI members. More than 50,000 retail outlets recommend that consumers contact their local InterNACHI inspector exclusively. PRO-LAB®, the leading provider of environmental laboratory testing services in the world, has re-packaged all of their millions of retail kits to include a recommendation to contact solely InterNACHI members for further professional inspections and testing.

PRO-LAB® consumer home safety test kits can be found at ACE® Hardware, CVS® Pharmacy, Distribution America, Home Depot®, Kroger®, Lowe's®, TrueValue®, Wal-Mart, and other stores. On the back of each kit is the recommendation that consumers with environmental issues visit www.InspectorSEEK.com and contact their neighborhood InterNACHI inspector. Find this InterNACHI-exclusive deal at: www.nachi.org/50000retailoutlets.htm Order a free PRO-LAB® catalogue here: www.nachi.org/prolabcatalogue

Hertz®

InterNACHI members now enjoy:

- 10% off all Hertz® rentals;
- up to 15% off weekend rentals;
- one car-class upgrade;
- $10 off weekly rentals; and
- free child-safety seats for weekly rentals.

The discount card is free. Visit www.nachi.org/hertz

Avis®

All members are entitled to enjoy the deep discounts on top of Avis'® already low promotional rates for vacation or leisure travel. The discount card is free. Visit www.nachi.org/avis

WellCard™

Get valuable discounts for yourself and your family on certain medical procedures, devices and prescriptions with the InterNACHI WellCard™. Get yours at www.nachi.org/wellcard

InterNACHI's Microwave Oven Leak Detector

Re-use it again and again. Get your first one free from InterNACHI at www.nachi.org/microwaveovenleakdetectors2006 Order additional leak detectors from www.InspectorOutlet.com

The Total Package for Inspectors

The Total Package for Inspectors helps new inspectors get their business off the ground and veteran inspectors make an upgrade. You'll receive a deeply discounted package of marketing pieces, inspector apparel and other gear to help you make a professional impression without worrying about making multiple orders for multiple items. It's available at www.InspectorOutlet.com

The Commercial Inspector Marketing Pack

Order the Commercial Inspector Marketing Pack at www.InspectorOutlet.com

InspectorPoints.com

See how you rate as a home inspector and fill out this online survey at InspectorPoints.com

Inspection Crossword Puzzles

Try one of InterNACHI's Inspection Crossword Puzzles. They're fun and educational. Check them out at www.nachi.org/inspection-crossword-puzzles

Cartoons

Enjoy inspection-related comic strips at www.nachi.org/cartoons

InterNACHI's Free Member Benefits

Read the entire list and their details online at www.nachi.org/benefits

Get Paid What You're Worth

Ask: Is Your Home Inspector Blind?

Licensing of home inspectors, where required, only sets a minimum standard. Much like being up to code, anything less would be illegal. Under this low bar, theoretically, children, psychics (who claim to "sense" if a house is OK), pets, and even the blind can be home inspectors. Other home inspection associations have no entrance requirements and, worse, encourage their associates to go out and perform actual inspections for poor, unsuspecting consumers as the only way to achieve full membership. InterNACHI finds this practice unconscionable. We turn down more than 60% of the inspectors who want to join InterNACHI because they can't pass our Online Inspector Exam, and we turn down 90% of those left because they can't fulfill our membership requirements.

Read this full article online at www.nachi.org/blind

Charging for Estimates

If you're getting too many requests for estimates that aren't converting into inspections, it might be that your estimates (in and of themselves) have value to the prospects, or that your prospects aren't really serious about having an inspection performed. These issues can be resolved by charging for estimates.

Some prospective clients often take advantage of offers for free estimates to check on the price of the inspector they actually intend to use.

Especially when times are tough, estimating for the people who will probably hire you can also eat up a lot of time.

Some inspectors are hesitant about charging for estimates, and some consumers are equally hesitant about paying for them. Charging for estimates is a way of screening prospects for their seriousness. You can easily offer to apply the cost of the estimate toward the cost of the inspection for prospects who become clients.

The success of charging for estimates will vary with the area, the client, the type of inspection, the local market, and the economic climate. You may have to spend some money to make some money.

Tip: Use InterNACHI's Home Inspection Fee Calculator at www.nachi.org/fee-calculator to determine the appropriate fee for your inspection.

Remind Your Prospective Clients That Paying a Little Extra for an InterNACHI-Certified Professional Inspector® Pays Off!

Post this article on your website:

Buying a home? It's probably the biggest purchase you'll ever make. And it's no time to shop for a cheap inspection. The cost of a home inspection is very small relative to the value of the home being inspected. The additional cost of hiring an InterNACHI-Certified Professional Inspector® is almost insignificant, by comparison.

You have recently been crunching the numbers—negotiating offers, adding up closing costs, shopping for mortgages—and trying to get the best deals. Don't stop now. Don't let your real estate agent, a "patty-cake" inspector, or anyone else talk you into skimping on the home inspection. InterNACHI inspectors perform the best inspections by far. They earn their fees many times over.

As the most qualified inspectors in the industry, InterNACHI inspectors do more, and—yes—they generally charge a little more. So, do yourself a favor and pay a little more for the quality inspection you and your family deserve.

Find this article online at www.nachi.org/smartchoice

That's a lot of money for only a few hours' work!

If you've been in the inspection business for a while, you've probably heard one of your clients say, "That's a lot of money for only a few hours' work!" As more and more home inspectors use time-saving report-generating software, including pictures (worth a thousand words), and even generate their reports on-site, they also start to make it look easy. When I was an inspector, I used to collect my fee on the job. I had a short but true story I printed on my letterhead and kept it with me to present to any client who questioned how much I was earning. The story goes as follows:

> The legendary artist Pablo Picasso was dining at a restaurant in New York City one evening. A fan approached his table and introduced herself, and gushed at how thrilled she was to meet the great master and how much she loved his work.
>
> Encouraged by his polite response, the fan begged, "Oh, Mr. Picasso, would you draw me a sketch?"
>
> Picasso grabbed some paper and a pen, and promptly sketched an image of the waiters passing by with their dessert trays.
>
> As the woman reached for the sketch, Picasso stopped her and said, "Madame, that will be $10,000."
>
> Shocked, she replied, "But that only took you five minutes!"
>
> "No, Madame," he answered. "It took me 50 years."

Picasso priced his service according to its value, not the cost of its manufacture. He did not price his sketch based on the cost of the paper, plus the cost of the ink, plus some hourly wage... and nor should an inspector. Keep your pricing up.

Pricing and Billing

The most important factor in any business is figuring out how much to charge for services. That's what we call pricing. It's crucial. Many inspectors have no idea how to go about it. They don't know what price is both competitive and profitable. That's why you need to develop a strategy for pricing your services.

Figuring out how to bill clients is also very important. In a home inspection business, you have to learn how to set competitive prices and also how to bill clients efficiently.

Let's learn about those two things: pricing and billing. They are two essential tasks for an inspection service business.

Pricing

Inspectors find it difficult to figure out how to price their services and what rate to use. Many professionals struggle in assigning a value to their time. You should know your hourly rate or how much you charge per hour. And remember, your hourly rate needs to cover not just your valuable time, but also your overhead. And it has to also bring you profits.

Two Ways

Figuring out how much to charge is not easy. And there is no standard way for how service businesses like yours do it. But there are two common ways you can consider. One way is to adjust your number of billable hours so that your revenue equals salary, overhead and profits. And the other way is based upon the local market. This means that you set your hourly rate based on what your local market will bear. Let's explore more in-depth explanations about these two methods: billable hours and market-based.

Billable Hours

The billable hours method is based on how many hours you work on your inspection service. The more time you spend doing an inspection, the lower your hourly rate. Given the same rate, the less time you work, the more you make per hour.

The goal here is to figure out your billable hours or your hourly rate. Then you'll multiply that rate by the number of hours it takes you to perform one home inspection. This will result in a number that we'll call your flat rate. The goal is to calculate your flat rate or what you charge for a home inspection on average. This flat rate can be adjusted up or down by a few other factors, including the size of the job or the amount of time spent doing the inspection.

For example, Inspector Mary may have figured out that her business is profitable when she charges an average of $400 for a typical home inspection. This flat rate represents her calculated hourly rate of $100 per hour, assuming that it takes Mary about four hours, on average, to do one typical home inspection. So, Mary's flat rate is $400, which can be adjusted up or down, depending on other factors. She figured out that, on average, she works four billable hours at $100 per hour to be successful—or profitable—in her business.

To figure out billable hours, let's consider how many total hours you work in a week. If you consider that there are 40 hours in a typical work week, and there are 50 working weeks a year, then you work a total of 2,000 hours a year. If you work 10 hours a day, that's 50 hours a week, and 2,500 hours a year. But how many of those working hours are billable? That's the question, and you'll have to do some figuring on your own to answer it. But let's make some assumptions about doing home inspections to come up with an example from which you can learn how to figure out your billable hours.

You may have no idea how many inspection jobs you'll have during the year, and, therefore, you really don't have a clue as to how many hours you'll actually be working for your clients. Brand new inspectors face this dilemma. You don't have any jobs scheduled, but you need to figure out how much to charge for your services, just like Mary did.

If you don't have any jobs scheduled, or maybe you just don't know how many jobs you will be scheduling in the future, you can calculate your billable hours to include the number of hours you desire or plan to spend, at most, per inspection job. This does not include business-related work, such as administrative stuff: filing paperwork, cleaning the office, marketing development, extra training, answering the phones, replying to emails, working on taxes, paying bills, research, shopping for tools, etc. You may think of billable hours as the maximum amount of time you want to spend per inspection job, including driving, inspecting, and report writing.

So, ask yourself: How many hours, on average, does it take you to do a typical home inspection?

Take that number you work per inspection job multiplied by the number of jobs you plan to work per year (hours per job x number of jobs), and that will be your billable hours. For example, let's say Inspector

John assumes that it takes him an average of five hours per inspection job, including driving to the job, doing the actual inspection, driving back to the office, and writing the inspection report. John plans to work five inspection jobs per week (that's 250 per year, assuming 50 work weeks per year). So, John's billable hours are 250 jobs x five hours per job = 1,250 billable hours. Now, you try this. Just for this exercise, pick some numbers to play with. You don't have to have the exact numbers, but do your own calculations, like John.

Again, to calculate billable hours is to think about how many hours you'll actually work on each home inspection job, even if you don't have any jobs scheduled. The hours would be only the time you spend working on the inspection itself. Assume each job takes five hours, including driving time, inspecting time, and report-writing time. And you expect to do one job per day. That's five hours per day of billable hours, 25 hours per week, and 1,250 billable hours per year.

Now that you've figured out your billable hours per job and per year, let's work on your flat rate, or your average fee for one inspection of a typical home in your market.

Billable Hourly Rate

To calculate your billable hourly rate (assuming you have no employees yet), use the following simple formula:

$$\textit{(Desired Annual Salary + Overhead + Desired Annual Profit)} \div$$
$$\textit{Annual Billable Hours = Billable Hourly Rate}$$

Let's review what the terms in the above calculation mean. Your "desired annual salary" is how much you want to make every year. This should be fairly straightforward. How much money do you want to earn annually? $50,000 per year? $100,000 per year?

The term "overhead" is the fixed costs of operating your inspection business. This usually includes rent and utilities (electric, HVAC, phone/Internet), computers and software, other office equipment, cameras and other inspection tools, vehicle and fuel, training and certifications, etc. These are the business-related expenses that you must pay for all the time, no matter what is going on or how your business is doing. Your overhead is your fixed costs.

The term "desired annual profit" is how much profit you want your business to make. A reasonable goal is 20%, and that's not including your salary or overhead.

Now, add everything together (desired annual salary + overhead + desired annual profit) and divide that result by your annual billable hours (the total number of hours you work doing the inspections; for John, it's 1,250). The result is the hourly rate you need to charge to cover your salary, overhead and profit.

Here's an example of Inspector John figuring out his billable hourly rate. John wants to make $100,000 per year in salary (that's his desired annual salary as gross income, before taxes). And he figured out that his overhead is $25,000 per year. So far, John's business needs to make a total of $125,000 to pay for his salary and overhead. Now, John sets his profit margin at 20%. Twenty percent of $125,000 is $25,000. Add that to $125,000 to get a new total of $150,000. Now, John's business needs to make a total of $150,000. John plans to work one five-hour inspection job per day. Assuming 50 work weeks per year, that's 1,250 billable hours per year. So, John takes $150,000 (salary + overhead + profit) and divides that by his annual billable hours of 1,250. The result is $120 per hour.

John should be pricing his inspections at $120 per hour. Assuming John's typical inspection takes five hours, John's home inspection service should be priced at $600. This is John's flat rate, the average fee for one inspection for a typical house in his market. John should do a home inspection for $600, give or take a little.

John figured out that $600 per inspection will cover his $100,000 salary and $25,000 overhead, and yield a 20% profit. John has successfully set his pricing.

Market-Based

Another way to figure out your hourly billable rate is to base it upon what the market will bear. This method is imprecise because you're not using any math. You're just using your understanding of the local market, including what other businesses with similar services are doing and what they're charging. It's also based upon what you have experienced in your business using different pricing.

Some inspectors simply price their services high and see if potential clients hire them. If they don't convert based on a certain price, they'll lower it until their market responds.

Some inspectors look at their competitors' websites to see how they price their services. Then they decide to price their own services based upon what they see their competition doing. To check out your competition, use InterNACHI's home inspector search engine at InspectorSeek.com

Combination

It's probably a good idea to set your pricing based upon both methods: billable hours and market-based. You may consider that doing the calculations of your billable hours will result in a number that will pay the bills, pay yourself, and yield a profit. And after using the formula, you can make adjustments to your pricing using the market-based approach.

For example, Inspector John's calculated hourly rate resulted in $120 per hour, which equals $600 for a five-hour inspection job. Now, if John's competitors are charging $400 per inspection, then John will have to work on his marketing strategy and communicate to potential clients why he charges more than everyone else and why he's worth it. For help with creating your own persuasive marketing materials, contact our Inspector Marketing Department at marketing.nachi.org

If a client hires John at $600 to do an inspection, and John realizes that the house is very large, then he can adjust his fee upward. If it takes him an extra hour, then John knows that, according to his hourly rate, he needs to charge an extra $100 dollars for a total $700 for the job. Likewise, if the job is extra small, and it takes John one less hour to do the inspection, John can have confidence in discounting his inspection service by $100 and still follow his hourly rate formula.

Fee Calculator

InterNACHI provides a free inspection fee calculator at www.nachi.org/fee-calculator Give it a try to figure out your pricing strategy. It's free.

Outsourcing Inspections

Sometimes an inspector has to hire another inspector to do all of the inspection services that the client wants. Maybe Inspector Mary does not perform mold inspections, but she wants to provide the service. If Inspector Mary hires her inspector friend Manny the Mold Inspector, the common approach is for Mary to charge a little more than what Manny would charge.

If you use another inspector to perform some services that your business offers but that you don't do yourself, then you should inform your client that you intend to hire another inspector to perform certain inspection services. Be transparent. You should also inform your client of the total price of the service, including the subcontracting work. Don't surprise your client with a big bill.

For example, let's say Inspector Mary is hired to do a home inspection and a mold inspection. Mary has figured out that to maintain profitability, she must charge an average fee of $500 for a typical inspection. Mary decides to hire Manny the Mold Inspector to perform the mold inspection. Manny charges $200 for a mold inspection. Mary will mark up the cost of Manny's mold inspection by 20%, a common approach to yield a profit. Mary's goal is to make a reasonable 20% profit for managing Manny and his mold inspection. Mary informs her client that the total fee is $740 for both the home inspection ($500) and mold inspection ($240). This calculation took into consideration Mary's annual salary, overhead, profit margin, and outsourcing management fee.

If you hire another inspector to provide services that your business offers but that you don't directly perform, then your pricing strategy must include your flat rate, the subcontractor's fee, and a management fee in order to yield your desired profit.

Summary

- Figure out your billable hourly rate by using a formula that factors in your desired salary, overhead and profit.
- Adjust your flat rate for your inspection service up or down using your hourly rate.
- Do market research on your competitors.
- If you outsource services, mark up your costs by your desired profit margin.

Every business owner—large and small—must calculate these figures in order to run a business that will not only sustain itself, but also provide some room to grow, whether you intend to fold your profits back into the business, expand your family, or elevate your lifestyle. Most business owners desire to do all three. It all starts with the numbers.

"3 Costly Mistakes"

Use this consumer brochure to remind your prospective clients of the importance of protecting themselves during their real estate transaction. Find it at www.InspectorOutlet.com

One More Time: Why InterNACHI?

InterNACHI is the world's largest nonprofit association of home inspectors, with members in every state and in 65 countries. InterNACHI provides training, education, certification and professional support for its members through its news, online courses, video instruction, informational articles, marketing materials, and member message board.

Far too many trade associations offer an impersonal online presence, collect dues, and offer generic, one-size-fits-all endorsements, with few, if any, practical benefits. InterNACHI provides its inspector-members with a multi-faceted organizational network based on the principles of education, collaboration, professionalism, and the highest code of ethics. Our dedicated staff of professionals is responsive, knowledgeable and encouraging. Our membership is a robust community that is truly interactive. Headquartered in Boulder, Colorado, we provide 'round-the-clock, personal support for questions relating to membership, training, marketing, and any other assistance a member (or prospective member) may require. Our website is the industry's powerhouse: www.NACHI.org has more than 275,000 pages and links, and it's updated several times a day with news, events, articles and courses that are timely, topical and relevant for the home inspector.

Additionally, we host seminars, training sessions, booths, fairs and chapter meetings all around the country, giving current and future members the opportunity to network and share insights as inspectors and as small business entrepreneurs. We champion our inspectors—whether they're new to the game or have been in it their entire careers—to strive for success in their individual businesses and as active representatives of our industry. We are their advocates. At InterNACHI, we believe that our strength is in our members.

Education

InterNACHI's online and video educational inspection courses have set the gold standard for the inspection industry. InterNACHI has developed its own proprietary course and test-taking system, which allows inspectors to take our free courses at their own pace and convenience. These courses are written by industry experts, edited by professional educators, and illustrated with original graphics and accurate drawings, as well as photos (many provided by our own members) showing defects that inspectors may encounter on the job. The courses challenge the inspector-student with quizzes that are automatically scored, and also permit the course-taker to review sections to reinforce new learning.

Each course concludes with a timed final exam which inspectors must pass (with specific minimum scores) in order to earn Continuing Education credits, as well as a customized and printable Certificate of Completion. Most of InterNACHI's courses are accredited by states around the U.S. as counting toward college-level Continuing Education credit hours, as well as state-mandated CE for licensing purposes, and we are awarded with new accreditations nearly every day.

InterNACHI's online inspection courses cover components, systems and issues, including: electrical; plumbing; HVAC; exterior; roof; structural; moisture intrusion; mold; radon; wood-destroying organisms; lead paint; septic systems; attic, insulation, ventilation and interior; water heater and discharge piping; pools and spas; deck inspections; foundation walls and piers; and much more.

InterNACHI leads the way with green courses, such as: green building inspection; log homes; energy audits; wind mitigation; building science and thermal imaging; and more.

In addition to our core training, InterNACHI offers courses which help the inspector develop his knowledge and specialty services, including: advanced residential code inspection exam prep; state exam prep; defect recognition and report writing; advanced commercial property code inspection exam prep; 25 standards every inspector should know; safety practices; Certified Master Inspector® application; and more.

InterNACHI is continually expanding its educational offerings. We now offer several of our online courses in the form of affordable, soft-cover books. Not only are these useful study aids, but their portability and durability make them handy enough to bring along on the job for easy reference. InterNACHI also provides them as downloadable PDFs—perfect for reading on a laptop or e-reader without having to be online.

NACHI.TV

Many of InterNACHI's core educational subject areas are also offered as advanced training on NACHI.TV With professionally outfitted studios at InterNACHI's headquarters, NACHI.TV produces episodes featuring guest instructors and industry professionals who take the student on a visual tour of both residential and commercial inspections. NACHI.TV also ventures out into the field to locations in the field, such as a warehouse, a bakery, a dentist's office, and other commercial properties, in addition to residential sites.

Some of NACHI.TV's more specialized episodes cover: Chinese drywall; portable fire extinguishers; crawlspaces; emergency egress; stucco and EIFS; vermiculite insulation; polybutylene plumbing; radiant barriers for windows; well meters; modular homes; and more.

With more than 100 episodes in its lineup, NACHI.TV is continually adding new episodes to give the inspector an in-depth look at systems, components and conditions before he encounters them on the job.

In addition to the basic and advanced training videos, NACHI.TV offers informational programming that features InterNACHI Director of Education Ben Gromicko and Founder Nick Gromicko, who welcome experts for technical guidance in the field and demonstrations in the studio, as well as for one-on-one interviews and roundtable discussions, to examine the industry's best practices for inspecting, marketing, home health and safety, energy efficiency, and a host of other topics of interest for the inspector and his clients.

Marketing

At InterNACHI, we believe that marketing your inspection business is as important as performing actual inspections, so we provide our members with literally hundreds of free, practical tools and tips that can be implemented today, which are designed to take the anxiety and guesswork out of this challenging but essential aspect of any small business. We want our members to continually improve and build on what they can offer their customers, on and off the job.

InterNACHI's customizable marketing arsenal includes: free logo, business card and brochure design; free optimized websites and web hosting; free search engine-optimization tracker; 200+ marketing tips for creating the best brochures, flyers and websites; free use of InterNACHI-trademarked logos, webseals and taglines for members' use on their own websites and marketing materials; free downloadable contract and agreement templates for inspectors to tailor to their specific requirements and jobs; free InterNACHI book displays, banners and trade show displays; free use of our downloadable, original images from our vast Images Gallery; free form-letter templates to customize for homeowners, Realtors and home buyers; free listing and phone notification through InspectorNow.com; free listing on CorrectInspect.com; free listing on FindAnInspector.us; free listing on InspectorSeek.com; free Client Satisfaction Survey; free decals and license plate holders; deeply discounted books for giveaways to current and prospective clients; free use of informational articles from the vast and regularly updated Inspection Articles Library www.nachi.org/articles; and more.

InterNACHI inspectors must maintain their membership in good standing by taking and passing a Code of Ethics course, annually taking and passing an online inspector exam, and meeting other membership requirements. We believe this commitment makes them the best in the business, and we're dedicated to helping them promote their education and services in ways that reflect their excellence and professionalism.

Support

We continually support our members with the means to succeed. The pillars of this support come in the form of our education and marketing tools, our tireless staff, the dedicated industry professionals and educators we engage for training and expert advice, and also—most importantly of all—the InterNACHI members themselves.

InterNACHI sponsors more than 400 events around the world every year. Members attend inspector and chapter meetings free of charge, and many events are free and open to non-members.

InterNACHI chapter and inspector meetings are a great way to network with other inspectors in your area. They provide mutual access for troubleshooting issues and brainstorming solutions to challenges you may be facing. And they're also the place to share and reinforce best practices. Most inspection businesses are one-man operations, and there's just no substitute for the camaraderie and fellowship that members experience when they get together under the InterNACHI banner.

On a daily basis, members and non-members alike can access the InterNACHI Message Board to read and participate in the many forums and discussion threads covering home components and systems, inspector news, marketing tips, legal issues, geographically specific regions, and many others. In this way, inspectors can instantly connect with other professionals to introduce themselves, ask for advice, offer assistance, and help uphold InterNACHI's culture of encouragement and cooperation. Those who need mentoring and those who are excited about sharing their knowledge and expertise will surely find each other on the InterNACHI Message Board. The Message Board is full of helpful advice, lively discussion and debate, and odd and unusual encounters experienced by inspectors on the job, as well as issues that affect them beyond the job.

Need emergency help from inspection experts while you're on the job site? Try out our Emergency Forum! This forum is for time-sensitive emergencies only. If you need help using the InterNACHI website, or for any other questions, email FastReply@nachi.org instead. Visit the Emergency Forum at www.nachi.org/forum/f79

Log in to InterNACHI.org each day for your chance to win one of our daily door prizes. Usually, it's some great tool that every inspector can use on the job.

Peruse InterNACHI's Inspection Articles Library www.nachi.org/articles, our extensive articles archive, to read up on the latest news about systems, components and trends that affect home inspectors.

InterNACHI's own legal counsel and legislative experts provide guidance on what to do to avoid legal liability, and what to do if you can't.

What makes InterNACHI the leader in inspection training and education is that it maintains the highest standards in the industry. Founder Nick Gromicko, CMI, has worked with other industry experts to develop its Standards of Practice for both residential and commercial inspections. InterNACHI also requires its members to uphold a strict Code of Ethics, putting integrity, safety and the client at the forefront of their service.

InterNACHI is truly the greatest advocate for the home inspector and the homeowner, offering more value and support than any other inspectors' association in the world. Visit www.NACHI.org and www.NACHI.org/benefits and see for yourself.

If you use social media, keep in touch with InterNACHI via LinkedIn, Twitter and Facebook.

To find the help you need from InterNACHI, visit www.nachi.org/contact

Become a Certified Master Inspector®

Do you have what it takes to become a Certified Master Inspector®?

Certified Master Inspectors® (CMIs) are the best inspectors in the world. CMI is a professional designation available to all qualifying inspectors in North America who wish to become Board-Certified by the Master Inspector Certification Board. All CMIs are experienced, dedicated to education, and have a proven record in the inspection industry.

Every Certified Master Inspector® must:

- have completed 1,000 fee-paid inspections and/or hours of education (combined);
- have been in the inspection business for at least three years;
- agree to abide by the inspection industry's toughest Code of Ethics;
- substantially follow a Board-approved Standards of Practice;
- agree to periodic criminal background checks; and
- submit the required application and the one-time, lifetime membership fee.

You need not be a member of any professional association. The Certified Master Inspector® professional designation is open to all qualifying inspectors in the United States and Canada.

If your application is approved, the Master Inspector Certification Board will issue you a certificate and list you as a Certified Master Inspector® on its website. You may then advertise yourself as a Certified Master Inspector® and/or Board-Certified.

Experienced.

All CMIs have completed at least 1,000 fee-paid inspections and/or hours of training and education combined.

Educated.

All CMIs have completed professional education prior to being approved.

Established.

All CMIs have been in the inspection business for at least three years prior to applying.

Vetted.

All CMIs have agreed to submit to periodic criminal background checks.

Professional.

All CMIs abide by the inspection industry's toughest Code of Ethics.

The Best.

Not everyone can become a Certified Master Inspector®. Hiring a CMI means hiring the best.

Certified Master Inspectors® are the very best of the best!

CMIs can get all kinds of free items for themselves, their businesses, and their clients—all at no charge. Here are some of the free items available exclusively to Certified Master Inspectors®:

- the InterNACHI member photo ID card with the words "Certified Master Inspector®" on it
- CMI name tag
- CMI ball cap (in red and blue)
- CMI t-shirt
- marketing rack cards
- embroidered patches
- full-size decals
- mini-decals
- awards for marketing purposes
- and more!

One great free item for CMIs to pass along to their clients includes "The Safe Home Book," a free PDF download.

Visit the Certified Master Inspector® website at www.certifiedmasterinspector.org/find and click on the "Download Safe Home Book" link (it takes a moment to download, as it is a large book).

Note the first page. Under the title of the book, it says: "Brought to you by..." and lists your name, city, state/province, website address, email address, and phone number.

Then, every other page of the book has your name and inspection business website address at the bottom, as well.

Each book is unique in that it has the particular Certified Master Inspector's® name and contact information embedded within it. This is an awesome book for consumers, and great for search engine optimization!

Read the entire list of free items and other resources at www.certifiedmasterinspector.org/resources

Visit www.CertifiedMasterInspector.org to find out how to apply now!

InterNACHI's Estimated Life Expectancy Chart for Homes

The following charts detail the predicted life expectancy of appliances, products, materials, systems and components.

Inspectors advising their clients should note that these life expectancies have been determined through research and testing, based on regular recommended maintenance and conditions of normal wear and tear, and not extreme weather (or other) conditions, neglect, over-use or abuse. Therefore, they should be used as guidelines only, and not relied upon as guarantees or warranties.

Surface preparation and paint quality are the most important determinants of a paint's life expectancy. Ultraviolet (UV) rays via sunshine can shorten life expectancy. Additionally, conditions of high humidity indoors or outdoors can affect the lifespan of these components, which is why they should be inspected and maintained seasonally.

Adhesives, Caulk & Paints	Life Expectancy in Years
Caulking (interior & exterior)	5-10
Construction Glue	20+
Paint (exterior)	7-10
Paint (interior)	10-15
Roofing Adhesives/Cements	15+
Sealants	8
Stains	3-8

Appliance life expectancy depends to a great extent on the use it receives. Furthermore, consumers often replace appliances long before they become worn out due to changes in styling, technology and consumer preferences.

Appliances	Life Expectancy in Years
Air Conditioner (window)	5-7
Compactor (trash)	6
Dehumidifier	8
Dishwasher	9
Disposal (food waste)	12
Dryer Vent (plastic)	5
Dryer Vent (steel)	20
Dryer (clothes)	13

Appliances	Life Expectancy in Years
Exhaust Fans	10
Freezer	10-20
Gas Oven	10-18
Hand Dryer	10-12
Humidifier (portable)	8
Microwave Oven	9
Range/Oven Hood	14
Electric Range	13-15
Gas Range	15-17
Refrigerator	9-13
Swamp Cooler	5-15
Washing Machine	5-15
Whole-House Vacuum System	20

Modern kitchens today are larger and more elaborate. Together with the family room, they now form the "great room."

Cabinetry & Storage	Life Expectancy in Years
Closet Shelves	100+
Entertainment Center/Home Office	10
Garage/Laundry Cabinets	70+
Kitchen/Bathroom Cabinets	50
Modular (stock manufacturing-type)	50

Walls and ceilings generally last the full lifespan of the home.

Ceilings & Walls	Life Expectancy in Years
Acoustical Tile Ceiling	40+ (older than 25 years may contain asbestos)
Ceramic Tile	70+
Concrete	75+

Ceilings & Walls	Life Expectancy in Years
Gypsum	75
Wood Paneling	20-50
Suspended Ceiling	25+

Natural stone countertops, which are less expensive than they were just a few years ago, are becoming more popular, and one can expect them to last a lifetime. Cultured marble countertops have a shorter life expectancy, however.

Countertops	Life Expectancy in Years
Concrete	50
Cultured Marble	20
Natural Stone	100+
Laminate	20-30
Resin	10+
Tile	100+
Wood	100+

Decks are exposed to a wide range of conditions in different climates, from wind and hail in some areas, to relatively consistent, dry weather in others. (See FASTENERS & STEEL section for fasteners.)

Decks	Life Expectancy in Years
Deck Planks	15
Composite	8-25
Structural Wood	10-30

Exterior fiberglass, steel and wood doors will last as long as the house, while vinyl and screen doors have a shorter life expectancy. The gaskets/weatherstripping of exterior doors may have to be replaced every five to eight years.

Doors	Life Expectancy in Years
Closet (interior)	100+
Fiberglass (exterior)	100+
Fire-Rated Steel (exterior)	100+

Doors	Life Expectancy in Years
French (interior)	30-50
Screen (exterior)	30
Sliding Glass/Patio (exterior)	20 (for roller wheel/track repair/ replacement)
Vinyl (exterior)	20
Wood (exterior)	100+
Wood (hollow-core interior)	20-30
Wood (solid-core interior)	30-100+

Copper-plated wiring, copper-clad aluminum, and bare copper wiring can be expected to last a lifetime, whereas electrical accessories and lighting controls, such as dimmer switches, may need to be replaced after 10 years. GFCIs could last 30 years, but much less if tripped regularly.

Remember that faulty, damaged or overloaded electrical circuits and equipment are the leading cause of house fires, so they should be inspected regularly and repaired or updated as needed.

Electrical	Life Expectancy in Years
Accessories	10+
Arc-Fault Circuit Interrupters (AFCIs)	30
Bare Copper	100+
Bulbs (compact fluorescent)	8,000 to 10,000+ hours
Bulbs (halogen)	4,000 to 8,000+ hours
Bulbs (incandescent)	1,000 to 2,000+ hours
Bulbs (LED)	30,000 to 50,000+ hours
Copper-Clad Aluminum	100+
Copper-Plated	100+
Fixtures	40
Ground-Fault Circuit Interrupters (GFCIs)	up to 30
Lighting Controls	30+
Residential Propane Backup Generators	12
Service Panel	60
Solar Panels	20-30

Electrical	Life Expectancy in Years
Solar System Batteries	3-12
Wind Turbine Generators	20

Floor and roof trusses and laminated strand lumber are durable household components, and engineered trim may last 30 years.

Engineered Lumber	Life Expectancy in Years
Engineered Joists	80+
Laminated Strand Lumber	100+
Laminated Veneer Lumber	80+
Trusses	100+

Fastener manufacturers do not provide lifespans for their products because they vary too much based on where the fasteners are installed in a home, the materials in which they're installed, and the local climate and environment. However, inspectors can use the guidelines below to make educated judgments about the materials they use.

Fasteners, Connectors & Steel	Life Expectancy in Years
Adjustable Steel Columns	50+
Fasteners (bright)	25-60
Fasteners (copper)	65-80+
Fasteners (galvanized)	10+
Fasteners (electro-galvanized)	15-45
Fasteners (hot-dipped galvanized)	35-60
Fasteners (stainless)	65-100+
Steel Beams	200+
Steel Columns	100+
Steel Plates	100+

Flooring life is dependent on maintenance and the amount of foot traffic the floor endures.

Flooring	Life Expectancy in Years
All Wood Floors	100+
Bamboo	100+
Brick Pavers	100+
Carpet	8-10
Concrete	50+
Engineered Wood	50+
Exotic Wood	100+
Granite	100+
Laminate	15-25
Linoleum	25
Marble	100+
Other Domestic Wood	100+
Slate	100
Terrazzo Tile	75+
Tile (ceramic, other)	75-100
Vinyl	25

Concrete and poured-block footings and foundations will last a lifetime, assuming they were properly built. Waterproofing with bituminous coating lasts 10 years, but if it cracks, it is immediately damaged.

Foundations	Life Expectancy in Years
Baseboard Waterproofing System	50
Bituminous-Coating Waterproofing	10
Concrete Block	100+
Insulated Concrete Forms (ICFs)	100
Post and Pier	20-65
Post and Tensioned Slab on Grade	100+
Poured-Concrete Footings and Foundation	100+
Slab on Grade (concrete)	100

Foundations	Life Expectancy in Years
Wood Foundation	5-40
Permanent Wood Foundation (PWF; treated)	75

Framing and structural systems have extended longevities; poured-concrete systems, timber/wood-frame houses, and structural insulated panels will all last a lifetime.

Framing	Life Expectancy in Years
Log	80-200
Poured-Concrete Systems	100+
Steel	100+
Structural Insulated Panels (SIPs)	100+
Wood/Timber-Frame	100+

The quality and frequency of use will affect the longevity of garage doors and openers.

Garages	Life Expectancy in Years
Garage Doors	20-25
Garage Door Openers	10-15

Home technology systems have diverse life expectancies and may have to be upgraded due to evolution in technology.

Home Technology	Life Expectancy in Years
Built-In Audio System	20
Carbon-Monoxide Detectors*	5
Doorbells	45
Home Automation System	5-50
Intercoms	20
Security System	5-20
Smoke/Heat Detectors*	less than 10
Wireless Home Network	5+

* Batteries should be changed at least annually.

Thermostats may last 35 years but they are usually replaced before they fail due to technological improvements.

HVAC	Life Expectancy in Years
Air Conditioner (central)	7-15
Air Exchanger	15
Attic Fan	15-25
Boiler	40
Burner	10+
Ceiling Fan	5-10
Condenser	8-20
Dampers	20+
Dehumidifier	8
Diffusers, Grilles and Registers	25
Ducting	60-100
Electric Radiant Heater	40
Evaporator Cooler	15-25
Furnace	15-25
Gas Fireplace	15-25
Heat Exchanger	10-15
Heat Pump	10-15
Heat-Recovery Ventilator	20
Hot-Water and Steam-Radiant Boiler	40
Humidifier	12
Induction and Fan-Coil Units	10-15
Chimney Cap (concrete)	100+
Chimney Cap (metal)	10-20
Chimney Cap (mortar)	15
Chimney Flue Tile	40-120
Thermostats	35
Ventilator	7

As long as they are not punctured, cut or burned and are kept dry and away from UV rays, cellulose, fiberglass and foam insulation materials will last a lifetime. This is true regardless of whether they were installed as loose-fill, housewrap or batts/rolls.

Insulation & Infiltration Barriers	Life Expectancy in Years
Batts/Rolls	100+
Black Paper (felt paper)	15-30
Cellulose	100+
Fiberglass	100+
Foamboard	100+
Housewrap	80+
Liquid-Applied Membrane	50
Loose-Fill	100+
Rockwool	100+
Wrap Tape	80+

Masonry is one of the most enduring household components. Fireplaces, chimneys and brick veneers can last the lifetime of a home.

Masonry & Concrete	Life Expectancy in Years
Brick	100+
Insulated Concrete Forms (hybrid block)	100+
Concrete Masonry Units (CMUs)	100+
Man-Made Stone	25
Masonry Sealant	2-20
Stone	100+
Stucco/EIFS	50+
Veneer	100+

Custom millwork and stair parts will last a lifetime and are typically upgraded only for aesthetic reasons.

Molding, Millwork & Trim	Life Expectancy in Years
Attic Stairs (pull-down)	50
Custom Millwork	100+
Pre-Built Stairs	100+
Stair Parts	100+
Stairs	100+

The lifetime of any wood product depends heavily on moisture intrusion.

Panels	Life Expectancy in Years
Flooring Underlayment	25
Hardboard	40
Particleboard	60
Plywood	100
Softwood	30
Oriented Strand Board (OSB)	60
Wall Panels	100+

The quality of plumbing fixtures varies dramatically. The mineral content of water can shorten the life expectancy of water heaters and clog showerheads. Also, some finishes may require special maintenance with approved cleaning agents per their manufacturers in order to last their expected service lives.

Plumbing, Fixtures & Faucets	Life Expectancy in Years
ABS and PVC Waste Pipe	50-80
Accessible/ADA Handles	100+
Acrylic Kitchen Sink	50
Cast-Iron Bathtub	100
Cast-Iron Waste Pipe (above ground)	60
Cast-Iron Waste Pipe (below ground)	50-60
Concrete Waste Pipe	100+
Copper Water Lines	70

Plumbing, Fixtures & Faucets	Life Expectancy in Years
Enameled-Steel Kitchen Sink	5-10+
Faucets and Spray Hose	15-20
Fiberglass Bathtub and Shower	20
Gas Lines (black steel)	75
Gas Lines (flex)	30
Hose Bibb	20-30
Instant (on-demand) Water Heater	10
PEX	40
Plastic Water Lines	75
Sauna/Steam Room	15-20
Sewer Grinder Pump	10
Shower Enclosure/Module	50
Shower Doors	20
Showerhead	100+ (if not clogged by mineral/other deposits)
Soapstone Kitchen Sink	100+
Sump Pump	7
Toilet Tank Components	5
Toilets, Bidets and Urinals	100+
Vent Fan (ceiling)	5-10
Vessel Sink (stone, glass, porcelain, copper)	5-20+
Water Heater (conventional)	6-12
Water Line (copper)	50
Water Line (plastic)	50
Well Pump	15
Water Softener	20
Whirlpool Tub	20-50

Radon mitigation systems have but one moving part: the radon fan.

Radon Mitigation Systems	Life Expectancy in Years
Air Exchanger	15
Barometric Backdraft Damper/Fresh-Air Intake	20
Caulking	5-10
Labeling	25
Manometer	15
Piping	50+
Radon Fan	5-8

The life of a roof depends on local weather conditions, building and design, material quality, and maintenance. Hot climates drastically reduce the life of asphalt shingles. Roofs in areas that experience severe weather, such as hail, tornadoes and/or hurricanes, may also experience a shorter-than-normal lifespan overall, or may incur isolated damage that requires repair in order to ensure the service life of the surrounding roofing materials.

Roofing	Life Expectancy in Years
Aluminum Coating	3-7
Asphalt Shingles (3-tab)	20
Asphalt (architectural)	30
BUR (built-up roofing)	30
Cellulose Fiber	20
Clay/Concrete	100+
Coal and Tar	30
Copper	70+
EPDM (ethylene propylene diene monomer) Rubber	15-25
Fiber Cement	25
Green (vegetation-covered)	5-40
Metal	40-80
Modified Bitumen	20
Simulated Slate	10-35
Slate	60-150

Roofing	Life Expectancy in Years
TPO	7-20
Wood	30

External, outdoor siding materials typically last a lifetime. Some exterior components may require protection through appropriate paints or sealants, as well as regular maintenance. Also, while well-maintained and undamaged flashing can last a long time, it is their connections that tend to fail, so seasonal inspection and maintenance are strongly recommended.

Sidings, Flashing & Accessories	Life Expectancy in Years
Aluminum Siding	25-40+
Aluminum Gutters, Downspouts, Soffits and Fascia	20-40+
Asbestos Shingle	100
Brick	100+
Cementitious	100+
Copper Downspouts	100
Copper Gutters	50+
Engineered Wood	100+
Fiber Cement	100+
Galvanized Steel Gutters/Downspouts	20
Manufactured Stone	100+
Stone	100+
Stucco/EIFS	50+
Trim	25
Vinyl Siding	60
Vinyl Gutters and Downspouts	25+
Wood/Exterior Shutters	20

Site and landscaping elements have life expectancies that vary dramatically.

Site & Landscaping	Life Expectancy in Years
American Red Clay	100+
Asphalt Driveway	15-20
Brick and Concrete Patio	15-25
Clay Paving	100+
Concrete Walks	40-50
Controllers	15
Gravel Walks	4-6
Mulch	1-2
Polyvinyl Fencing	100+
Sprinkler Heads	10-14
Underground PVC Piping	60+
Valves	20
Wood Chips	1-5
Wood Fencing	20

Swimming pools are composed of many systems and components, all with varying life expectancies.

Swimming Pools	Life Expectancy in Years
Concrete Shell	25+
Cover	7
Diving Board	10
Filter and Pump	10
Interior Finish	10-35
Vinyl Liner	10
Pool Water Heater	8
Waterline Tile	15+

Aluminum windows are expected to last between 15 and 20 years, while wooden windows should last nearly 30 years.

Windows	Life Expectancy in Years
Aluminum/Aluminum-Clad	15-20
Double-Pane	8-20
Skylights	10-20
Window Glazing	10+
Vinyl/Fiberglass Windows	20-40
Wood	30+

REMEMBER:

Life expectancy varies with usage, weather, installation, maintenance, and quality of materials. These charts should be used only as a general guideline and not as a guarantee or warranty regarding the performance or life expectancy of any appliance, product, system or component.

A Final Word: Re-Investing Revenue Back into Your Business

After you pay yourself each month with the bare minimum that you need to live on, you should plow back or re-invest every last available penny into marketing until you exceed capacity, which is your company's ability to service the number of prospects trying to hire you.

When you get to the point that you simply can't pack your schedule any tighter, you can:

1. market less and keep that reduction in expenditure as profit;

2. expand capacity (hire help); and/or

3. raise prices.

In the inspection business, it is nearly impossible to save your way to prosperity.

Best Wishes,

Nick Gromicko

BONUS: Inspection Riddles

Riddle #1

I'm not a wheel, but I have lots of spokes.
My name sounds like a flower to quite a few folks.
I'm colorful, but flat as can be.
Before you build a runway, you'd better build me.
What am I?

Riddle #2

For me to work correctly, I need a fresh batch.
Lift me straight up, that's the catch.
I'm used to test consistency.
But what you'll like is my simplicity.
What am I?

Riddle #3

I have a can, but it's not for beer.
One of my inlets is hopefully near.
I'm installed during construction, with any luck.
You'll think I'm great, though I really suck.
What am I?

Riddle #4

I look for leaks,
but I'm not a home inspector.
I love balance,
but I'm not an art collector.
Sometimes I'm frustrating to find.
Sometimes I'll save your behind.
What am I?

Riddle #5

I have a first name for a last name,
and not much can stop me.
And, unlike a level,
you're welcome to drop me.
What am I?

Riddle #6

I keep a low profile,
but pop up now and then
to help with the fish dinner
on my island.
What am I?

Riddle #7

If you open me up,
I disappear.
Replacing my parts
is a pain in the rear.
What am I?

Riddle #8

Near the beginning of the inspection,
you'll use me once or twice.
But you'll need another way
if you use me more than thrice.
What am I?

Riddle #9

Southern builders would not select me.
That would make no sense.
GFCIs need not protect me
if high and a nuisance.
What am I?

Riddle #10

I'm a durable product, and never break down.
I'm both an adjective
and a noun.
I'm found on some government buildings
and hotels deluxe.
I'm a malleable material
and cost a few bucks.
You'll never see me rot, stain or rust.
Recycling me is an absolute must.
What am I?

Riddle #11

I'm a miniature version
built into the full.
Open me first
to make sure it's cool.
What am I?

Answers: **#1** A Compass Rose; **#2** A Slump Cone Test; **#3** A Central Vacuum System; **#4** A GFCI;
#5 A Plumb Bob; **#6** A Retractable Island Range Hood; **#7** A Pocket Door; **#8** A Doorbell;
#9 A Roof Ice-Melt System; **#10** Gold; **#11** A Speakeasy Door

Would you like a FREE business logo as professional as these?

InterNACHI
Marketing Department

Brochures
Business Cards
Rack Cards
Flyers
Vehicle Magnets
Stickers
Business Card Magnets
Retractable Banners
Folders
Postcards
and more!

Contact us to get started:

720-369-3229   marketing@internachi.org   marketing.nachi.org

InterNACHI
Marketing Services

FREE Logo and Marketing Design Services for InterNACHI Members

How It Works (3 Easy Steps)

Step 1
Order any custom marketing from Inspector Outlet (business cards, brochures, etc.).

Step 2
Work closely with InterNACHI's design team to create a custom logo and design for your company.

Step 3
Receive your custom promotional materials within 10 days of your approval!

We provide InterNACHI members with custom print marketing to promote their home inspection business:

- Brochures
- Business Cards
- Rack Cards
- Flyers
- Vehicle Magnets
- Stickers
- Business Card Magnets
- Retractable Banners
- Folders
- Postcards
- and more!

View additional logos and marketing that we've designed for InterNACHI members at <u>marketing.nachi.org</u>

Have us design your logo, brochure and matching business card — free writing and editing are included!

What Inspectors Are Saying...

Thanks for the outstanding design and printing services! I recently received my first order of business cards with my new logo. The quality of the card is terrific. The designers managed to get everything on the card that I wanted. They even made some suggestions that really had a nice impact. The colors and paper are also top-quality. It's great to have these services available through InterNACHI.

— P. Dennis Murphy, Greater Peoria Property Inspections

Jessica at InterNACHI was an excellent resource! I have dealt with many people and places over the years for business cards and brochures, and Jessica and InterNACHI are the best! They worked very hard to make sure I was getting the best service, from the design to the printing. The final cards and brochures that came in the mail are excellent. I am very happy with the entire experience and I will be going back again in the future, for sure!

— Ryan Eberhardt, Premier Home Inspection & Analysis, LLC

The teamwork of Levi and Jesse boosted my startup to the top of the stack and gave me the competitive edge I needed. My logo is easy to understand and, most importantly, memorable. I've gotten feedback from several leads saying they saw my logo, which has translated into business. I'm definitely keeping this winning marketing strategy!

— Erik Coplin, EDC Professional Home Inspections

InterNACHI Print Services has done a great job with our print materials. While we were quite specific about our logo image and colors, Levi turned our idea into a unique, attention-getting device. Jessica then created awesome cards, brochures and vehicle signs. We simply filled out a one-page questionnaire and they took it from there. They are very talented and responsive, and have created a look we feel reflects our style. Well worth the money!

— Steve Wisenbaugh, Blue Lizard Home Inspections

Not being too artistic, I had zero idea of what to do. With one call to InterNACHI Print Services, I gave them all my information. The next day, a great business card and company brochure were sent to me for my approval. Helpful, fast service—I'm now a lifelong customer!

— Tom Little, Tom Little Property Inspections

I just want to express my gratitude for the help I have received from the InterNACHI staff in regard to the wonderful and extremely professional marketing materials they have designed for me. They have really helped me build my business and made it possible for me to present my business in a professional manner. I get nothing but compliments from everyone who has received the material. If you are looking for people to help you create professional marketing materials, I highly recommend InterNACHI Design & Print Services.

— Nathan Fairchild, Safe Investment Home Inspections LLC

InterNACHI
Marketing Services

720-369-3229   marketing@internachi.org   marketing.nachi.org

INSPECTOR OUTLET

YOU'LL BE SHOCKED AT OUR LOW PRICES!

Inspector Outlet is your source for all things home inspection-related. We are the official store for InterNACHI publications, equipment and apparel. We strive to provide the best products at the lowest prices in the industry.

Find an outstanding selection of original training manuals, checklists, articles and PDFs, as well as publications for clients, including the best-selling home-maintenance guide, *Now That You've Had a Home Inspection*.

We offer a great line of protective outerwear and customized apparel for home inspectors, including shirts, jackets and hats.

InterNACHI's Inspector Marketing Department can design and print a variety of custom marketing materials for your home inspection business.

Protect yourself and your clients on the job with our specialized safety and inspection equipment that help make your inspections easier and safer.

Are you an InterNACHI member? Inspector Outlet offers free inspector decals and embroidered patches to all eligible members!

"Inspector Outlet is officially endorsed by InterNACHI for the best prices in the business for our members."
—Nick Gromicko, Founder of InterNACHI

www.InspectorOutlet.com　　　　Sales@InspectorOutlet.com

EDUCATION & TRAINING BOOKS

Whether you're new to the business, an inspector seeking more information, or a veteran of the industry looking to expand your knowledge, these official InterNACHI publications—companion guides to InterNACHI's accredited online courses—will help you become the best inspector you can be!

Find these books plus more tools to grow your inspection business at **www.nachi.org/go/books**

Inspecting the Attic, Insulation, Ventilation & Interior
Item Number: 0109

The purpose of this publication is to provide accurate and useful information for performing an inspection of the attic, insulation, ventilation and interior at a residential property. This book is also a useful tool as a portable guide for inspectors on the job. It also serves as a study aid for InterNACHI's online *Inspecting the Attic, Insulation, Ventilation and Interior* course and exam.

How to Inspect the Exterior
Item Number: 0094

The purpose of this publication is to provide accurate and useful information to home inspectors for the inspection of the exterior of residential properties. This manual covers the components and materials of the exterior at a typical residential property, including: siding types; site drainage; moisture intrusion; windows and doors; flashing; garages; exterior structures; and other exterior systems and components. This book also covers the inspection process and InterNACHI's Residential Standards of Practice.This publication is a useful tool as a portable guide for inspectors on the job. It also serves as a study aid for InterNACHI's online *How to Inspect the Exterior* course and exam.

Residential Plumbing Overview
Item Number: 0064

The purpose of this publication is to provide accurate and useful information for home inspectors in order to perform an inspection of the plumbing system at a residential property. This manual covers the components of common residential plumbing systems, and also refers to the InterNACHI Residential Standards of Practice with regard to recommended inspection protocols. This publication is a useful tool as a portable guide for inspectors on the job. It also serves as a study aid for InterNACHI's online *Residential Plumbing Overview* course and exam.

Safe Practices for the Home Inspector
Item Number: 0038

The purpose of this publication is to assist the inspector in recognizing the conditions which can lead to personal injury, and provide safety guidelines for such situations. It also provides basic information and useful tips for operating a safe and professional home inspection business.

Structural Issues for Home Inspectors
Item Number: 0059

The purpose of this publication is to help prepare the home inspector to observe and report on structural components and their conditions in a residential dwelling.

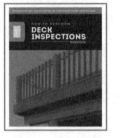

How to Perform Deck Inspections
Item Number: 0029

Because decks appear to be simple to build, many people do not realize that decks are, in fact, structures that need to be designed to adequately resist certain stresses. Like any other house or building, a deck must be designed to support the weight of people, snow loads, and objects. A deck must be able to resist lateral and uplift loads that can act on it as a result of wind or seismic activity. Deck stairs must be safe and handrails graspable. And, finally, deck rails should be safe for children by having proper infill spacing. This book explains how to properly inspect a deck.

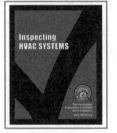

Inspecting HVAC Systems
Item Number: 0061

The purpose of this publication is to provide accurate and useful information for home inspectors in order to perform an inspection of the heating, ventilation, and air-conditioning, (HVAC) system at a residential property. This manual covers the components of common residential HVAC systems, including: warm-air, hydronic, steam and electric heating systems; air-conditioning systems; and heat-pump systems. This guide also refers to the InterNACHI Residential Standards of Practice with regard to recommended inspection protocols.

How to Perform Electrical Inspections
Item Number: 0023

This book teaches the home inspector how to perform the electrical portion of a residential home inspection. A must for every home inspector!

How to Inspect Pools & Spas

Item Number: 0076

The purpose of this publication is to provide accurate and useful information for home inspectors in order to perform an inspection of pools and spas at residential properties. This manual covers the following topics: how pools and spas work; the circulation, heating and filtering systems and components; the electrical components; water chemistry; safety issues; maintenance recommendations; and an inspection procedural checklist. The focus of this book and its corresponding online course is on the water of residential pools and spas, and the systems and components that move or change it. This publication is a useful tool as a portable guide for inspectors on the job. It also serves as a study aid for InterNACHI's online *How to Inspect Pools and Spas* course and exam.

How to Perform a Mold Inspection

Item Number: 0022

Mold inspection is a specialized type of inspection that goes beyond the scope of a general home inspection. The purpose of this publication is to provide accurate and useful information for performing mold inspections of residential buildings. This book covers the science, properties and causes of mold, as well as the potential hazards it presents to structures and to occupants' health. Inspectors will learn how to inspect and test for mold both before and after remediation. This textbook is designed to augment the student's knowledge in preparation for InterNACHI's online *Mold Inspection* course and exam. This manual also provides a practical reference guide for use on-site at inspections.

How to Perform Roof Inspections

Item Number: 0042

This book will teach the inspector how to perform roof inspections of various types of roof coverings and other components. It also serves as a study aid for InterNACHI's online course, as well as a reference manual on the job.

How to Perform Radon Inspections

Item Number: 0028

This very comprehensive book explains how to perform radon measurements and how to inspect radon mitigation systems.

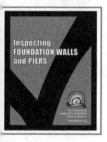

Inspecting Foundation Walls and Piers

Item Number: 0065

This publication is designed to help the home inspector evaluate foundation walls and piers. Additionally, it provides insight into newer innovations pertaining to products and their usage. This book is offered as a learning tool to prepare for successful completion of the online course and final exam. This manual also provides a useful on-the-job guide for inspectors.

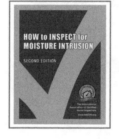

How to Inspect for Moisture Intrusion

Item Number: 0073

This publication is designed primarily for residential and commercial property inspectors who will learn how to inspect for moisture intrusion in buildings, structures and homes. This publication discusses the design, construction, maintenance and other details of homes and buildings in order to look for defects that may cause moisture-related problems, and to help property owners manage moisture effectively.

25 Standards Every Inspector Should Know

Item Number: 0037

The purpose of this publication is to teach 25 building standards and best practices related to inspecting systems and components in a residential dwelling. Learning and understanding these standards will allow the inspector to effectively recognize defects in condition and installation.

International Standards of Practice for Inspecting Commercial Properties

Item Number: 0016

These comprehensive standards have been written by experts and adopted worldwide. Protect yourself by including this book with your commercial inspection report.

Now That You've Had a Home Inspection

Printed Hard Copies (one case of 20 books)

To help reduce liability, an inspector should give the client as much information as possible about how to maintain the home and look for issues after the purchase. That's why we wrote the ultimate home maintenance book.

Each chapter references the InterNACHI Standards of Practice and reinforces the homeowner's responsibility of maintaining their home.

InterNACHI's WDO Inspection Field Guide

Item Number: 0027

This is the ultimate reference manual for inspectors who perform wood-destroying organism/insect inspections. This field guide includes several high-resolution photos, illustrations, comparative charts and diagrams of possible entry points, as well as information on habits, habitat, descriptions and prevention. The guide is meant to be used on-site at inspections and is color-coded for easy flip-to reference.

Order your books today at www.nachi.org/go/books

INTERNACHI'S HOME MAINTENANCE BOOK: "NOW THAT YOU'VE HAD A HOME INSPECTION..."

$2.70 each
(ENGLISH VERSION)

$2.70 each
(SPANISH VERSION)

USE OUR HOME MAINTENANCE BOOK TO GROW YOUR BUSINESS:

Add the book to your inspection report. It will dress up your inspection report, impress real estate agents, and get you more referrals. It is 3-hole-punched for a 3-ring binder. Give one to your favorite real estate agent, too.

Advertise on your website: "My inspection report come with this free home maintenance book." Put a picture of the book cover on your website. Gain a competitive advantage with this book.

Drop one off at every home for sale. Every seller is likely a buyer in your local service area. Introduce yourself by saying, "Hi, I'm a local home inspector and I noticed that you are selling your home. I'd like to give you this free book. My business card is attached. Call me if you need an inspection of the home you are moving to, or if you would like me to inspect the home you are selling."

Reduce your liability. The book is also written specifically to reduce your liability by reminding your clients that a home inspection does not reveal every defect that exists, that certain issues fall outside the scope of a home inspection, and that the homeowner is now responsible for maintaining their home.

Sell your additional inspections. Inside this maintenance book, there are 22 very good reasons to hire you again. The book makes the recommendation to hire an inspector every year as part of a complete homeowner maintenance plan. It promotes your ancillary inspections, too.

Visit www.nachi.org/go/nowbook to order yours today!

THE SPECTOSCOPE

Get the new **SPECTOSCOPE VERSION 2.0** from Inspector Outlet to safely inspect and photograph roofs!

The **SPECTOSCOPE VERSION 2.0** is taller, lighter, thinner and easier to use.

This 38-foot-tall telescoping pole camera allows you to safely take high-quality pictures of roofs from the ground. Simply connect a wireless camera to your iPhone, iPad, iPod Touch or Android-enabled smartphone or tablet, extend the pole, and start capturing photos! You can purchase our WiFi-enabled digital camera that allows you to see on your smartphone or tablet what the camera is seeing at the top of the pole. No wireless network is needed. The camera and smartphone or tablet work together without the need for external WiFi.

Here are the great features of the **SPECTOSCOPE**:

- The 38-foot-tall telescoping fiberglass **SPECTOSCOPE** pole collapses to only 6.8 feet and weighs only 7.5 pounds!
- The pole has swivel mounts at the top for your camera, and a universal mount at the bottom for your smartphone. You can use your own wireless camera, or purchase our camera for an additional charge. You can also purchase a universal tablet holder for an additional charge.
- It comes with a 6-inch PVC hard-pipe carrying case, with a screw cap on one end.

Easy to use to safely take pictures of steep, slippery and unsafe roofs!

Get yours at **www.nachi.org/go/spectoscope**

I purchased a Spectoscope a few months ago and have been very happy with it. Easy to set up and use. I really like the idea of staying off the roof and going home to my family at the end of the day.

—Dennis Pelczynski

SATISFACTION GUARANTEE

If you are dissatisfied with the Spectoscope for any reason, you may return it to us in like-new, unused condition within 30 days from the date of sale for a full refund. This does not cover damage to the pole or any included parts from operator use.

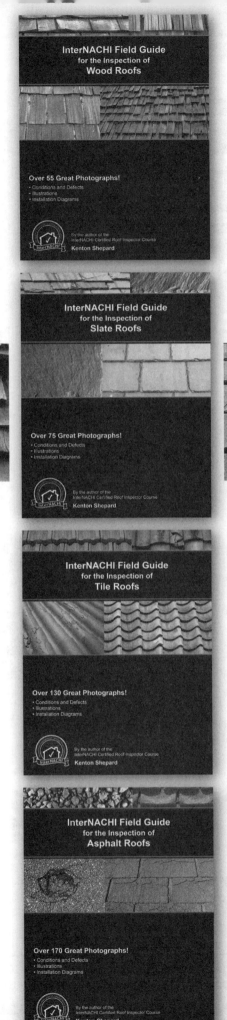

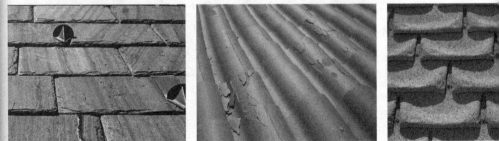

WE'LL BUY YOUR HOME GUARANTEE

FULL PURCHASE PRICE · BACKED BY INTERNACHI

★ IF WE MISS ANYTHING ★
WE'LL BUY YOUR HOME BACK

If the participating inspector misses anything,

WE'LL BUY THE HOME BACK!

And now for the "fine print":

 Honored for 90 days after closing.

 Valid for home inspections performed for home buyers by participating InterNACHI members.

 We'll pay the homeowner whatever price they paid for the home.

→ Excludes homes with material defects not present at the time of the inspection, or not required to be inspected per InterNACHI's Residential Standards of Practice.

LEARN MORE AND SIGN UP AT:

www.nachi.org/buy

Get a Custom Online Video Ad
to Help Promote Your Inspection Business!

Here's how it works:

1. Place your order.

2. Within three business days, we'll contact you to get some information about your inspection business, such as:
   - your company name;
   - your phone number;
   - your website address;
   - your email address;
   - your qualifications;
   - the ancillary services you offer;
   - your inspection business logo (if you have one);
   - your service area; and
   - any unique selling points.

3. We'll produce an awesome video ad that will generate lots of business for you.

4. We'll search engine-optimize (SEO) your video to promote your inspection business in your local markets.

5. We'll add translated custom captions to your video. Because Google owns YouTube, captions are an important tool for video SEO and YouTube visibility for businesses. Custom captions are indexed by Google, making your video searchable by a larger audience.

6. We'll upload your custom video to InterNACHI's YouTube channel for an additional SEO boost. You do not need your own YouTube channel.

7. We'll upload your custom video to Facebook for an additional SEO boost. You do not need your own Facebook page.

8. We'll send you a simple YouTube link with your video already uploaded. You can then:
   - email your video to your potential and past clients;
   - download your custom video as an FLV or MP4 video file;
   - embed your video on your website;
   - add the video to your Facebook page;
   - add your custom video link to your InterNACHI message board signature for an additional SEO boost; and
   - simply use the YouTube link we give you.

CUSTOM INSPECTION VIDEOS

We'll produce a custom video for you that is search engine-optimized (SEO) to promote your inspection business in your local markets. We'll make your inspection business look great, and the process is easy.

Check out some videos we've created for other inspectors at:
www.nachi.org/go/custom-video

Questions? Email:
erik@internachi.org

Order yours today! www.nachi.org/go/custom-video

Notes: